The Asian Grocery Store Demystified

The Asian Grocery Store Demystified

Linda Bladholm

RENAISSANCE BOOKS
Los Angeles

For Joel

Library of Congress Cataloging-in-Publication Data
Bladholm, Linda.
    The Asian grocery store demystified / Linda Bladholm.
        p.   cm.
    Includes index.
    ISBN 1-58063-045-6 (alk. paper)
    1. Food—Dictionaries. 2. Cookery—Dictionaries.   I. Title
TX349.B53   1999   98-55397
    641.3'095'03—dc21   CIP

10 9 8 7 6 5 4 3

Design by Lisa-Theresa Lenthall
Illustrations by Linda Bladholm
Typesetting by Jesus Arellano
Chart on page 17 by James Tran

Distributed by St. Martin's Press
Manufactured in the United States of America
First Edition

Contents

Foreword

Cooking well is the product of a number of complex steps towards a gustatory goal. Planning must go into the preparation of any meal, and even the simplest sandwich requires some sort of plan. Not all preparations take place in the kitchen, since most meals begin in the market.

As cooks, we gather our palette of materials from one or more markets. All of us are familiar with large American-style supermarkets, and the shelves of our local grocer or delicatessen. But by limiting your home's pantry shelves to ingredients found in those stores, you are missing out on hundreds of different spices, products, and flavors that are available at shops with a particular ethnicity. In *The Asian Grocery Store Demystified,* Linda Bladholm gives you the information you need to cruise the aisles of your local Asian food shop with confidence and a sense of adventure.

Like anything new, you'll need to develop some skills particular to the handling and cooking of Asian products. You will also need to stock your kitchen cabinets with a number of ingredients that might be unusual. As a professional cook I spend as much time as possible in food markets—markets of any kind. I have just returned from a trip through Thailand, Vietnam, and Bali, much of which was spent touring the shelves of exotic shops and markets. I have found the inspiration for most of the dishes served in my restaurants while walking the aisles of sundry markets.

If you like to cook at home, or are a professional cook, I urge you to spend time in unfamiliar markets, especially Asian grocery stores. The flavors of Asia are incredibly diverse and have thousands of years of history behind them. With just a little inspiration, a few good recipes, and a little direction from this book, I'm sure you will be on your way to a new world of cooking and eating pleasure.

—Jonathan Eismann, restaurateur
Pacific Time
Miami Beach, Florida

Acknowledgments

Countless unknown Asian people contributed to this book by allowing me to share their lives and learn about their cultures when I lived in their countries. Thank you for the experience. Certain people who helped make this book possible deserve a special mention: Angelina Phillips in Singapore for pre-editing my rough draft, compiling the index, and lending advice on the herbal soup recipes; Quinn Martinelli of Miami Beach for help with Chinese herbs; Phil Chan of the Chinatown Chamber of Commerce in Chicago; and the many patient and helpful Asian grocery store owners. These include Edward S. Lin of the Thai Grocery in Chicago, Tim and Soa Chi Leung of Tim's Oriental Grocery in Homestead Florida, Ms. Loc Trang of the Vinh An Market in North Miami Beach (who commented "you eat more Chinese food than I do!" on one of my almost weekly visits) and Ann Verrilli of the Asia Market in Miami. Thanks also to Elizabeth Sim of the Kung Ju Korean Restaurant, and the Chung Hing and PK Oriental Marts, all in North Miami Beach. Thanks to Dawn Reshen-Doty and Neil Reshen who believed in my talent and Richard F. X. O'Connor for believing in the project and bringing it to reality. Special thanks also to the staff at Renaissance Media, Masakazu Asakawa, Barbara Gillman, Jonathan Eismann, Phung Chung, Chris Ho, Andy Bui, Asako Severn, Rith Khem, and Lou Hong and to Ann and John Bladholm and my wonderful mother-in-law, Freda Weltman.

Introduction

Asian cuisine is an evocative mingling of many ingredients and contrasting flavors, uniting robust, spicy elements and delicate, subtle nuances. This book is meant to give anyone wishing to try their hand at Asian cooking an accessible guide to identifying and using a variety of these ingredients used in recipes found in your Asian cuisine cookbooks.

While the ingredients are readily available in more than 5,000 Asian markets dotting America's landscape, many potential cooks give up in confusion because they can't figure out what all the items cramming crowded shelves are or can't understand how to use them. If you are one of these people, I have designed this book to meet your needs by anticipating questions and explaining what you will find, what it will look like, taste like, and be used for. I want to share with you what I learned living in many Asian countries.

This book is a guide to the typical Asian grocery. Its purpose is to help you, the reader, use your Asian recipes and cookbooks.

For ten years, I prowled the markets, cooked meals, snacked, slurped, and munched my way from Singapore, Malaysia, Indonesia, and Thailand to Japan with trips to the Philippines, Hong Kong, China, Korea, and Taiwan and tramps through Laos, Cambodia, and Vietnam. I embraced all these cultures, especially their markets and foods.

Asian markets can seem forbidding with all those strange jars, bottles, and bags, piles of weird looking vegetables and smelly dried fish,

but you can learn to guide yourself by using this
book. Here, entries are organized from most to
least important and follow the shelf plans of the
many grocery stores I researched while working on
the guide.

Keep two things in mind. If it's in the produce section, it's a vegetable or fruit. And since it's in a food market
you can assume it's something edible. Next, keep an open mind. Be
willing to experiment. Explore. Ask. Taste and try new things. Take
your time and be patient. Keep in mind that the store owners want to
see you there—it's in their interest to get a new customer.

The Store Near You

Wherever you live, it is certain that some type of Asian grocery is
nearby. In large metropolitan centers such as New York, Chicago,
Houston, Los Angeles, or San Francisco with sizable Asian communities—and Chinatowns—you will find the largest stores. Authentic and
versatile, these markets have a network of food production industries
to provide them with freshly made noodles and dumplings, roasted
meats, and live or freshly caught seafood. There will be tiers of fresh
produce crates out front on the sidewalk with a scale hanging nearby.
Piles of fat Chinese cabbage, bunches of bok choy, huge hunks of
fuzzy winter melon, boxes of neatly arranged lotus roots, and pyramids
of oranges or whatever else is in season, will tempt you. Inside the
store will be aisles filled with goods from all over Asia. One will be
heavy on the Chinese imports and another will feature more Thai or
Vietnamese products, depending on the owner's ethnic background or
the predominate Asian group in the local community. There will be
small shops along with multi-storied mega-markets to pick from.

The huge shopping complexes stock wares from all over Asia,
with whole floors selling only dried products, other floors just canned
and bottled items and yet others, household goods. Some produce is
grown locally and trucked to city wholesale markets. Much comes by
air or truck from California and Florida. The fresh noodles, tofu, pickled vegetables, preserved meats, and Asian sweets will be made in shops
within the Chinatown, and sold through the network of markets.
Neighborhood butchers and fishmongers provide fresh, high quality
meat, poultry, and seafood. Outside of large metropolitan areas, Asian
grocery stores tend to be smaller, but stock a broad range of goods.

Obviously, you know where the nearest Asian grocery is to you.
But before you go there, make a list of what you want to buy. Deter-
mine your purchases around a menu or a specific recipe.

Food & Philosophy

Or, think like an Asian. In basic Asian philosophy, food, as everything
else in life, must be in balance. Therefore when preparing meals, a
harmonious balance of the two opposing life forces—yin and yang—
is the goal. Yin foods are cooling, moist, soft foods such as winter

melon or crab. Yang foods are hot, including garlic, chili, ginger, fried foods, or red meat. To achieve the ideal is to achieve a balance of color, flavor, aroma, and texture. There should be an interplay of salty, sweet, sour, bitter, and spicy-hot—the primary flavors of Asian cuisine. Color and texture are added for variety: soft, tender, crisp, smooth, and crunchy elements in proportion, combined with complementary flavors and contrasting pale or bright colors create a dynamic harmony of all the ingredients. The senses of sight, smell, and taste fuse in each dish. (See the note on balancing yin and yang at the beginning of chapter 17.)

It may sound complex, but once you begin cooking with Asian ingredients, this balancing act becomes instinctual and natural. To aid you, Asian markets are generally stocked according to the principles of balance. Shelves are organized into sections of goods by their properties. Hot, spicy, chili sauces and curry pastes are all in one place; salty items are together in one row; and bitter, sour, or sweet things are in other sections.

But first, you will want to purchase your staple: rice. Build around this base, adding the back-up starch: noodles. Think of them as your neutral main element.

1

A Walk through Mr. Lin's Grocery Store

亚洲烹调的基本必备品

Chinese for "stocking the basic Asian kitchen"

The small grocery store where I shop is a typical mom-and-pop Asian grocery. Once inside, you are in another land, surrounded with exotic looking provisions, colorful wrappers and labels, mysterious smells of incense, musty medicinal herbs, pungent dried fish, mysterious citrus, cooked curry, and tinkling sounds of tea cups in a tiny kitchen area in the rear. But you need no passport or visa to enter this place!

THE LINS

The store's owners are Mr. and Mrs. Lin. The Lins are Thais of Chinese descent who arrived from Bangkok long before I had moved to the neighborhood. I can't imagine it without them and I consider them my extended family.

Mr. Lin, "Sam" (Americanized from his Thai name Samorn), his wife Arun (Dawn), 12-year-old daughter Noi and 14-year-old son Tim form the nucleus of the grocery. The family is hardworking but each member always takes time to chat with customers. Mr. Lin opens early each morning, hosing down the front sidewalk and helping unload crates of produce or iced fish from delivery trucks. He is in his mid-fifties with a receding hairline, big wide-toothed grin, and gentle demeanor. When I practice my Thai with him, his dark eyes light up in encouragement, but his English is perfect. Mrs. Lin, wearing an apron, her salt-and-pepper tresses up in a twisted french bun, puts on a tea kettle and busies herself in the tiny kitchen in back of the store. She is petite and very graceful, having studied classical Thai dance at the Royal Dance School of Bangkok. She is like a mother to me, and brings home-made chicken, ginger, and garlic soup when I'm ill. She cooks a selection of daily specials and barbecues her delicious ribs and other treats. The red-glazed strips of pork, rib slabs, and mahogany ducks dangling on metal hooks above the tiny deli counter are testimonials to her culinary skills. This deli counter is wedged between a fish tank and a refrigerator case. In the aquarium swims pomfret, carp, and sea bass. Customers choose a fish and Mrs. Lin bops it on the head with her cleaver, cleans and guts it, and then wraps it in paper, often with a cooking suggestion. The Lin kids help out after school and on weekends.

As we take a quick tour of the store, don't concern yourself with the exotic names and goods, all of which will be fully covered in ensuing chapters. You might find it convenient to follow along by referring to the store layout on page 17.

The Layout

FIVE AISLES

Upon entering the store, you face five jam-packed aisles running the length of the grocery, with numbered paper markers strung above each one. Pegboards are at the front of the center aisles with snacks in plastic bags hanging on hooks. Little wrinkled preserved plums, dried sweet mango, peaches, and ginger beckon next to packets of red and black dried watermelon seeds, spiced almonds, beef, pork, fish and squid floss, candies, rice crackers and dried honey olives, green peas and tamari flavored potato chips. Crates of fruit—Asian pear apples, green papaya, and starfruit, nestled in tissue and cardboard trays—are on the floor below the snack foods. A tangerine pyramid is piled in front of shelves 7 and 8, with a basket of pineapples below.

Rice bags dominate the front window with burlap 25-pounders stacked like sandbags against the pane. Across from those, on a shelf fronting shelves 1 and 2, are the smaller sacks of rice.

Open refrigerated produce bins are around the corner from the rice, along the east wall, or right side, of the store. The bins are divided into dozens of compartments, each one filled with fresh, lightly water-spritzed vegetable greens and herbs. Included are jade green bok choy, mustard cabbage, water spinach, flowering mustard and chilies, coriander, pale Chinese chives, and mint leaves. Further down the case are slim lavender and tiny pea eggplants, giant daikon radish, long beans tied in loose knots and, in plastic sieves, pea shoot tendrils, water chestnuts in papery brown skins, whole bamboo shoots and sausage-like lotus roots. Beansprouts are in a large plastic tub with tongs nearby to put them in smaller plastic bags pulled off of a roll.

After the produce bins, stretching to the back of the store (the north wall), is a freezer case. Pull open the top and look down into a

The Lin Family's Grocery Store Floor Plan

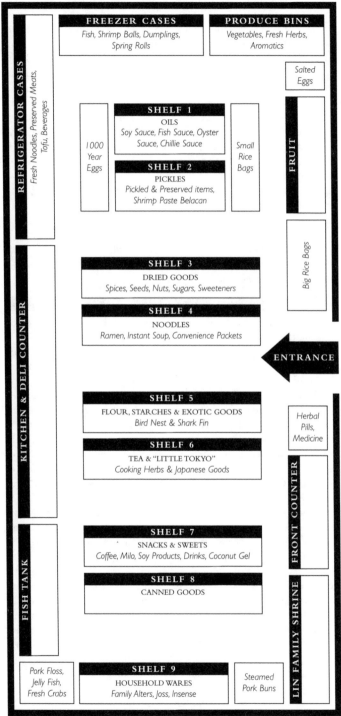

REFRIGERATOR CASES
Fresh Noodles, Preserved Meats, Tofu, Beverages

FREEZER CASES
Fish, Shrimp Balls, Dumplings, Spring Rolls

PRODUCE BINS
Vegetables, Fresh Herbs, Aromatics

Salted Eggs

SHELF 1
OILS
Soy Sauce, Fish Sauce, Oyster Sauce, Chillie Sauce

1000 Year Eggs

Small Rice Bags

FRUIT

SHELF 2
PICKLES
Pickled & Preserved items, Shrimp Paste Belacan

SHELF 3
DRIED GOODS
Spices, Seeds, Nuts, Sugars, Sweeteners

Big Rice Bags

SHELF 4
NOODLES
Ramen, Instant Soup, Convenience Packets

ENTRANCE

KITCHEN & DELI COUNTER

SHELF 5
FLOUR, STARCHES & EXOTIC GOODS
Bird Nest & Shark Fin

Herbal Pills, Medicine

SHELF 6
TEA & "LITTLE TOKYO"
Cooking Herbs & Japanese Goods

FRONT COUNTER

SHELF 7
SNACKS & SWEETS
Coffee, Milo, Soy Products, Drinks, Coconut Gel

SHELF 8
CANNED GOODS

FISH TANK

LIN FAMILY SHRINE

Pork Floss, Jelly Fish, Fresh Crabs

SHELF 9
HOUSEHOLD WARES
Family Alters, Joss, Insense

Steamed Pork Buns

swirl of water vapor to find whole or chunks of frozen fish, pig brains, ears, and tails, shrimp and fish paste balls, tubs of tiny rice paddy crabs, ducks, salmon and flying fish roe, boxes of squid, bags of wonton noodles, and all sorts of wrappers. There are also packaged frozen dumplings, siu mai, pork buns, and egg rolls to reheat and serve at home. Half of the back wall is lined with floor-to-ceiling glass refrigerator cases fitted with metal shelf racks. Doors swing open from each case letting out a blast of frosty air. The racks are full of everything from kim

beer

chee and sour bamboo pickles, Chinese sausage links, preserved duck eggs, styrofoam containers of fermented soybeans, miso paste, and tubs of tofu to bags of fresh egg or rice noodles, spicy boiled chicken feet in aspic-filled pouches, cans of coconut water, sugarcane soda, soybean milk, and coffee. You will also find Japanese fish paste cakes, smoked pressed geese, spring and egg roll wrappers, fried beancurd puffs and lotus or red bean paste-filled mooncakes wrapped in plastic. You can't miss the selection of imported Asian beer: Singha from Thailand, Tsing Tao from China, Bintang brewed in Indonesia, or Tiger brand from Singapore.

wonton dumpling

THE KITCHEN

The refrigerator cases end midway across the back wall. There you find the tiny take-out counter where Mrs. Lin prepares her specials. A one-wok mini kitchen that resembles a mobile hawker's cart from the streets of Bangkok is just behind the counter. Cooked food is displayed behind glass in metal steam pans. On a given day there could be green curry pork, chicken in red coconut curry, or fried catfish with a side of green papaya salad, but her popular pad thai noodles (see a recipe in the appendix) are always on the menu. While you wait for your order, you can watch fish glide around in the tank sandwiched between the deli counter and a narrow row of shelves. This nook is stocked with jumbo-sized plastic containers of pork floss. On the lower shelf space are foil packets of "instant" prepared jellyfish.

Long shelves run almost the length of the grocery, toward the front counter. They are packed with household merchandise: dishes, teacups, pots, pans, woks, dome lids, rice cookers, cleaning brushes, knives, bamboo steamers, mesh noodle strainers, bundles of chopsticks, balls of cotton string, multicolored plastic sieves, and bathroom slippers. There are also bamboo skewers for satay, mats for rolling sushi, wooden tongs, soup dippers, clay stew pots, Mongolian fire pots for

soup, stone mortar-and-pestles and chopping boards that resemble round slices of tree trunks. At one end are small, red, tin family altars, wired to light up when plugged in. Stacks of paper money, incense coils, joss sticks, and candles are here, too, to be burnt or lit as offerings in Asian homes to appease any upset spirits, placate kitchen gods, or honor deceased ancestors.

The Lin's family altar glows with red electric lights in an alcove above the front counter, on the left side of the store. A plump orange or a sprig of blossoms is placed there daily when the Lins open for business. They pause at the altar, clasp their hands in prayer and burn a stick of sweet incense, which sends a curl of smoke into the air. They have a cup of tea and their day begins.

Lin Family altar

Behind the counter are shelves filled with vials of herbal pills, medicines, ointments, balms, creams, and face powders.

*a medicine
powder label*

With her satin smooth complexion, Mrs. Lin has me convinced that Pearl Cream is the answer to beautiful skin. Have a headache? Mr. Lin will sell you a paper packet with a picture of an elongated man's head on it, filled with aspirin powder. For general good health he suggests Bao ji wan pills, sold in little capsules, ten to a box. "All natural herbs and roots, can't hurt!" he adds. Next to the cash register is a carton of tiny glass "poppers" of ginseng extract that Mr. Lin urges tired customers to take for an energy rush. And there is a cup filled with miniature silver ear picks, a sort of Asian impulse item. You can also spring for a pack of licorice or ginseng chewing gum. Near the register is an antique set of scales used to weigh produce, chopped barbecue meats, and pickles from earthenware crocks. On top of the counter, in a glass steamer box, pork char siu bao and red bean paste–filled buns keep warm. Below are plastic wrapped styrofoam trays of chow fun (sheets of oiled pliant rice pasta). On the floor you will see a basket full of jiggling live crabs and a crate of shrimp packed in ice chips.

steamed buns

Now let's tour the aisles and check out the contents of each shelf.

Spices

Just opposite the produce and freezer cases is shelf 1. Salty flavorings lead off: bottles of soy sauces, fish sauce, teriyaki marinade, oyster sauce, noodle dipping sauces, jars of hoi-sin, and salted yellow and black bean sauce. Next is a section of squat jars and ceramic crocks of red and white fermented beancurd. About mid-aisle are slender bottles of pale golden rice vinegar and black vinegar, sweet cooking wine, and Chinese wine, which is similar to sherry. This is followed by a section of tart and sweet-sour flavorings: tamarind concentrate in jars or bricks of pulp, plum, duck, and sweet-and-sour sauce, even a tangy Thai dipping sauce for fruit.

If you are a chili addict, you won't be able to resist the next section: hot and spicy flavoring ingredients that add tongue-tingling heat to recipes. There are big fat jars of pickled ground chili peppers,

ketchup shaped bottles of hot banana sauce and sambal seafood sauce, siracha, sambal olek, and chili powders and pastes in tubs or jars. Moving along, at the end of the aisle are cooking and flavoring oils. For deep-frying and cooking choose peanut or corn oil. Add the sesame and chili oils for flavoring. Now you are at the end of the row. Turn the corner and slowly stroll up aisles 2 and 3.

Pickles & Preserves

SHELF TWO

Here you'll find pickled and preserved goods. Cans and jars will be on the upper shelves, with brine-filled plastic pouches of "wet"-pack pickles and "dry"-pack salt-preserved ones on the lower shelves. Take

your pick from mustard cabbage greens, radish in strips or shreds, turnips, tiny hot chilies in vinegar, sour spicy bamboo shoots, green mango pickle slices, or ping-pong ball-sized Thai eggplants—all used as seasoning ingredients or as condiments. You'll notice a pungent spicy aroma coming from a large crock on the floor. It's Sichuan preserved vegetable. At the end of this aisle are jars of pale purple fish paste and potent smelling dried fish paste cakes wrapped in paper. This is called belacan, and the overpowering rotten odor dissipates after roasting or cooking.

pickle crock

Dried Goods

SHELF THREE

Enticing odors waft down this aisle: the spicy scent of curry powder, black and white pepper, and coriander seed mingles with fragrant star anise, cinnamon bark, dried citrus peel, and lime leaves. We are in the dried goods area of the grocery, and beyond the spices are dried seeds, nuts, berries, beans, sheets and rolls of beancurd skin, chilies, and mushrooms—both the little shriveled cloud ear fungus and the black Chinese sort. Don't overlook the dried spongy looking pulp of the inside of bamboo stalks or plastic containers of fried red onions and shallots. Dried seafood products fill a large section and are important flavoring ingredients in Asian cuisine, adding an intense dimension of richness. Fancy whole or sliced abalone in expensive boxes are on the top shelves. Middle and lower ones are filled with bags of shriveled oysters, scallops, salt encrusted sheets of jellyfish, squid, fish slabs, and sun dried silvery anchovies.

Keep an eye out for the dried shrimp that look like pinkish-orange crustacean fossils. The jars of pink sawdust are shrimp flakes and the dark reddish substance nearby is dried shrimp roe, both used as garnishes. The rest of the shelf space is filled with sweeteners and sugars. You'll find tumbler glasses of golden Chinese honey, some lychee-scented honey, and fat tubs of liquid amber maltose sugar. Yellow lump sugar crystals, used in savory slow-cooked dishes as well as in sweet ones, will be in bags or boxes. That large layered "toffee candy" is actually brown slab sugar made of compressed layers of two sugars and honey. At the very end of the row are jugs of semi-soft creamy-tan palm sugar and cylinders of dark coconut sugar.

Noodles

SHELVES FOUR & FIVE

On the right are oodles of noodles stretching almost to the end of the aisle. They are grouped on the shelves by content. Rice stick noodles, vermicelli, and flat round packages of rice papers fill one section. Next are wheat flour-and-egg noodles. In another section are cellophane and Korean yam and mung bean starch thread noodles. And yet another has Japanese buckwheat soba, somen, and udon noodles. The whole upper shelf is stacked with ramen and instant soup noodles.

Powders & Mixes

FAST FOOD

In the last section you'll find convenience packs of powdered mix for soups, noodle sauces, marinades, satay seasoning, Chinese roast duck and barbecue spices, and much more. The most popular brand stocked in the Lin's grocery is Asian Home Gourmet from Singapore. Available mixes range from Thai tom yam soup, Cantonese fried rice, and Indonesian tamarind fish to Indian briyani rice, herbal spare rib, and coconut curry noodle. You'll also find bouillon cubes and powdered soup stocks, Vietnamese beef noodle broth mix in cube and powder form, jars of instant Thai coconut ginger, and hot-sour seafood soup pastes and packets for Filipino guava soup. This section is your friend. Stock up on these time-saving mixes for authentic Asian meals in a flash.

Flours & Starches

FLOURS & EXOTICA

At the front section of shelf 5 are bags of flours and starches. These are used in making noodles, dumplings, and steamed cakes and as sauce binders and thickeners. Good old cornstarch is found here, in the familiar yellow-and-blue box and in bags of Asian brands. There is also wheat starch and flour, long-grain and glutinous rice flour, potato and water chestnut flours, mung bean starch, tapioca and sago starches and pearls. The little pellets of these root starches are also sold in pastel tints for use in puddings and desserts. You will find Japanese roasted soybean flour and cinnamon-colored Thai toasted rice powder.

Here too is where to find Vietnamese pancake powder for making rice flour crepes, boxes and small plastic bags of tempura batter mix and panko to coat foods for deep-frying.

Where the various types of flour end, the truly exotic begins. For here are beautiful boxes of bird's nests and sharksfin, both very pricey and almost tasteless but prized for their gelatinous texture—and as a symbol of luxury. Here's where to find fish maw, the puffy dried air bladders of a deep-dwelling fish, also a textural delicacy, but without the high price tag. Then there are all those withered-looking leaves— dried lotus leaves, screwpine, or pandan, and so on. Lastly you'll see bags of black "hair clippings." This is fat choy, a dried black sea moss. And for more exotica such as blood pudding, duck feet, and devils tongue jelly check the refrigerator cases.

Tea

SHELVES SIX & SEVEN

Now we wend our way up shelves 6 and 7. On your left is a great wall of tea, stacked in boxes, tin canisters, and paper-wrapped blocks. All the main tea types are represented—blacks, slightly fermented oolongs, and greens—from Japan, China, Taiwan, India, and Indonesia. Browse here, too, for jasmine, chrysanthemum, or ginger teas, slimming beauty brews or healthy herbal ones. Here too are Chinese medicinal cooking herbs, including caterpillar fungus and ginseng. Mid-aisle are the teapots, metal and bamboo strainers, and little china cups for serving the brew.

Little Tokyo

JAPANESE STAPLES

The other half of shelf 6 is "Little Tokyo" as the Lins call it. Here are found nonperishable Japanese products. Tubes and small cans of sinus-blasting green wasabi, an ocean of seaweed from black sheets of nori and strips of dark green wakame to stiff olive-green konbu and the black, twig-like hijiki. In this section is sansho and seven spice peppery powders in small shakers and hon-dashi instant soup base, packets of instant miso soup, sushi rice mix powder, and dried shavings of boni-to fish. Sake, ponzu, and seasoned rice vinegar in glass bottles are here too, while Japanese pickles, salted umeboshi plums, sushi ginger, and fish paste products are over in the refrigerator cases.

Now turn around and face shelf 7. Shelf 7 is a mixed bag of items. First is a section of typical Asian hot beverage mixes. There are big green cans of Milo, Ovaltine, and other malt-based drinks, Thai spiced coffee, and Malaysian roasted coffee powder blended with dehydrated margarine. Then there are the unfamiliar drink powders: soybean cheese, almond, sesame and peanut soup pastes, and mango or straw-berry dofu mix. These are all high-protein "health" drinks. In this area are almond and fruit flavor agar-agar dessert mixes, pudding, custard and gelatin powders, and tinted clear jellies in tiny plastic cups.

Snacks

SWEETS & CRACKERS

A snack section is mid-aisle. You will find toothsome curry and green onion pop pan crackers, tins of biscuits, soda crackers, cookie rolls that look like cigarettes, almond cakes, popped rice candy pieces made of puffed rice in a hardened sugar-honey syrup, sesame brittle, peanut cookies, and soft thin pancakes made of melted sugar and sesame seeds. Fancy some ginger? Choose from ginger bon-bons, red pickled ginger, and crystallized chunks. There's also tamarind and prune chewy candy, date-walnut soft candy, sugar-coated almonds, Sichuan toasted honey glazed walnuts and sizzling rice crusts to deep-fry and drop into soup.

Japanese senbei fills another section of this shelf. They are toasted rice crackers in lots of sizes and shapes both savory and sweet; glazed with soy sauce, wrapped in seaweed, spiced, or sugar coated. Nearby you can pick out chocolate swizzle sticks and bags of puffy pink shrimp crackers or seaweed flavored potato chips. Other treats to discover are dried roasted coconut chips, crystallized pineapple, melon seeds, and papaya milk taffy. The last section of this shelf has a row of tiny bottles of extracts used to flavor desserts and drinks: banana, rose, pandan, jasmine, and orange flower. Next to these are jars of syrup-preserved fruits, sugar palm seeds, and coconut gel balls and shreds. That jar of vivid purple puree is a sweet jam made from a Filipino purple yam. You'll also find jars of sweet chick peas in syrup, chunks of yellow-orange jackfruit and a fruit mix labeled "halo-halo." All of these are used in desserts or served over shaved ice.

Canned Goods

SHELF EIGHT

Rounding the corner of shelf 8, the eye is greeted by a solid wall of rows of neatly stacked canned goods. Cans of fish and seafood are first: sardines in hot sauce, grass carp, clams, cockles, oysters, crabmeat, squid-in-ink, and grilled eel rolls. You will also find canned vegetable items including pickled lettuce and cucumber, bamboo shoots, baby corn, water chestnuts, and straw mushrooms. These are handy to store in your pantry for throwing together fast meals, and will keep almost indefinitely. More canned items to consider are tiny boiled quail eggs, ginkgo nuts, lotus seeds, and mock meats made of

fried, boiled, and braised wheat gluten. Unusual canned things you will see are Ai-yu jelly, banana flower buds, green jackfruit, and kaya, a coconut and egg jam. Cans of coconut milk fill the next section, an essential and convenient item you should stock up on for adding flavor and creaminess to spicy soups and curries as well as desserts. Keep on hand for instant dessert some of the many tropical fruits in stock: lychees, longans, rambutan, soursop, small red bananas, pineapple, and mandarin orange segments.

At the end of the last aisle, you are now back at the front counter. You will get to know Lin's grocery in more detail as you go through this book. We will use the floor plan just described in each chapter as a guide, referencing where to find a particular item, what it is, and how to use it. If you get lost along the way, just take a look at the floor plan . . . and, have fun!

2

Rice

Japanese for "rice"

Rice is the fundamental grain that feeds half the world's population. It is the principal food of Asia—the filling starch of almost every meal, eaten with fish, meat and vegetable garnishes, or side dishes.

Soup and curries are other flavoring agents to be spooned over rice throughout a meal. Rice provides a plain foil for the rich sauces, pungent, salty, or spicy seasonings and various textures of the courses served over it. A meal without rice is almost a joke in most Asian cultures—anything else, such as noodles, is considered a snack, even if it comes in a meal-size bowl!

Rice & Soul

MYTHIC FOOD

In Asian culture rice symbolically represents fertility and life. Rice is embedded in the Asian psyche as something essential, with almost magical properties. It weaves through people's life, diet, art, politics, and even religion. Rice is income, nourishment, security, versatile, fun, and has soul.

Besides its role as a staple, rice is ground into powder and used to make confections, cakes, and puddings and as a coating for meats and fish before cooking. Rice flour is used to make rice stick noodles and steamed whole sheets of rice pasta. A plethora of other food products are also made from rice including: rice paper—thin round sheets of dried rice dough used as wrappers for spring rolls; rice flakes—broken pieces of rice paper; rice cakes—deep fried cakes of puffed rice added to soups; and rice crackers—Japanese roasted and glazed crackers.

Then there is rice vinegar, rice wine, and toasted rice tea—a mixture of toasted rice and green tea with a nutty flavor.

Asia still grows most of the world's rice. What produces the distinct flavors, aromas, and textures of each type are differences in growing conditions, together with seed stocks' complex heritages. Even a few years ago, the range of rices on store shelves was mainly plain long or short grain white and perhaps brown. Not anymore. There has been a rice boom. Now you will find many types of rice. They are classified as short-grain, medium-grain, or long-grain and come as red, blackish-purple, brown, and white rice.

Depending on the type, rice can be sticky, fluffy, crispy, hard, or chewy after being boiled, steamed, fried, stewed, baked, or grilled over coals wrapped in banana or lotus leaves.

Rice inspires festive celebrations, influences the Buddhist calendar of events, and is used to purify and bless everything from a wedding couple to a new car. It is offered to friends, family, and the gods to cement relationships. All Asian countries have folk tales and mythology involving rice or rice goddesses and offer rice in ceremonies to the spirit world.

Types of Rice

This chapter lists types of rice from long-grain to short-grain to brown to sticky types. In the typical Asian grocery, the first items you are likely to see in the shop are the huge family size 25-pound

bags of rice in the front windows. Focus on the more modest 5- to 10-pound bags or a 3- to 10-pound sack. There are even smaller 1- and 2-pound bags, good for test tasting different types.

There is rice from India, China, Japan, Thailand, Vietnam, California, Louisiana, Texas, and an aromatic jasmine from Florida to choose from. Some are packaged in cotton sacks or rough brown burlap, while others are in thick jute bags or stiff, clear, or white plastic. You can identify the type of rice by looking at the grains through the plastic and reading the labels—there is always a description of the content and kind of rice in English someplace on the package. "New crop" on the label indicates the most recently harvested rice, thus the most fragrant.

In most Asian groceries you will find four or five main rice varieties: long-grain, medium-grain, short-grain, basmati, glutinous, and maybe a specialty rice, such as Wehani. There's also brown rice for the health conscious. White rice comes from polishing off the outer layers of bran and oil, so that the rice will keep longer. Asians prefer white rice and are aware that the grains have less vitamins, but feel the sauces, vegetables, and other additional ingredients will compensate nutritionally for what is lost in the polishing process. All rice should be stored in a cool dry place and will keep for a very long time.

Refrigerate leftover cooked rice in a well-sealed container. Most rices will harden if exposed to cold. Reheat cold rice with a few spoonfuls of water in a microwave or in a covered pot over low heat. Use leftover rice dropped into soup or broth or stir-fried to create another meal.

LONG-GRAIN RICE

This is by far the most popular rice eaten in China and throughout Southeast Asia. Kernels are about five times as long as they are wide. Long-grain rice is the least starchy of all rice and cooks up dry and fluffy with grains that separate easily. It is the best type for making plain steamed rice, pilaf, and fried rice dishes.

long-grain rice

There are many brands and varieties to choose from, including naturally fragrant jasmine from Thailand called khao hom mali, aged basmati from India, and American labels such as Carolina, Patna, and Louisiana Pecan. An aromatic jasmine from Florida is Sem-Chi brand, which comes in a light blue bag with an orange half-sun on it. Good Thai jasmine brands to look for are Asian Best, Dragonfly Milagrosa "Rice King," Peacock, and Bangkok Elephant.

Other good Thai jasmine brands are Ba Con Nai with a blue and red deer head logo on a white bag, Farmer Boy, Jasmine Hong Thong, and King Elephant with a green elephant wearing an orange crown on the 25-pound bag.

The Lin's use one 25-pound bag of jasmine rice a week. Each morning, Mrs. Lin starts a huge pot of rice in her tiny kitchen area. When you enter the store, fragrant smells of steamed jasmine rice mingle with curry and incense to permeate the air. You can also buy cartons of fresh-cooked rice from the deli counter to take home when you don't have time to make your own.

> For me, the most important thing about rice is an invitation to "eat rice," which is an introduction to friendship. This leads to a dining experience with everyone sharing from a communal pot or bowl of rice. An extra guest can always be accommodated and given some rice. Friendships form and people bond over this rice eating ritual. The word "rice" means meal from Bali to Vietnam, so if you are ever asked to eat rice in Asia, it is an offer to dine, make friends, and be spiritually nourished.

BASMATI

basmati rice

An aromatic long-grain type with very slender kernels, this rice is grown in India, Iran, and Pakistan. It is aged for at least a year after harvesting to let it develop its full flavor. Both brown and white types are available and they have a nutty aroma and taste. Basmati rice expands

greatly, especially lengthwise, as it cooks, creating distinct, dry, fluffy grains. Ideal for Persian and North Indian dishes as well as an excellent everyday rice.

Look for brands from India and Pakistan in brown burlap bags, often with colorful lettering and sewn-on handles. Royal Basmati in 11-pound burlap bags is good. Texmati is a Texas grown type of basmati, similar in character to the ones from Northern India.

MEDIUM-GRAIN RICE

This is another all-purpose rice. Kernels are shorter and a bit wider than long-grain varieties. This rice type is useful for making rice porridge and cooks up soft with a slightly sticky texture. It is also good as an everyday plain rice. Look for the Calrose brand, the U.S. premium grade Nishiki, and Asian Best Milagrosa medium-grain Thai rice.

SHORT-GRAIN RICE

The most popular rice in Korea and Japan, often called sushi rice, is the variety used, mixed with sugar and rice vinegar, to make sushi. Kernels are stubby with a plump almost round shape. Short-grain rice is slightly stickier than long-grain, making it easier to eat with chopsticks. When properly cooked it tends to form clumps of soft grains that cling together and have a shiny texture. Short-grain rice is commonly used for making rice porridge (congee) or enjoyed as a plain table rice.

short-grain rice

Look for the Japanese Nishimoto and Hikari Imperial Quality brands or Assi Korean brand. The American-grown Kokuho Rose and Calusa are also excellent. Use short-grain rice to make the salmon with rice tea recipe on page 216.

BROWN RICE

This is the natural rice with the outer layers of bran and an inner layer of germ left intact. The bran and germ contain many of the rice grain's vitamins, fiber, and protein making it chewier, more filling, and more nutritious. Brown rice should be stored in a tightly closed jar in the refrigerator to prevent oils in the husk from turning rancid.

Brown New Crop rice is available in the Oriental Mascot brand in a white, yellow-orange, and black bag. Look also for Nishiki brown rice in 2- or 5-pound bags; Home Village; and Pear Blossom natural brown Calrose rice, in 5-pound bags.

RED YEAST RICE

This is harvested throughout Asia and is similar to brown rice in taste and flavor. It is eaten mainly by poor farmers and the health conscious. As it is in the glutinous rice family, it has to be soaked at least two hours prior to cooking. Some strains are grown in California and are sold in commercial blends of rice. Look for Oriental Mascot red rice from Thailand in 5-pound plastic bags with a chef in a circle logo.

Did you ever admire those glowing red ducks and spare ribs in Chinese restaurants? The red color comes from powdered red yeast rice which is an ingredient in the marinade and barbecue sauce. This rice powder is being made into capsules after a recent clinical study at UCLA found people taking the powdered grain lowered their cholesterol significantly.

GOBINDUVOG RICE

This rice comes from Burma and is a long-grain white rice on a mini scale, sort of a baby basmati. It is a good everyday plain rice and good for use in pilaf. Look for Shapla brand (in white cloth bags).

GLUTINOUS RICE

Called khao niao in Thai, gao nep in Vietnamese, and mochi in Japanese. This is also known as sweet or sticky rice because of its texture when cooked. The broad, short grains are an opaque milky-white when raw and become translucent after cooking or steaming, just the opposite of other rice. Glutinous rice has to be soaked for at least 8 and up to 24 hours before being steamed. The cooked grains are tender, slightly sweet and chewy, but not gluey. It is the daily rice in Northeast Thailand, Laos, and parts of Vietnam and Cambodia, where it is squeezed into balls with the fingers and dipped in sauces or used as a scoop to pick up other foods. It is also used in making Asian sweets, snacks, and ceremonial foods, and often is steamed in lotus or banana leaves to make dumplings. Stuffings for dumplings range from braised chestnuts or spiced braised pork to Chinese sausage and dried shrimp, sweet azuki beans, or stewed preserved plums.

Look for Thai rice brands in burlap-textured plastic or cloth sacks. The labels will have the words "pin kao" or "gao ked" printed on them. Good ones include Thai Rice King, Plum Blossom brand, Three Rings sweet rice "sanpatong," and Praproma with a four-handed blue Buddha on the bag. Also good is Sho-Chiku Bai sweet rice from Koda farms and Chaoten, both from California and in 5-pound bags.

Rice is a culture in Japan. The first rice of the year is very, very special. It is called shinmai (new rice) and in the old days farmers brought some to a shrine, to give thanks for the harvest before eating any themselves. If you live in the countryside of Japan, you will find more than water in the tub. Warm bath water is used to soak rice seeds. When they crack, they will be planted close to together in one field.

FERMENTED SWEET RICE

Made by fermenting cooked grains of glutinous rice. It resembles a rice gruel and is used to make desserts and sweet rice pudding, often mixed with palm sugar and coconut milk. It is found in the refrigerated cases, in glass or plastic containers. Look for Fermented Sweet Rice Sauce in 16-ounce jars with a cartoon face logo on an orange label and Oriental Mascot in 13-ounce tubs.

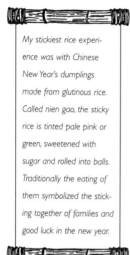

My stickiest rice experience was with Chinese New Year's dumplings made from glutinous rice. Called nien gao, the sticky rice is tinted pale pink or green, sweetened with sugar and rolled into balls. Traditionally the eating of them symbolized the sticking together of families and good luck in the new year.

BLACK THAI STICKY RICE

This is an unpolished, long-grain rice with a chewy texture when cooked. The black bran coating keeps the grains separate and gives the rice a slightly sweet, mild, earthy flavor. In Thailand black rice is soaked and cooked together with white glutinous rice, creating a beautiful purple color when they blend, then mixed with coconut milk to make desserts.

Because of the bran layer, black rice needs extra cooking time—about 10 minutes or more. Thai Rice King is a good brand to seek out.

WEHANI

This hybrid rice, developed in Northern California by Harlan Lundberg, is a reddish brown, long-grain type with Indian basmati in its ancestry. It has a distinct nutty aroma and, when cooked, resembles red-tinted brown rice with a hearty somewhat chewy texture.

Since it is unpolished it requires a longer cooking time. It is used in robust dishes like stews or served with grilled or roasted meats and thick curries. Sold in small boxes and 2- to 5-pound plastic bags.

BROKEN RICE

These are bits of long-grain rice, and are used to make soup, rice gruel, and porridge. Try the Select Food brand in convenient 1-pound bags with orange trim on clear plastic. Look also for Asian Best Thai broken rice in 5-pound bags.

STOCKING UP

Choose a rice for your everyday table rice—long-grain or medium-grain would be most versatile. You might also want a bag of short-grain rice on hand if you like sushi or Korean-style food. The other varieties of rice could be picked up as you need them, for instance, glutinous rice if you're trying a sticky rice pudding or traditional Laotian meal. Experiment with what looks interesting and explore the different shapes, colors, aromas, textures, and tastes. Keep in mind that rice is incredibly versatile and can be served with just about any type of food.

3

Noodles

국수

Korean for "noodles"

Hand-thrown noodles are part of the night's entertainment in some Chinese restaurants, but the ones you'll see in Lin's grocery are machine-made. Noodles and pasta are second only to rice in the Asian diet. Noodles are enjoyed throughout Asia as a snack, a side dish, or a one-dish meal. They are popular because they are accessible, easy to prepare, inexpensive, nutritious, and can be consumed hot or cold. Noodles also symbolize longevity. Slurping is the accepted way to enjoy noodles as, in Asian custom, it's bad luck to cut them, and the noise shows you are relishing the taste.

Noodles are made from rice, wheat flour and water, buckwheat, mung bean starch, yam starch, cornstarch, tofu, and flour-water-and-egg dough and sold in an amazing variety of sizes, shapes, and textures. Because of their infinite variety of shapes, noodles can be an accompaniment to fish, meats, and vegetables or make a complete meal on their own. Noodles are added to soups and stir-fries, served plain or with sauces, boiled, steamed, or deep-fried. The list below starts with rice noodles (rice is the grain most often milled for pasta). This is followed by wheat flour noodles, egg and wheat flour noodles, down to less frequently encountered noodles, or those specific to certain countries such as Japanese soba, bean thread, and Korean yam starch. This is the display plan used in most stores.

Shopping for noodles can be confusing because of the numerous names for the same noodle in different Asian countries. I've listed all the main noodle types by what they are called in Chinese, Thai, Lao, Vietnamese, and Tagalog (the language of the Philippines). Country specific ones are listed under the Tagalog or Japanese name and by country such as Korean or Cambodian. More important than name is selecting what you want by the ingredient the noodle is made from: rice, wheat, egg, bean or potato starch, and whether it is in fresh or dry form. Also pick by strand size. Do you want very fine threads, round medium noodles, or thick flat ribbons?

The least frustrating way to shop for noodles is to buy what appeals to you visually and, ultimately, how it tastes.

R i c e   N o o d l e s

RICE STICK NOODLES

Also called dried rice sticks. These noodles are made from ground long-grain rice powder and water. They are sold in looped skeins of dried, flat, stiff, and brittle semi-transparent noodles in various widths and lengths. The noodles turn opaque white after cooking. Rice sticks are available in three sizes. The thin ones are used primarily in stir-fried dishes but may be added to soups. These are called sen yai (in Thai), bun (in Vietnamese), and palabok (in Tagalog). The classic Thai noodle stir-fry is made with slim rice sticks swirled in a wok in a sweet-sour sauce. Medium rice sticks are all-purpose noodles, used in Vietnamese pho soup, stir-fries, and salads. These are called lai fen and mi fen (in Chinese), Mekong rice stick and sen lek (in Thai), and banh pho (in Vietnamese). Use boiled and chilled in salads. Try them tossed in a creamy peanut or spicy sesame paste sauce or a lemon, garlic, and soy sauce dressing with blanched Chinese greens and cooked shredded chicken. You can also serve grilled meats or seafood nestled on a bed of lightly dressed warm rice noodles.

The wide type are best used in stir-fried dishes or soup and are called shan shui ho fun and sha ha fun (in Chinese) and sen chan or jantaboon noodles (in Thai). Rice stick noodles need to be soaked in warm water before using, about 20 minutes. They can be stir-fried with combinations of meats, seafood, or vegetables and added to soup and broth (before adding to soup, boil separately a few seconds and rinse or they will cloud the stock). Use these noodles stir-fried with marinated

strips of beef and garlic, chili peppers, scallions, and soy sauce. The wide flat noodle edges become crispy when seared in the pan, adding contrast to the tender meat. There is no standardized label for rice sticks, so it is best to just look at the noodles through the cellophane wrappers and select by what you see.

Rice sticks are found in 8-ounce and 1-pound packages. In selecting rice sticks look for Mount Elephant, Summit, and Erawon brands from Thailand as well as the excellent Double Swallow brand from China, and Oriental Style Noodle brand from
rice stick noodle Thailand in orange- or red-trimmed bags with a photo of a big bowl of noodles with chopsticks lifting

some strands. Caravelle offers Mekong rice sticks in 12-ounce bags. Golden Sail, Fan Ho Fun quick serve, and Dana Rose brands come in all sizes. Rice stick noodles are used to make the Thai fried noodles recipe on page 210.

RICE VERMICELLI

Rice vermicelli are also called mi fen (in Chinese), sen mee (in Thai), mai fun (in Japanese), bun and banh hoi (in Vietnamese), and pancit bihon (in Tagalog). These are dried skinny wire-sized semi-transparent noodle threads made from rice powder and water which become opaque white after cooking. They are sold in 8-inch long looped skeins of wispy looking strands packaged in layers in cellophane bags.

rice vermicelli

These are used to make sour-hot mee siam, a popular breakfast dish in Malaysia. They are used stir-fried with a touch of curry powder and nuggets of barbecued pork, shrimp, and vegetables, then tossed in a seasoned sauce to make Singapore curried noodles. In Thailand spicy hot coconut cream is spooned over boiled vermicelli and vegetables with pieces of fish.

In Vietnam boiled vermicelli (bun) is used as an accompaniment to main course dishes in place of rice, stir-fried, added to soup, spring roll stuffings, or salads. Bun is especially good with grilled meats and curried dishes.

In the Lin's grocery and many Thai markets you will find fresh rice vermicelli called khanom jeen. These are thin, round white noodles made from rice flour and water. They are sold in wads that look like bird's nests, in plastic bags. Use steamed and serve with curry or coconut milk sauces or topped with grilled meat or fish. Look for them in the refrigerator case or freezer.

Rice vermicelli must be soaked until softened, about 15 minutes before using in stir-fries. For soup or plain noodles, drop dry noodles into boiling water for 2–3 minutes and rinse under hot water to remove excess starch. Lift and separate the strands with a chopstick to prevent clumping. Rice vermicelli can also be deep-fried into a crunchy mass to use as a bed for stir-fried dishes or as a garnish to add a crispy element to salads and vegetable dishes. Try rolling up strips of spicy stir-fried beef with deep-fried vermicelli bits and toasted sesame seeds in a lettuce leaf. Eat with a soy, chili, and bean paste dipping sauce. The extra thin ones work best for deep-frying, but slightly thicker strands can be used too.

For thin rice vermicelli look for CTF Thai brand, Quon Yick "mai fun" rice noodles, and Newton "pancit bihon" in 8-ounce bags. Oriental Mascot makes thicker round rice vermicelli in long looped skeins, two to a package.

For extra fine rice vermicelli look for Caravelle Guilin thin rice sticks from China with a sampan logo, Wai-Wai Thai "instant" brand, and Summit brand in 1-pound bags with eight swirled square cakes. These just need to be plunged in boiling water a few seconds and rinsed to use.

RICE FLAKES

Also called kuay chap noodles, these are large 1- to 2-inch chips of broken rice papers and are used in soups, or soaked until soft then stir-fried. Look for the Thai Family Elephant and Caravelle brands. Also good are Combine Thai Food Co. and Number One banh pho thuong hang rice flakes.

"Across the bridge rice noodles," a famous Yunnan dish can be made made with dried rice sticks or fresh rice noodles. According to legend, this dish was created by the wife of a scholar studying for the Imperial exams who isolated himself on an island connected to shore by a long hanging bridge. The meals she delivered were always cold by the time she got across the bridge. One day she came up with the idea of carrying a pot of broth kept hot by the layer of oil she poured over the surface. Nourished by hot meals, he passed his exams.

RIVER RICE NOODLES

River rice noodles are also called fen noodle, sha ho fen, chow fun guo tiao (in Chinese), kuay taew (in Thai), and khao pun (in Lao). They are made from long-grain rice flour, wheat starch, and water. This opaque white, pliable pasta is steamed in whole sheets and folded or cut into thick or thin ribbons coated with a light layer of oil to prevent sticking. Before using, rinse gently in boiling water to soften the noodles and remove oily coating.

The whole fresh sheets can be cut into any width and are usually served with a sauce, in soup, or stir-fried. These noodles have a bland taste, so they go best with a flavorful sauce.

Fresh pre-cut river rice noodles are rare to find in small Asian groceries, but most sell the uncut sheets called fun. While they are fun to eat, "fun" means powder, in this case rice powder. Guon fun is a Chinese roll. The wide flat sheets are rolled up with meat, vegetables, and seasonings and cut into 2-inch lengths, served with oyster sauce for dipping. Hom fun is rolled sheets filled with dried shrimp, scallions, and sesame seeds and sliced into small pieces. A popular dim sum dish is ha cheung, rice noodle sheets rolled up with shrimp, steamed, and served with a light soy and cilantro sauce drizzled over them.

fen noodles

Fun sheets will be found on styrofoam trays wrapped in plastic. For soup, just cut the sheets into ribbons, place them in a bowl and pour hot broth over them. A dry version is also sold in plastic bags. Use fresh or dry river rice noodles to make the sweet sesame noodle recipe on page 215.

SILVER PIN NOODLES

Silver pin noodles are also called mee tye bak, nen dzem fen, loh shee fun, and "rat-tail" noodles. These are hand rolled cylindrical white noodles about 2 inches long made of compressed, cooked rice coated with oil which resemble fat bean sprouts or rat's tails. You don't need to boil them, just add them directly to the pan. Cook just until heated through, about 5 minutes, and don't crowd the pan or they will stick. Good stir-fried with meats and seafood.

A Cantonese classic combines these noodles in a stir-fry with chicken and scallions seasoned with black pepper and soy sauce. They are sold fresh in 1-pound plastic bags or sealed pouches in the refrigerator case. Best used within two days of purchase. Look for Seng Cheang Food Company brand, Sincere Orient Foods Vietnamese "banh canh," and Bayon brand pure rice noodles.

You may also find bags of long white, spaghetti shaped fresh rice noodles, sold in bags in the refrigerator case or freezer. These are laksa soup noodles. To use, blanch them in boiling water. They are then bathed in a spicy coconut milk broth to make laksa lemak or the variation, asam laksa Penang, a fragrant, hot and sour broth.

Wheat Noodles

CHINESE WHEAT-FLOUR NOODLES

Known as lo mein, gan mian, and mee swa (fresh thin round ones), or sun mian (loose nests of thin round or broad flat fresh ones), these noodles are made from wheat flour and water and are the most ancient form of all noodles, originating in Northern China. The ones hand-thrown from fresh soft dough are prized for their silky texture. They will only be found in large Chinatown groceries or sold in Chinese restaurants that make their own.

What you will find are dried wheat noodles, made from hard or soft wheat. They vary in thickness and can be round or flat in shape. The very thinnest are called mian xian or "dragon's beards," labeled "Amoy-style" or "Chinese somen," and are used in soups. The thicker wheat noodle varieties are shaped like fettucine and linguine and hold up when stir-fried or added to thick stews and clay pot casseroles. These are called bian-de, ji-mian, or gan-mian, and are flat. You may also find crab, fish, spinach, shrimp or chicken flavored wheat noodles in various tints. Packages will be plastic wrapped and the noodles either in straight cut strands or flat sticks, coiled nests, or compact square cakes.

The fresh type should be boiled for 2 to 4 minutes while the dried need about 5 minutes. Add another minute or two if using frozen noodles. Try stir-frying the flat, spinach-flavored sort with bean sprouts, scallions, carrot julienne, and sliced mushroom, with a dash of oyster sauce. You may wish to add some strips of ham or seasoned, fried pork too.

A famous street hawker food in China's Sichuan Province are Dan-Dan noodles. Vendors balance pails of fresh wheat noodles and spicy sesame sauce on bamboo poles slung on their shoulders. The name comes from the "dan-dan" sound the pails make banging together as the vendors make their rounds.

Good brands to look for are Twin Marquis in plain or spinach, Canton Noodle Factory (in cream, shrimp, crab, or fish flavors), Sun Shun Fuk, and Wu Hsing Foods Company. Mong Lee Shang brand makes vegetable "instant" noodles in carrot, spinach, and yam flavors.

There are also Oriental Mascot in 13-ounce bags with green dragons labeled "Baton noodles," Chef Bowl brand in 5-pound boxes, and Iron Man in red and white 1-pound boxes. Sunlight brand makes "long life" noodles in a long looped skein of very thin noodles tied with a red band.

Other Noodles

CHINESE EGG NOODLES

This is the most common all-purpose Asian noodle with an elastic texture and egg-rich flavor. They are also called dan mian (thick round fresh ones), shi dan mian (thin tangles of fresh noodles), xi or cu (in Chinese), ba mee (in Thai), mii (in Lao), mi soi and mi xao (in Vietnamese), and are available fresh or dried. They are made from wheat flour, water, and egg dough, and range in color from neon to pale yellow. Some brands are colored with yellow food dye and may not contain any egg, so check the label. Fresh pliable soft noodles are found in plastic bags in the refrigerator case. You will find them sold in two widths: thin, thread-like strands and thick, round yellow noodles.

Shake the noodles loose to use. The round type are used to make what could be considered the national dish of Singapore: fried Hokkien mee. Noodles are stir-fried with shrimp, squid, lots of garlic, and sambal belacan, seasoned with a squirt of lime juice. Malaysia's national dish might be mee goreng, egg noodles fried with spices, scrambled egg bits, and vegetables. In Indonesia bakmi goreng is popular—spicy stir-fried egg noodles topped with a fried egg and garnished with bean sprouts and lime wedges. Mi xao gia is a Vietnamese dish made by stir-frying egg noodles with bean sprouts and scallions seasoned with sesame oil, sugar, and fish sauce. And in Thailand pork balls are wrapped in softened egg noodles and deep-fried to make moo sarong, eaten dipped in a sweet-and-sour sauce.

Dry noodles are found in compressed round cakes or nests. Some have been precooked by steaming and just need to be dropped into boiling water for a few minutes. The package label should state

In Singapore I used to listen for the tick-toc man. He wore an old peaked straw hat, baggy samfoo pants and, like the dan-dan men, balanced a portable noodle kitchen on bamboo poles. His specialty was mee swa soup, wheat noodles in a pork broth with ground fish and pork balls. To advertise his approach he tapped two long chopsticks together, making the "tick-toc" noise that brought housewives dashing out of their flats to purchase soup. You either brought your own bowl or he provided one, to be picked up later. All my neighbors had little stacks of soup bowls outside their doorways waiting his collection.

this information and give cooking times. Popular uses include chow mein dishes, soups, stir-fries, and pan-frying. Try the following for a fast and tasty meal. Tenderize thinly-sliced tender beef with corn flour and water, then season with light soy sauce, pepper, and sugar. Have some lightly scalded Chinese leafy greens too. Stir fry beef, set aside, and then toss the softened noodles in the pan juices, add a little light sauce made of oyster sauce, water, and soy sauce. Throw back beef and veggies, mix well, and serve. "Two sides brown" is a popular Cantonese fried egg noodle cake, soft inside and crispy-brown outside, with a variety of meat, seafood, or vegetables on top. You probably know this dish as chow mein or pan-fried noodles on your local Chinese restaurant menu.

egg noodles

Look for the Long Life and Gold Key quick cooking brands, both in square cellophane wrapped blocks of four cakes. More examples are the Hong Kong-style Pan Fried Noodle brand, STR Quick-Cooking flat Chinese noodle nests (eight to a package) in a red and yellow wrapper, and Taksan Fine Mee dried steamed round egg noodle cakes from Singapore (two long flat ones).

You may also find frozen ones, including Maruchan's Yaki-Soba (fried noodle) with seasoning in 17-ounce bags. Fresh noodles in nests or loose strands will keep a week in a sealed bag in the refrigerator or can be frozen. Dried egg noodles keep for months if stored in a covered glass jar.

noodle nest

WONTON NOODLES

Wonton noodles are another type of egg and wheat flour noodle found in the refrigerator case and freezer. These yellowish-brown noodles are sold in fine strands or ¼ inch wide flat strips. Drop fresh or frozen into boiling water about one minute before using. They are best known for their use in wonton soup, but they can also be used in fried noodle dishes, or served with meat, vegetables, and a sauce.

Look for the Twin Marquis brand in 12-ounce plastic-wrapped styrofoam trays or big 5-pound bags, frozen. Wonton Specialist makes 16- and 14-ounce packages of plain and chicken-flavored wonton noodles, fresh and frozen. Both are the thin strand type in nest clumps. Chicken powder is added to the dough for extra color and flavor in the chicken kind. Yung-Kee brand fresh wonton noodles in 1-pound bags are in the refrigerator case.

YI NOODLES

Also called yifu noodles and yi mien, yi noodles are round egg noodles woven into cakes, then deep-fried. In China they are called "noodles of the yi house" after a scholar-official and noodle gourmet, Mr. Yi Ping-Shou, who invented them in the 18th century. To use, break cakes into 3 or 4 pieces, then drop into boiling water and boil 1 minute or until noodles are tender but not soggy.

Drain off the water. Yifu noodles are stir-fried with strips of vegetables and meat and maybe à light gravy, or in a soup broth. Try them with strips of leftover roast duck, bean sprouts, carrot julienne, and scallions. Mr. Yi also came up with dry-braised yifu noodles. Chopped dried shrimp, garlic, ginger, and crab are stir-fried in a wok in peanut oil. Next, add a cup of clear chicken stock

yi noodles

and bring to a boil. Add a boiled, drained noodle cake and cook until the stock has been absorbed. Serve sprinkled with scallions and oyster sauce.

They are sold dried in 8-ounce, cellophane-wrapped packages about 10 inches in diameter. After purchasing store in a cool place or refrigerator. If left out too long they can become rancid.

FILIPINO NOODLES

These come in several varities. All are Chinese noodles called by Filipino names. Pancit Mami are flat Chinese-style egg noodles. Pancit Miki are eggless Chinese-style wheat noodles. Pancit Miswa are very fine wheat noodles that cook in a few seconds.

Still More Noodles

BEAN THREAD NOODLES

Also known as fen si (in Chinese), woon sen (in Thai), bun tau (in Vietnamese), pancit sotanghon (in Tagalog), glass, jelly, slippery and sil-ver, or cellophane noodles, bean thread noodles are dried semi-trans-parent noodles made from mung bean starch. The soaked beans are ground into a smooth paste, mixed with water, and strained. This liquid starch is then dried into sheets and cut into threads.

You should soak bean thread noodles in warm water until softened before using in soup or spring roll stuffing. They are good stir-fried with a spicy sauce, or served chilled in a salad with rice vinegar dress-ing. Thai yam wun sen is a Southern style salad made with bean thread noodles tossed in a spicy chili and lemongrass flavored dressing and topped with seafood. They are used in "lo-han chai" a braised vegetable dish containing dried Chinese mushrooms, cabbage, gingko nuts, and dried oyster. A simpler dish involves stir-fried cabbage and carrot strips, braised with the noodles and dried tofu in a light sauce. They have more texture than flavor and will absorb the flavor of the sauce or broth in the dish. To deep-fry, separate a bundle over a wide bowl (to catch

bean noodles

broken bits) and toss into hot oil in small hand-fuls. The puffed, crispy result is good as a gar-nish and added to seafood or chicken salads.

You will find bean thread noodles in pink plastic net bags containing six to eight individual plastic-wrapped bundles, each tied with string. Look for Goods brand Lungkow bean thread vermicelli with twin red dragons bordering a green or aqua logo.

BEANCURD NOODLES

Also known as gan si, beancurd noodles are usually only sold in markets near sizable Asian communities. They are made by cutting pressed tofu into thin strips and you will find them in the refrigerator case. Thin, dried tofu noodles, light beige in color should be softened in a mixture of baking soda and water, then rinsed. Used mainly in cold dishes and salad platters, they are also good stir-fried with meat, bean sprouts, and scallions, seasoned with soy and chili sauce.

You can make your own noodles by putting a cube of bean curd in a sieve and leaving a weight on top until most of the liquid drains out. Cut the compact square into noodle-like strands. Look for Chan Kee, Phoenix bean products, or AFC brands, fresh or frozen.

TIENTSIN FEN PI

These are dry, transparent, brittle round sheets made from ground mung beans and potato starch, about 9 inches in diameter with a slightly indented striated pattern on them. Fen pi literally means "the skin of the flour." They need to be soaked in hot water for about half an hour before using, then cut into the required size. They have a slippery texture—sort of a cross between rice noodles and cellophane noodles. Use in stir-fries, add to soup, or roll whole sheets around a meat, vegetable, or seafood stuffing and serve hot or cold.

A delicious Northern Chinese salad dish is cold shredded chicken served on folded pieces of boiled, chilled fen pi with a tangy mustard, rice vinegar, and sesame oil dressing poured over it.

They are found in large flat plastic wrapped packages, stacked in thin sheets and tied with string or gold cord. Look for the 8.8-ounce size Tian Jin brand in a bright yellow wrapper with a photo of the starch sheets on it.

PANCIT CANTON NOODLES

Also called flour sticks, pancit mian, and chuka soba (in Japanese), these are pale yellow, dried noodle cakes made in the Philippines from hard wheat flour, water, coconut oil, salt, and a yellow coloring. They have been pre-cooked by steaming, baking, and drying so are quick to prepare and don't even need to be boiled first. Add dry to soups and stews, pour curry gravy over them, or add to stir-fries with a little extra liquid. They soak up the sauce or broth and expand while retaining their chewy, light texture.

Look for Newton, Excellent, Golden Goose, Happiness "yung chung," and Jo-Na's brands in 1-pound bags. Use within several weeks of purchase.

PANCIT LUG-LUG NOODLES

Also called cornstarch noodles, pancit lug-lug noodles are long, skinny, semi-transparent, dried white noodle loops made in the Philippines from cornstarch and water. They are similar in texture to bean thread noodles and need to be soaked in hot water until soft before using in salads, casseroles, as an egg roll stuffing ingredient, or added to spicy soups and stews. They readily absorb the flavorings of any dish they are used in and have a slippery smooth texture. Look for Jo-Na's and Newton brands in 8-ounce packages.

CAMBODIAN NOODLES

These are called nom ban chock in Khmer. They resemble wide rice stick noodles but are made from tapioca starch, salt, and water. In Vietnam flat tapioca starch noodles are called hu tieu dai or mein and are labeled "my-tho." They are used in the same way as rice noodles but are slightly chewier. Look for Asian Boy tapioca sticks and the Hu Tieu Nam Vang product from Vietnam, available in two flat noodle nests. For a tasty one-dish meal try them stir-fried with pork and eggs in a light sauce made from soy, fish sauce, and garlic thickened with cornstarch. In Cambodia I ate these noodles smothered in a coconut milk sauce flavored with tumeric, galangal root, and fermented fish paste (pra hok). In Vietnam I had them pan-fried with beef, tomatoes, and celery, seasoned with fish sauce and white pepper.

KOREAN YAM NOODLES

Called tangmyon or sweet potato noodles, Korean yam noodles are similar to cellophane noodles and are made from a mixture of yam and mung bean starch. They become translucent when cooked and absorb the flavors of the ingredients they are cooked with. Soften in hot water for about 10 minutes before using. Good in stir-fries, stews, soups, chilled served with a pungent dipping sauce, or in salads. Look for off-white wiry strands in little bundles wrapped with gold tie twists in plastic bags with Korean lettering. Look for Assi brand, which has a cartoon smiling circle face logo, and Wang brand.

KOREAN BUCKWHEAT NOODLES

Also called naengmyon, Korean buckwheat noodles are pale brown and made from buckwheat flour and potato starch. These noodles are similar to Japanese soba, but have a chewier texture. Use noodles cooked and chilled in salads or in soup with a soy-based dipping broth on the side. Ja-jang-myun is made with buckwheat noodles served in a dark rich sauce made from miso (fermented soybean paste), beancurd, meat, and scallions. The noodles only need to be boiled for about 3 minutes before using. They are sold in extra long plastic bags, sometimes with pouches of soup stock powder included. Look for the Assi brand with the circle smiley face.

Korean noodles

UDON NOODLES

Also called U-Dong and kal guksu (in Korean), udon noodles are off-white fat flat strips, about ⅛ of an inch wide, made of wheat flour and water. Some varieties are round, about the thickness of spaghetti. Broad flat strips are called kishimen in Japan where they are popular in Osaka and the southern regions. Use in soup, dip in broth, or stir-fry. They need to be boiled for 10 to 12 minutes. Udon can be used interchangeably with soba and Chinese wheat noodles in recipes.

These dried Japanese and Korean noodles will be found in plastic packages, divided into segments with colored bands. Look for Hoshi Maru Udon in 3-pound packages of ten bundles, Futomaru Udon in 17-ounce bags and Hana brand in various sizes. In the freezer case look for fat Japanese-style San-Ukiya udon made by Shirakiku brand in 44-ounce (five servings) bags. In the ramen instant noodle section

udon noodles

you can find vacuum-sealed pre-cooked udon noodles with soup base flavoring packets. Good for quick meals, but the texture tends to be overly soft. Look for Myojo, Nama, Nikomi, Rokko, and Six Fortune brands.

SOBA NOODLES

These are Japanese noodles made from buckwheat flour; they are light brown and have a unique nutty flavor and slightly chewy texture.

Buckwheat came to Japan around the 8th century through Korea from China. It was eaten as gruel, mixed with rice. In the 17th century a visiting monk from Korea hit on the idea of mixing soba flour with a little wheat flour to give it more body. This way the dough held its shape and could be made into "sobakiri," cut soba noodles.

u-dong noodles

The best quality brands come from Japan and are sold in dried bundles, each wrapped in a colored band with about 3 bundles to a plastic wrapped package. The highest quality soba is called "ni-hachi," meaning 2 parts wheat flour to 8 parts buckwheat flour. Fresh soba may be found in plastic sealed packs in the refrigerator case and will be loose, not in bundles.

Soba noodles are good used in soups, stir-fries, or chilled as mori-soba. Traditionally this is served on a bamboo rack in a lacquer box with a small dish of cold broth made from soy sauce, mirin, sugar, and dashi stock and small dishes of chopped scallion and wasabi. The condiments are mixed into the broth and the noodles dipped in the mixture before eating. Sprinkle thin strips of nori (dried seaweed) over the cold noodles and you have zaru-soba. These are popular summer dishes. Hot soba comes in the same broth, but heated and topped with tempura shrimp, fried tofu, or fried crumbles of tempura batter (agedama). You will also find soba flavored with green tea (cha soba) and lemon zest or black sesame seeds. Dried soba needs to be boiled 4 to 5 minutes while fresh takes 1 to 1½ minutes.

Look for Shinshu Hachiwari brand in 7-ounce bags, Hadson (Toko) Trading Co. in 17.6-ounce bags labeled "obinata" omori soba, and JAS, 3 bundles to a package, wrapped in brown and white checked bands.

soba noodles

SOMEN NOODLES

These are called "khanom chine" in Thai, or angel hair. The delicate, white, hair-like strands are the thinnest of all Asian noodles. Somen are dried extra thin Japanese noodles made from wheat flour dough with a bit of oil. Hiyamugi are slightly thicker somen. These are delicious served cold with a soy and rice vinegar dipping sauce, in salads, or added as a light garnish to soups. They need to be boiled 2 to 3 minutes.

They are sold in beautifully wrapped packages of 5 to 6 bundles tied with colorful ribbons. Good brands to look for are JFC. Hime and Tomoshiraga from Japan and Wu Mu Alimentary paste (somen) from Taiwan with a bearded sage on the wrapper.

somen noodles

HARUSAME SAI FUN

The name means "spring rain." These Japanese noodles made from potato starch, cornstarch, and water resemble stiff white threads and when soaked, are similar to bean thread noodles. They are good added to soups, or cooked, then chilled, for salads with a soy and rice vinegar dressing. A beautiful tempura dish I had in Japan was a patty of minced shrimp with strips of harusame noodle pressed into it. After deep-frying, the patty resembled a chrysanthemum flower with the puffed noodles becoming petals. Look for Wel-Pac Maloney, Dynasty, and Hadson (Toko) Trading Co. brands.

RAMEN NOODLES

Also called chuka soba, this ubiquitous curly instant noodle, made from wheat flour, egg, and water, is sold in dried one-meal packets with assorted flavors of soup stock base usually loaded with MSG (monosodium glutamate) and other chemical seasonings. They are convenient, quick cooking, and you can use the noodles without adding the soup flavor pack. Just drop into boiling water for 3 to 4 minutes and add

ramen noodles

your own condiments, meats, and vegetables. You may even want to mix them with leftover curry.

Ramen is sold in individual size packages and in huge jumbo bags, with several dozen individually wrapped single servings in the package. There are numerous brands including Sapporo ichiban, Kung-Fu, Maruchan, and Ve Wong. You will also find the halal (meaning containing no pork, and suitable for Muslims) Indo-Mie brand and Vietnamese rice pho and bean thread ramen.

STOCKING UP

With such staggering varieties of noodles available, it is best to sample each of the main groups: rice, wheat, and egg. Decide which one you like best. Some people adore the thick, bright yellow egg noodles with their strong flavor. Others prefer the more subtle flavor of wheat or wonton noodles, the crunch of rice vermicelli, or the smooth slipperiness of udon or ho fun noodles. It's very much an individual preference, and most noodle recipes work just as well with your favorite sort. The important thing to remember is that noodles for stir-frying should not be boiled too long or they will stick to the pan.

Noodles are a versatile food, swirled in soup, twirled with chopsticks, sizzled into woks, topped with curry, dipped in sauce, and always slurped with gusto.

· 4 ·

Starches & Flour

과자

Korean for "cookies"

Throughout Asia various grains, beans, tubers, and roots are milled and ground into starches and flours. They are used as thickening agents, binders, and to make batters, buns, flat breads, noodles, dumplings, steamed cakes, puddings, and egg roll or wonton wrappers.

In Asian cooking, sauces are light, just barely coating the food, never thick. Corn, tapioca, and water chestnut starches are commonly used because they thicken faster and bind longer, giving the desired lightness and translucent glossy effect. Starches are also added to marinades, helping to coat foods properly and impart a smooth texture called "velveting." Certain starches and flours also protect food during deep-frying by sealing in the juices. Lastly starches are used to blend minced ingredients for stuffings or in fritters.

Starches and flours are found on shelf 5 in the Lin's grocery. You'll see piles of small pillow-like plastic bags filled with white powders. Most show pictures of dumplings on them, with both English and Asian characters describing the contents. You will find tempura batter mixes, Japanese breadcrumbs for coating foods to be fried, roasted soybean flour, and Vietnamese crepe mix in this section too.

WHEAT STARCH

Sometimes labeled as wheat flour, this soft, all-purpose flour has had the proteins (gluten) removed. It is a white powder with a fine texture, and it is used to make dim sum dough and delicate pastry wrappings.

wheat flour

When steamed, wheat starch becomes soft, shiny, and opaque white. Wheat starch may come ready mixed with another starch or flour such as potato or cornstarch. This makes a very crispy batter and is usually a combination of wheat flour, corn flour, and glutinous rice flour, in the ratio of 3:3:1. The label printed on the bag will give the flour content and often provides a recipe—steamed shrimp cakes, or Canton sponge cake, for example. Commonly found brands are Golden Bell, D & D Gold, Hawk, Caravelle, Polar Bear, Jumbo, and Asian Boy.

CORNSTARCH

Often labeled as corn flour, this is a fine white starch extracted from corn. It is possibly the starch most commonly used to thicken sauces and coat foods in marinades. Cornstarch is blended with equal amounts of cold water into a smooth paste and added at the last moment to sauces. It will look milky at first, then becomes clear and shiny as the sauce thickens. When used for marinating, it is blended with water and mixed with the meat before any other seasonings are added. This helps seal in the meat flavor. It gives a velvety texture to the cooked food. Cornstarch is used to dust food for deep-frying, and it produces a crisper result than wheat flour. Look for Golden Bell, Hawk, and Asian Boy brands in bags, and Argo in a box.

TAPIOCA STARCH

tapioca pearls

This can be either a fine powder or small round balls, called pearl tapioca, which are made from the tuber of the cassava plant. This starch is almost as popular as cornstarch for use as a thickener. Sometimes it is mixed with other flours to make dim sum and to dust wonton and egg roll wrappers, giving them a translucent sheen after steaming and keeping them from sticking together in the packages. The pearl type is used in desserts and as a texture ingredient in sweet or savory soups, puddings, and steamed tapioca balls with a spicy minced pork filling. Pastel-tinted pearls are also made for use in desserts such as Vietnamese che chuoi, a sweet soup made with coconut milk, tapioca, and bananas. Tapioca flour is seldom used in desserts except as a binder, often with coconut milk and sago or tapioca pellets in thick puddings. The flour is made by Golden Bell, Caravelle, Asian Boy, Erawan, and Hawk brands. For pearls, look for Summit, Farmboy, and Mount Tai brands in large, medium, and small white or pastel pellets in 16-ounce bags.

TAPIOCA FLAKES

Hard clear and color tinted bits and little squiggles that resemble legless centipedes are made from tapioca starch and used in jelly and coconut milk desserts. They expand slightly and become soft and chewy after soaking and boiling. Tapioca flakes add an element of texture and splash of color to creamy-smooth puddings and drinks. Look for Rotary, Bot Khoai, and Double Parrot brands.

RICE FLOUR

Sometimes called rice powder, this is made from finely milled raw long-grain rice. Rice noodles, pasta sheets, and dim sum wrappers are made from this flour, as are steamed cakes, pastries, and sweets. Rice flour is also used to make a batter for deep-fried sweet potato or banana fritters. Sweet pancakes are made from a rice flour and coconut milk batter, rolled up with palm sugar syrup and coconut shavings. Look for Tienley, D & D Gold, and Thai World brands.

tapioca flakes

GLUTINOUS RICE FLOUR

Also called sweet rice powder or flour, it is made from short-grain "sticky" or glutinous rice. Dumplings, buns, and pastries made with this flour have a chewy texture. A delicious sweet is onde-onde, balls made of mashed sweet potato and glutinous rice flour. A piece of coconut sugar is placed in the center of each ball, which is then dropped in boiling water to cook. The final touch is to roll the cooked balls in fresh grated coconut. Che bap is a Vietnamese sweet coconut milk and corn pudding thickened with glutinous rice flour. Fancifully shaped Japanese tea cakes and sweet bean jam stuffed dumplings are made from shira-tamako, refined glutinous rice flour. This flour is sold in 1-pound packages. The more common brands are Thai World, Erawan, Peacock, and Mochiko from Japan.

CHENG MIEN FLOUR

Also called tang fun, this is a gluten free rice flour used in Chinese pastry, dumpling, and noodle making. It becomes translucent when mixed with water making almost clear dough and dumpling wrappers. It is also used to make silver pin noodles and sheets of fun pasta. Sold in plastic bags. Look for Wu Hsing brand. You can substitute the more readily available potato flour.

ROASTED RICE POWDER

Known as khao kua pon in Thai and thinh in Vietnamese, this pale cinnamon-colored powder is a traditional seasoning and binding agent. Roasted rice powder is mixed with seasoned minced meat, fish, or vegetables in Northeast Thai-style and Laotian salads, called laab or laap, and is sprinkled over spicy soups. The powder binds shrimp paste grilled on sugar cane sticks and meat paste balls barbecued on skewers. It is made from raw glutinous rice that has been toasted in a hot skillet until nutty brown. It is

roasted rice powder

then ground into a sawdust-like powder. This is sold in small 3-ounce plastic packets. Look for the yellow Vietnam Food and Drink Co. and D & D Golden Bell labels. You can also make your own by grinding toasted rice in a spice or coffee-grinder and storing the powder in a glass jar.

Laap is Lao minced fish salad mixed with green onions, roasted rice powder, mint, lime juice, and lots of chili. It's eaten with your hands, scooped and folded in lettuce leaves from the communal dish. The word "laap" in Lao means luck. If you win the lottery, you eat laap. If you hope to win, you eat laap—and eating laap with a stranger might bring the luck to win!

POTATO FLOUR

Also labeled potato powder or starch, this flour is made from cooked potatoes. It is used as a thickening agent or binder, for making batters and marinades, and for dusting food before frying. It is more glutinous than cornstarch and gives a subtle glossy finish to sauces. Potato starch can be used interchangably with cornstarch in any recipe requiring a light sauce. In thickening the same amount of liquid, use about two-thirds the amount of potato flour as you would cornstarch. It also thickens hot-and-sour soup, is used to coat clams and other foods for frying, and is added to meatballs and Vietnamese pates as a binder and to yield a slightly springy texture after cooking. Look for Hawk, Golden Bell, Wel-Pac Katakuri-ko, and Wu Hsing brands.

WATER CHESTNUT FLOUR

A slightly grayish flour made from ground water chestnuts, this is used when a lighter thickening agent is needed for a savory or sweet dish.

The Chinese make a steamed cake with this flour, boiled together with sugar and finely chopped water chestnuts. The result can be kept in the refrigerator and slices cut off, dipped in egg and fried as desired. It can also be used to thicken delicate soups such as sharksfin. Other similiar thickening agents are lotus root or arrowroot starch. For water chestnut flour, look for Chi Kong and Li Hu brands in 8-ounce boxes. Pantang brand makes arrowroot starch. For lotus root starch look for Chekiang West Lake or Golden Lion brands.

MUNG BEAN STARCH

Also called salim in Thai and hoon kwe among the Hokkien-speaking Chinese, this is the starch extracted from the tiny green mung beans. It is mainly used as a thickening agent and in making sweet steamed cakes and desserts, often mixed with coconut milk. Cendol is a desert made with boiled mung bean starch strands mixed in palm sugar syrup and coconut milk served over crushed ice. Mixed with rice flour, it is used to make spongy, light steamed cakes. Look for the Pine Tree and Thai World brands.

SAGO STARCH

This starch is milled from the pith of the sago palm, a type of cycad. It is available in powder form and in small pellets. The powder is used as a thickening agent in sauces and, with coconut milk, in steamed desserts, such as kuih lapis, a chewy cake made by steaming colored layers of flavored batter. When sliced, the cakes look like little rainbow chunks. The pellets are used mainly to make puddings and sweets such as Gula Melaka, smooth sago pearls in creamy coconut milk and palm sugar syrup. Look for Asian Boy and Thai World brands.

KINAKO

A Japanese soybean flour, this is a light tan powder made by roasting and grinding soybeans. This flour is mixed with sugar and used to coat mochi (pounded rice cakes), ohagi (rice balls), and wagashi, a type of confection. Look for the Shirakiku brand and Assi roasted soybean flour, both in 1-pound bags.

VIETNAMESE PANCAKE FLOUR

Labeled Saigon Pancake Mix or bot do banh xeo, it is a prepared mix of rice flour and cornstarch with an attached pouch of ground turmeric. The powders are mixed together with water and coconut milk to make a thin egg-yellow tinted batter. Crispy crepes stuffed omelette-style with shrimp, pork or vegetables, called banh khoai or banh xeo, are made from this batter. Look for the D & D Gold brand in 12-ounce bags. The recipe is given on the package.

Vietnamese crepe mix

TEMPURA MIX

tempura mix

This is a prepared mixture of wheat starch, rice flour, salt, egg powder, and stabilizers. The mix is dissolved with cold water to make a thin coating batter. Shrimp and vegetables are dipped in this batter before being deep-fried. Look for Tung-I in 10-ounce boxes, Tippy, GoGi, or Lobo Thai brands in 5-ounce plastic packets, Caravelle in an 8-ounce box, and Zui Fa Food Co. tempura fry powder in a red and yellow bag. Instructions for mixing and using these mixes are found on the back of the packages.

PANKO

These are Japanese-style breadcrumbs used for breaded and fried foods. The crumbs are coarse and irregular-shaped and, after frying, give a golden-brown, crisp texture with a tasty toasted flavor. They absorb less grease and stay crunchy after sitting awhile. Try pork chops, oysters, squid rings, or shrimp dredged in panko and deep-fried. Serve with lemon wedges. Panko are sold in cellophane bags or boxes. Look for

panko (breadcrumbs)

Nishimoto Honey, Hana, Hadson Toko, and Oriental Mascot brands in 7- to 10-ounce bags and Rokko brand in 6-ounce packets.

STOCKING UP

You should add a box or bag of cornstarch to your shopping basket. It is a basic staple and the best all-purpose binder and sauce thickener in Asian cooking. Panko is a handy addition, and the tempura and Vietnamese pancake mixes are great for greaseless fried foods and fast-to-make, fun-to-eat crepes.

Finally, depending on how ambitious you are, you could get the necessary flours and try making breads, desserts, and cakes. Just reading some of the recipes printed on the bags may inspire you to whip up some dim sum dumplings, tapioca pudding, or rice noodle dough.

5

Flavorings
& Condiments

고추장

Korean for "flavorings and condiments"

It's hard for me to think of Asia without recalling the heady blend of aromas which permeate the air of marketplaces: the scent of curry paste in pungent mounds, smoking coconut oil and ripe fruits mingled with a fishy redolence and frangipani blooms. Then there are the delicious smells of sizzling food in huge woks from tiny kitchen stalls on the market's fringes—simple food, yet each bite packed with complex flavors. It is this blending of unusual aromatic and pungent seasonings that produces some of the world's most sensual and flavorful food.

To start, go to shelf 1. Here you will find shelves crammed with rows of jars filled with red chili pastes, tall bottles of salty liquid soy and fish extracts, shrimp pastes, bean sauces, distilled rice vinegar and spirits, cans or tubs of curry pastes, fermented beancurd, and nut or sesame seed pastes. You'll know you are in the right section by the faintly pungent odor of fermented fish and chili pepper wafting from the containers.

Salty Flavorings

HEALTH & FLAVOR

In the hot tropical climates of Southeast Asia pungent flavorings such as fish sauce are popular not only for the punch they add to food but also because they are believed to ward off diseases like malaria and cholera. Strong brands of this amber liquid made from salted, fermented fish are used liberally throughout the region from

Thailand to the Philippines. Fish sauce adds a salty taste as a table condiment and in cooking melds with other ingredients like palm sugar, citrus juices, coconut milk, and chilies, heightening and balancing a dish's flavor. Cooking dissipates the pungent aroma, mellowing the fishiness to a caramelized light salty taste. For other salty flavorants you can choose from many fermented, salted shrimp and fish pastes and soybean-based products. Oyster sauce is also an all-purpose seasoning with a distinct sweet, salty, and smoky flavor.

FISH SAUCE

Called nuoc mam (in Vietnam), nam pla (in Thailand), tuk trey (in Cambodia), and patis (in the Philippines), fish sauce is found in tall plastic and glass containers with the best quality found in glass containers. It is the basic salty, savory flavoring agent of Southeast Asia, replacing soy sauce. A thin caramel-colored liquid, it is made from the extract of fermented anchovies or other fish, has a distinctive pungent, almost rotten, odor, and is very salty. It may also be made from crab, shrimp, or squid. Used to season foods, it adds a special richness and fragrance; it is diluted in dipping sauces and used at the table like salt. Good brands to look for are Golden Boy, Aroy-D, Narcissus Fish Gravy, Tiparos, and Caravelle. Store away from direct sunlight and it will keep indefinitely, even in warm climates.

fish sauce

ANCHOVY PASTE

Called mam nem (in Vietnam) and bagoong bala yan (in the Philippines), this is a thick, grayish paste, much thicker than fish sauce. It is made from ground, salted, and fermented anchovies and is used as a seasoning in cooking—from soup stock to stir-fried vegetables, and to flavor plain rice. It is also strained in a sieve to extract a clear liquid which is diluted with fish sauce and lemon juice. This is mixed with pineapple pulp and juice and a paste made from pounded chilies, garlic, and sugar to make a delicious Vietnamese dipping sauce (nam nem pha san) for grilled or fried fish. Look for Asian Boy and Newton brands anchovy sauce. For Vietnamese Fish paste–pineapple sauce look for Two Golden Fish and Que Huong brands.

SHRIMP PASTE

Kapi (in Thai), terasi (in Malay), and mam ruoc (in Vietnamese). This fragrant but pungent smelling pale purple paste is made from ground, salted, and fermented shrimp. It smells worse than it tastes, and adds authentic flavor to Southeast Asian cooking. There are several types: one is soft textured, milder, and pinkish-lavender to grayish in color. It adds a distinctive flavor to many dishes, sauces, and curry pastes. Cooking tones down the odor and salty taste. The one from Penang, Malaysia, is a thick syrupy, brown-black paste labeled "petis udang." It is very strong, pungent, and slightly sweet. One delicious use is for rojak—a salad which features a dressing made of this shrimp paste, sugar, pounded chili, tamarind water, and lots of crushed peanuts. It

The Malaysian fish sauce chinchalok was probably first made in Malacca, a historic town on Peninsular Malaysia's west coast, ruled by the Portuguese in the 15th century, then the English and Dutch. A large Eurasian community thrives there, descendents of Europeans, Malays, and Chinese. The cuisine reflects this mixed heritage in such dishes as Devil Curry, spiced-up stews, and Portuguese baked fish.

can also be used as a dipping sauce for any raw vegatable or fruit, but may need some thinning down with a little water. Both soft shrimp pastes are found in glass jars and small plastic tubs. For the dark type, look for Wah Thai from Penang, Por Kwan, or CTF Thai thick paste in small round containers. Caravelle makes crab paste. Good brands to seek out for the pinkish-gray paste are Cheng Ki Kee, Lee Kum Lee, and Peony Mark. Kept in the refrigerater, both kinds will keep indefinitely.

Shrimp paste is used in the Thai red curry paste recipe on page 217.

SHRIMP SAUCE

Mam ruoc (in Vietnam), bagoong (in the Philippines), and chinchalok (in Malay). Near the shrimp paste you will see some products that look like they belong in a science lab. These are bottles of baby squid suspended in what appears to be cloudy pink formaldehyde and murky bottles packed with tiny pinkish-blackish, briny things—whole shrimps goggling you with their tiny pin-sized eyes! This is shrimp

shrimp sauce

sauce, a sort of liquidy version of shrimp paste, made from salt cured, fermented teeny shrimp or small squid packed in the fermenting brine. This pungent salty sauce is used to flavor soups, salads, dipping sauces, fried rice, and beef or pork dishes. Look for Kum Lee Kee and Mam Ruoc Ba Giao Thao brands. For chinchalok look for Sunrise Elephant in glass bottles, found in the refrigerater case. Kee Wee Hup Kee brand offers the squid sauce labeled "sotong cuttlefish-Tanjang Malacca" in 10.5-ounce bottles. Store in the refrigerator and it will keep indefinitely.

SHRIMP FRY

A Filipino product called Bagoong alamang, this is a shocking purplish-pink or pinkish-gray thick paste made from tiny salted, mashed, fried, and fermented shrimp. Very salty and pungent. Used to make dipping sauces or as a cooking seasoning. Look for Dagupan and Newton brands in glass jars.

Another similiar paste is called sauteed shrimp fry, or ginisang alamang. The salted shrimp mash is sauteed in oil and fermented with vinegar. Onion, garlic, and spices are added to some types, making a tangy-spicy-salty dip or seasoning sauce. Look for Newton and Rapenco brands for the pale pink plain type and Kamayan for the thick brown spiced kind. Lastly, there is bagoong padas, whole, salted, small anchovy-like fish in a pickling brine. Used to season stir-fries and soups and eaten with plain rice as a salty condiment. Look for Newton brand.

BELACAN

This is a dry, firm and dark-brownish cake made from sun-dried shrimp paste. Also has a very ripe, pungent aroma, and salty flavor. It is used in many sauces, sambals, and curry pastes. The chunks of dry paste are sold wrapped in foil and paper. It has to be roasted before using to release the flavor and temper the strong taste. It is used to make sambal belacan, a condiment made by pounding together roasted shrimp paste, red

hard shrimp paste-belacan

chilies, and lime juice—a must for authentic Malaysian or Indonesian dishes. To roast belacan, wrap a square in foil and grill or cook in a dry pan for a few minutes per side. It should be dry and crumbly. The best brand is Two Happy Swallow from Malacca. Store tightly wrapped in a cupboard or the freezer.

MUD FISH

Called Pla ra (in Thai), padek (in Lao), mam ca sac (in Vietnamese), and prahok (in Khmer). Mud fish is often labeled "Gouramy fish sauce." It is made of fermented chunks of freshwater fish preserved in a thick, gray, salty paste made from fermented rice husks and roasted rice "dust." It tastes potently fishy and salty. Found in glass jars and small cans. To use, break off a small piece, rinse off the paste and add to curries, soups, and vegetable dishes. It can also be made into a less intense liquid seasoning by diluting with water, boiling, and straining the fish chunks by pressing in a sieve and discarding the solids. This fish sauce is called tuk prahok in Cambodia and is indispensable to Khmer cuisine. Delicious and well worth making to use as a flavoring agent or dip. If you are adventurous, pep up the tuk prahok with finely chopped red or green chilies, garlic, and lemon grass, add lime juice and sugar, and mix into a dipping sauce. Serve with quickly seared paper thin slices of beef and a selection of raw vegetables. Also good in omelettes with holy basil. Look for Pantai, Sun Wah, and Asian Boy brands, all in 16-ounce jars. There is also Dragon & Horse cream-style (a thick pale creamy paste); Que Huong mam ca sac, a thick, dark brown sauce with chunks of mud fish; and pickled mud fish with papaya added, called mam thai du chau doc from C.TY, Vietnam. Store tightly closed to prevent the odor from scenting your kitchen or refrigerator.

mud fish sauce

PICKLED SALTED SHRIMP & FISH

Called mam tom chua (shrimp) and mam ca thu (fish). Similiar to fish paste and shrimp sauce, but made with salted and fermented whole de-headed medium-sized shrimp and fish slices in brine. The pickling solution contains fish sauce, oil, and sugar. Has a sour, salty, and pungent flavor, and is used to season soup, curries, and stir-fries. Sold in

16-ounce jars. For the shrimp type, look for Asian boy and Viet My. For the fish type, look for Queens brand pickled catfish and Asian Boy pickled mackerel steaks.

SOY SAUCE

This is a dark, salty liquid made from a mixture of soybeans, wheat, and water, which is then naturally fermented, aged, and distilled. Available in three main grades, light, medium, and heavy. Light is delicate and subtle in flavor and is served as a dipping sauce and used in light colored dishes and with seafood or poultry. Medium or thin soy sauce is saltier and darker than light, and full flavored. It is an all-purpose cooking or seasoning sauce. Dark heavy soy sauce has molasses added, is sweeter, full-bodied, and is often labeled as "superior soy sauce." This type is best used in hearty stews, in marinades, and to coat meats for roasting or barbecuing, as it gives them a deep mahogany color. All types are sold in various sized and shaped glass bottles. Good brands to look for are Kikkoman, Yamasa, Tung Chun thick or thin soy, and King Imperial Golden Light soy.

MUSHROOM SOY SAUCE

This is a smoother type of soy sauce with a rich, almost meaty, taste and woodsy essence. It is made from dark soy sauce infused with dried straw or shitake mushrooms. This is used as a seasoning, splashed into stews, or poured over stir-fries to add depth to the flavor, or added to marinades to give a light golden color to roasted meats and poultry. In Cambodia whole chickens are marinated in mushroom soy sauce and grilled to make mouan ang. Good brands are Pearl River Bridge, Foshan Superior Mushroom Soy, and Hai Tian.

KECAP MANIS

Pronounced "ketjap," it is a dark, thick, sweet soy sauce used in Malaysian and Indonesian cooking and as a table condiment. It is sweetened with palm sugar and seasoned with star anise and garlic. Kecap means "sauce added to food to enhance flavor" and it is where the word ketchup comes from. This is sold in glass and plastic squirt bottles with red plastic caps. Look for ASA and ABC brands.

KOREAN BULGOGI SAUCE

The traditional Korean seasoning for marinating meats which are grilled, pan-fried, or barbecued. Based on soy sauce, sesame, and carmelized sugar with liberal additions of chopped garlic, onions, and ginger to make a chunky liquid. Use as a flavorful all-purpose marinating and stir-fry sauce. Look for Lee Kum Lee and Assi brands in 8-ounce jars.

EEL SAUCE

Called unagi no tare, this is a syrupy grilling, broiling, and basting sauce made from soy sauce sweetened with corn syrup, sugar, or caramel, and flavored with mirin and sake. Made especially for grilled eel (unagi) but good with any grilled fish or poultry. Look for Assi and ANA brands.

OYSTER SAUCE

A concentrated savory sauce made from oyster extracts and soy sauce, this is a very rich and thick dark brown sauce with a slightly sweet smoky flavor. A popular and versatile seasoning, it is used in cooking or diluted as a dipping sauce. Also used as a condiment with meats and vegetables, especially sauteed greens. You can pour it directly from the bottle over stir-fried noodles or blanched vegetables. Found in glass bottles. Expensive brands are worth the price as they are better quality and contain more oyster extract. Look for Lee Kum Kee, Sa Cheng, and TRA Maekrua Co. brand from Thailand, with a picture of a woman pouring oyster sauce into a wok.

oyster sauce

HOISIN SAUCE

A sweet, tangy, dark reddish-brown bean sauce made from soy mash, sugar, flour, vinegar, and salt with garlic, chili, and sesame added. Often used to make barbecue marinade and as a glaze for roasted meats. This versatile, thick, rich paste is used in cooking and as a condiment, lending a spicy-sweet flavor. It is also made into a dipping sauce mixed with sesame oil for Mandarin pancakes served with Peking duck and Moo Shu pork. Different brands vary in texture from creamy thick to thin. It is sold in small glass jars or cans. Look for Koon Yick Wah Kee and Wei-Chuan brands.

hoisin sauce

CHAR SIU SAUCE

Also called barbecue sauce, it has a thick jam-like texture and rich reddish-brown color. It is made from fermented soybeans, vinegar, tomato paste, garlic, sugar or honey, chili, and other spices. This sauce adds a sweet, tangy flavor to grilled and roasted meats. Look for Bull Head, Lan Chi, and Yellow Lantern brands. Sold in jars.

SARSA ROAST SAUCE

An all around Filipino hot and spicy sauce for roasted meats, fish, and poultry. Use as a marinade and basting sauce. It is a thick, light brown liquid made from breadcrumbs, water, sugar, vinegar, soy protein, onion, garlic, and black pepper. Look for Mang Tomas brand. Mama Sita makes sarsa ng lechon, a marinade sauce for roast pork in glass bottles.

Vinegar, Wine & Sauces

VINEGAR

Asian vinegars are made from fermented, distilled grains and are lighter and slightly sweeter than Western white or cider vinegars—which do not make good substitutes. The main types found are: white (clear), red, and black. In this section of the grocery you will also find rice wines, tart tamarind concentrate, and a variety of sweet-and-sour dips and sauces which are used to balance or enhance flavors in a dish. These are the piquant notes that add a tangy spark and play against spicy hot, rich, smoky, and salty seasonings.

WHITE RICE VINEGAR

A clear, slightly sweet vinegar made from fermented glutinous rice, it has a mild flavor. Use like any vinegar in cooking and salad dressings, for pickling brines, sauces, or to add a dash to soups. This is essential in sweet-and-sour dishes. It is sold in clear glass bottles. Look for Pearl River Bridge, Great Wall, and Oriental Mascot brands. Store at room temperature.

BLACK VINEGAR

Also called Chinkiang vinegar, it is a product of Chekiang Province in China. It is made from fermented glutinous rice, which is then aged. Less tart than white vinegar, this is a thick, very dark brown vinegar with a complex, smoky, sweet mild taste and distinctive fragrance somewhat like balsamic vinegar. It is used in braised dishes, with noodles, as a dip or a seasoning, and is good added to soups just before serving. Black vinegar is sold in clear or green glass bottles. Look for Gold

black vinegar Plum, Koon Chun Sauce Factory, and Great Wall brands.

RED RICE VINEGAR

Red rice vinegar is clear, pale to dark brownish-red with low acidity. It has a slightly sweet, salty, and tart flavor and is used as a dipping sauce for seafoods, especially crabs and fried noodles, or added to soups. It is made from fermented and distilled red rice, barley, and sorghum. The Chinese believe red vinegar aids in digestion. Sold in tall clear or brown glass bottles. Look for Koon Chun Sauce Factory, Golden Bell, and Wu Tai Mountain brands.

SWEET RICE VINEGAR & COOKING WINE

This amber to brownish-black vinegar is thicker than plain rice vinegar. It has been processed with sugar and seasonings (anise, cloves, cinnamon, and cardamom) and has an aromatic and caramel-like taste with little tartness. Used in dipping sauces, marinades, and braised pork dishes. Sold in glass bottles with metal caps. Look for Pearl River Bridge and Phun Chun brands. Chinese sweet cooking wine, a little stronger than vinegar, is made by Mi Chui, Shenyang Lao Long Wine Factory, and Pagoda brands. Add a dash of this wine and pinch of sugar to stir-fried Chinese broccoli.

Every Chinese woman in confinement after delivery is expected to eat pork trotters and gingerroot braised in black vinegar. This is supposed to help with the healing process and to dispel the wind in the body.

COCONUT PALM VINEGAR

A popular sour flavoring agent in Filipino dishes, it is made from the fermented sap of coconut palms. It looks cloudy white in the bottle and has a lower acid content than most vinegars. Some brands have tiny pickled chilies, papaya, and onion shreds added. Used to marinate fish and meats, in soups, dipping sauces, and salad dressings. Look for glass bottles of Mama Sita's, Sarap, or Sukang Iloco, or any brands from the Philippines.

SHAOXING WINE

Made in Shaoxing, a city in Eastern China, it is a famous Chinese rice wine made from a blend of fermented glutinous rice, millet, and yeast, and aged at least 10 and up to one hundred years! It has a rich amber color, a full-bodied bouquet, and alcohol content similar to dry sherry, with a rich flavor and aroma. Served as a drink chilled or warmed up, it is essential at banquets. This wine is also used in cooking and added to marinades and sauces. It is sold in earthenware jugs that should be tightly corked after opening and kept at room temperature. Found also in clear or brown glass bottles. Look for Pagoda supreme Shao Hsing and Quing Hu Fine Shaoxing Chiew brands.

shaoxing wine

PLUM SAUCE

Also called Duck sauce, this golden to amber colored jam-like sauce is made from a puree of salted plums, apricots, yams, rice vinegar, and chilies. It has a spicy, sweet, tangy flavor and resembles a fine chutney. The chunky sauce is often served with roast duck in restaurants, thus the name "duck sauce." Also popular as a dip served with deep-fried appetizers and barbecued spareribs. Try mixing a little plum sauce with honey and pour over cold silken tofu. Add chopped spring onions and eat cold for a delicious, refreshing dish. It is sold in small glass jars and different brands vary in thickness and flavor intensity. Look for Pearl River Bridge, Zu Miao, and Tung Chung brands. Thai sweet prune sauce made from preserved prune paste, sugar, and vinegar is made by Nguan Soon Hand brand. Great as a dip for egg rolls.

SWEET & SOUR SAUCE

This well-known sauce is made from vinegar, sugar, chili, ketchup, and sometimes ginger. Used in a variety of sweet and sour dishes and as a table condiment and dip for fried egg rolls. Sold in glass jars. Look for Wei-Chuan, Por Kwan, and Amoy brands.

LEMON SAUCE

A thick sweet-sour translucent sauce made from lemon and tangerine peel, lemon oil, sugar, and cornstarch, seasoned with ginger, licorice, white pepper, turmeric, and star anise. It is used to add a sour note to dishes and is heated and poured over deep-fried or grilled chicken strips. Look for Wei-Chuan brand in 8-ounce glass jars.

HONEY GARLIC SAUCE

A thick, pale yellow creamy sauce with a sweet tangy flavor. Used as a dipping sauce or marinade for roasted foods. Good with egg rolls, chicken wings, or shrimp toast—triangles of bread spread with a seasoned paste made from shrimp and deep-fried. Can also be used as a dip for steamed dumplings or thinned into salad dressing with rice vinegar. Look for Lee Kum Lee brand.

TAMARIND

This comes from the fat, brown, bean-shaped fruit pod of the tamarind tree. The pod is filled with seeds and a sticky dark brown pulp. The sour juices extracted from this pulp are used as a flavoring agent in cooking. In Southeast Asia it is used as we use lemons, to add a fruity tart note in curries, soups, stews, and dipping sauces. Shrimp stir-fried in tamarind sauce with ginger, garlic, and ground turmeric is delicious. You will find it in two forms: in plastic wrapped bricks or in jars of strained concentrate. If you get the pulp kind, soak several seeds in water, then press through a sieve and use the collected brown liquid. Tamarind concentrate is more convenient as it has no seeds and is used straight from the jar. If you can't find either, substitute lemon or lime juice, sweetened with a little brown sugar. Look for Erawan and Super Brand of Bangkok in semi-soft packets or Caravelle brand "Fruit Candy" pulp bricks. CTF Thai Food Co. offers pure concentrate in plastic tubs. You will also find jars of chili-tamarind paste (nam phrik pao), a thick spicy seasoning made from fried garlic, shallots, and chilies blended with tamarind concentrate. It is used to make hot-and-sour soups, salad dressings, and dipping sauces, or added to stir-fries. Look for P. Pra Teep Thong brand.

FRUIT DIPPING SAUCE

This sweet-sour spicy dip for raw fruits such as guava and mango is made from palm sugar, salt, and crushed chilies. It is thick and golden colored and can also be used as a table condiment, added to fried rice noodles or used to make hot-and-sour soup. It is delicious with slices of green mango or papaya. Look for Por Kwan Thai brand with a photo of fruit and a bowl of dip on the label.

Nut & Seed Pastes

SESAME PASTE

Zhi-ma-jiang is a thick, rich, creamy, pale brown paste or "nut butter" made from toasted white sesame seeds. It adds a nutty taste and aroma to

sesame paste

food. Sesame paste is used in dressings for cold or hot noodle dishes, vegetables, and salads, mixed with a little oil and water. Also used as an ingredient in cooked dishes or sauces. If the paste has separated in the jar, blend contents in a food processor or blender. After using a portion of the paste, cover with a protective film of fresh oil to prevent contents from drying out. Will keep indefinitely if refrigerated. Look for Pearl River Bridge, Lan Chi, and Zebra brands, all in small glass jars. Use in the sweet sesame rice noodles recipe on page 215.

In Kuala Lumpur I used to enjoy eating sticks of satay grilled by hawkers that set up around dusk in a car park across the Klang River from the fairytale domes and moorish minarets of the Jame mosque. Smoldering charcoal fires and kerosene lanterns lit the Jalan Benteng parking lot as it turned into a huge outdoor restaurant. Satay men sweated over coals waving palm leaf fans over skewers of basted meats and shrimp.

SATAY SAUCE

This is a rich, spicy, time-saving sauce—made from ground peanuts, palm sugar, coconut cream, tamarind, and a spice paste. It is mainly used as a marinade and dip for Southeast Asian satay—skewered bits of meat, seafood, and vegetables grilled over charcoal. Satay sauce is always heated and served warm. The heated sauce is also tossed with cooked rice noodles, boiled seafoods and blanched greens. Look for Ayam brand in cans from Malaysia, with a rooster on the label. More choices are Bambu, Yeo's, Who Hup, and Bangkok Cuisine peanut sauce dip, all in jars.

satay sauce

GADO-GADO DRESSING

Similar to satay sauce, it is a creamy, coconut and peanut paste flavored with shrimp paste, lemongrass, and spices. In Malaysia and Indonesia, it is poured over a combination of shredded chicken, boiled eggs, and vegetables and topped with puffed shrimp crackers or potato chips. It is sold in glass jars and cans and looks like a thin, pale, peanut butter. Look for Ayam and Bambu brands.

Chili & Hot Sauces

Eating garlic is believed to ward off mosquitoes in hot tropical climates, and great amounts are consumed. Garlic is also added to fiery hot chili sauces, another staple of Southeast Asian cuisine. Spicy hot foods are said to cool a person by taking heat from the body through evaporation. You sweat, then feel cooler as even tepid air hits your sweaty skin. So, stay cool and add some volcanic heat to your cooking with any number of chili products in the hot sauce segment of shelf 1.

CHILI SAUCE

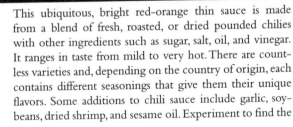

This ubiquitous, bright red-orange thin sauce is made from a blend of fresh, roasted, or dried pounded chilies with other ingredients such as sugar, salt, oil, and vinegar. It ranges in taste from mild to very hot. There are countless varieties and, depending on the country of origin, each contains different seasonings that give them their unique flavors. Some additions to chili sauce include garlic, soybeans, dried shrimp, and sesame oil. Experiment to find the

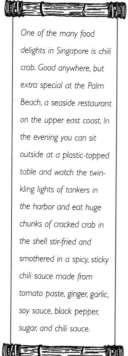

One of the many food delights in Singapore is chili crab. Good anywhere, but extra special at the Palm Beach, a seaside restaurant on the upper east coast. In the evening you can sit outside at a plastic-topped table and watch the twinkling lights of tankers in the harbor and eat huge chunks of cracked crab in the shell stir-fried and smothered in a spicy, sticky chili sauce made from tomato paste, ginger, garlic, soy sauce, black pepper, sugar, and chili sauce.

flavor that you prefer. Look for Yank Sing chili pepper sauce, Lan Chi brand, or Sun Wah Best. Other hot chili sauce brands include ABC Tropical, Lee Kum Lee, Yeo's, ABC Tropical, and Koon Chun.

GINGER CHILI SAUCE

The basic chili, salt, and sugar mix with a hefty dose of crushed ginger added. This is made to accompany Hainanese chicken rice (steamed chicken served in slices with rice cooked in stock), but can be used as a table condiment, dipping sauce, seasoning ingredient, marinade, or sauce for steamed foods. Smear some on a whole fish, scatter scallions over the top, and steam. Finish with a drizzle of hot peanut oil and garnish with sprigs of cilantro. Look for Delichoice Hai Nam Ginger Chili Sauce and Kee Wee Hup Kee.

SRIACHA SAUCE

First made in the seaside town of Sriacha in Southern Thailand, it is a mixture of chili, tomato, salt, garlic, sugar, and vinegar with a bright red color and the consistency of ketchup. It makes a good all-purpose chili sauce and table condiment. Sold in 17- and 24-ounce plastic squeeze bottles with green caps and a rooster logo, made by Huy Fong Foods, Inc., in California, following the original Thai formula. Imported brands include D & D Gold and Shark Sriacha.

PICKLED GROUND RED CHILI

Also labeled "Ground Fresh Chili Paste," this is a Thai concoction of red chili, garlic, and vinegar. It is a thin, bright red sauce with chili

seeds and is used as a dipping condiment or for adding hot-sour touches to stir-fries and noodle soups. Look for Combine Thai Foods Co. and Mae Ploy brands.

Mr. Lin, who was born in Krabi on the west coast of Southern Thailand makes a specialty of the region, yellow curry, when he feels homesick. He simmers fish steaks in a turmeric heavy curry paste thinned with tamarind water. He adds pickled red chili sauce, some bamboo strips, and a squeeze of lime to create a delicious, deeply flavored hot and sour dish.

pickled ground red chili sauce

SWEET CHILI SAUCE

Called nuoe cham ga in Vietnamese, it is a thick red translucent sauce made from ground red chilies with the seeds, sugar, garlic, vinegar, and salt. This is used mainly as a dipping sauce and glaze for grilled and fried chicken or seafood. It has a hot, sweet, and tangy taste. Sold in glass ketchup-shaped bottles. Look for Mae Ploy Thai brand with a photo of grilled chickens and a bowl of sauce on the label.

KOREAN KIM CHEE PASTE

Called gochu-jang and kim chee base, this is a thick, brick red, salty paste made from ground red chile peppers mixed with fermented soybean paste and glutinous rice flour. It is used to season layers of baechu (Chinese cabbage) salt pickled to make kim chee. Koreans also use this as a table condiment and to flavor stir-fried and simmered dishes. It has a hot, salty, but mellow taste. Found in glass jars and plastic bottles. After opening, store in the refrigerater for up to several months. Look for Momoya brand in 6-ounce jars.

BANANA SAUCE

This bright red, thick, pureed sauce is like ketchup in consistency. It is made from bananas, water, sugar, vinegar, ground red chilies, salt, and spices. It is a popular Filipino table condiment and is used to color and flavor fried rice or noodles. Look for ketchup-shaped glass bottles of Ju Fran Hot and Papa brands from the Philippines.

banana sauce

SAMBAL BADJAK

An Indonesian and Malaysian style chili paste (thicker than chili sauce) made with roasted chilies, onions, soy oil, and garlic. It is very thick, dark reddish-black, and very hot with a smoky undertone. Look for Huy Fong Foods Rooster brand with a gold foil label in 8-ounce plastic jars with bright green caps. A Thai, reddish-black version called nam prik pao is made by Mae Ploy and Maesri brands, both in 16-ounce jars.

SAMBAL OELEK

An Indonesian thin chili sauce used throughout Southeast Asia, it is bright red and made from ground chilies (seeds included), vinegar, and garlic. It is very spicy and slightly sour, and is used for seasoning stir-fries, or added at the table to noodle soups or other dishes. This is also used in making acar, a type of pickled vegetable condiment. Look for Huy Fong Foods Rooster brand with a gold foil label in plastic 8-ounce jars with green lids.

sambal oelek

SAMBAL BELACAN

This Malaysian paste or sauce is made from red chilies, dried roasted shrimp paste, water, and lime juice. It is very pungent, with a smoky-hot taste. Used as a condiment or added to various dishes in cooking. Pound and chop some dried shrimp, fry until fragrant with belacan, and use to stuff small spring rolls. Found in small plastic or glass jars. Look for Tan Kim Hock and Glory brands.

CHILI PASTE WITH SWEET BASIL

This thick Thai paste made from ground chilies, oil, sweet basil leaves, and salt, is used to flavor coconut curries and soups or to season stir-fries. It is very hot, spicy, and aromatic from the basil. Sold in 8-ounce jars. Look for Cock brand from Thai World Imports & Exports.

NAM PRIK

The name means "hot or spicy water" in Thai, and this is a staple of Thai cuisine. It is a liquid paste made by pounding together tiny hot chilies, garlic, shrimp paste, fish sauce, lime juice, sugar, and small crushed pea eggplants. You will find ready made nam prik paste in small

Thai nam prik paste

tin cans or jars. To use, mix several teaspoons of paste with enough water to make a thin dip or sauce. Mainly served with platters of raw vegetables and fried fish with rice to soak up the heat. It is delicious but extremely hot! Look for Maesri brand in 4-ounce cans.

Curry Pastes

The Curry pastes of Southeast Asia should not be confused with the yellow Indian curries, which are made from a mix of spice powders. Thai, Indonesian, and Malaysian curry pastes are intense, thick, moist blends of aromatic herbal ingredients and spices.

The curry pastes are classified by their color, which ranges from brick red and yellow-orange to deep green, and how they are used. Red and yellow-orange pastes are used in many dishes, while others, like the green, are very specialized, and used in only a few. The mildest of the pastes is Massaman or Muslim curry paste, and the green is by far the hottest. While it is pleasurable to make them by hand, much more convenient (and time-saving) are the wide range of pre-mixed pastes sold in small cans and jars and large plastic tubs. All of the following types are made by Mae Ploy, Maesri, and Asian Home Gourmet brands. They will last almost indefinitely if you keep a thin layer of oil over the surface to prevent mold. The pastes can also be frozen.

GREEN

Gaeng kiow wan in Thai, this is made from a mix of two types of fresh green chilies, lemongrass, coriander root, garlic, shrimp paste, kaffir lime leaves, and salt. It is hotter than red and used in coconut curry sauces and with beef, pork, or chicken dishes.

green curry paste

RED

Gaeng pet in Thai, this is the classic, most widely used and versatile curry paste. It is made from dried long red chilies, coriander roots and seeds, garlic, shallots, kaffir lime leaves, lemongrass, shrimp paste, and galangal root. Although hot, it is slightly milder than green. Popular uses are in red chicken, duck, beef, pork, or shrimp curry, and soupy noodle curries, dips, and marinades. To make your own red curry paste see the recipe on page 217 and use in the shrimp coconut curry dish on page 211.

YELLOW CURRY PASTE

Krung kaeng kari in Thai, it is a mellow sweet-spicy paste blend based on mild yellow turmeric and curry powder pounded together with coriander seeds, lemongrass, shrimp paste, dried red chilies, and shallots. This mild paste is commonly used with chicken, onions, and potatoes in yellow chicken curry and fish stews.

COUNTRY-STYLE CURRY PASTE

Nam phrik khing or chow na in Thai, this paste has a smooth peppery flavor and concentrated taste. This is used to make "dry-style curries," blended with just a small amount of chicken broth to make a thick sauce and "country-style" dishes made with pork, chicken, or fried fish. The secret ingredient in this paste is the crushed pork crackling blended into a mixture of dried red chilies, shrimp paste, and spices.

SOUR CURRY PASTE

Krung kaeng som in Thai, this is an orange, slightly sour, curry paste made from a combination of tamarind concentrate, vinegar, red chilies, shrimp paste, shrimp, salt, and garlic. It is used mainly to make tangy seafood soups, fish, and vegetable curries or with steamed fish.

In Southeast Asia various mouth-watering blends of curry paste are made fresh daily, mashed and pounded in a stone mortar and pestle. This rhythmic sound of stone thumping against stone emanates from kitchens in the late afternoons from Bangkok to Ubud in Bali as women pound together herbs and spices to enrich the evening meal. They mash a multitude of herbs, including coriander roots, kaffir lime zest and leaves, and lemongrass, with shrimp paste, gingerroot, garlic, peppercorns, and of course chilies. Varying proportions of chilies and other ingredients create the various taste differences.

PANANG CURRY PASTE

Known as krung kaeng Panang in Thai, this paste is named after the island off the west coast of Malaysia, just south of Thailand. This paste is popular in both Thai and Malaysian cooking. It is a distinctive smooth, well balanced, mellow, and moderately hot curry paste made from large dried red chilies, shrimp paste, kaffir lime juice and leaves, coriander seeds, stems and leaves, lemongrass, galangal root, garlic, and sometimes crushed peanuts. Look for Ayam Malaysian brand.

MASSAMAN

Krung kaeng Massaman or Muslim curry is a rich mild paste named after the Muslim people of South Thailand and Malaysia. It exudes an exotic aroma from sweet fragrant spices mixed with dried, de-seeded (so less hot) red chilies, coriander seeds, cumin, cinnamon, cloves, star anise, cardamom, garlic, and shrimp paste. The result is a rich, intense, but very mild curry when blended with coconut milk. Often used to make a stew-like curry with beef, potatoes, and peanuts or made into a broth for egg noodles, or blended with ground peanuts to make satay sauce. Look for Ayam brand in small cans.

STOCKING UP

Although there is a bewildering array of sauces, pastes, and condiments to choose from in this section, there are certain basic items the Asian cook always has in stock. You should pick up some soy sauce—both light and dark if desired, but at least a light one. A bottle of oyster sauce and another of rice vinegar are essential. For table use, it is good to have a bottle of chili sauce, either a sweet one or a chili-garlic one. If you like Thai food or seafood soups, do have some fish sauce on hand as well. Finally, be adventurous, add some curry paste, sambal belacan, and maybe some bean paste.

star anise

6

Oils

Korean for "oils"

Are you wondering what you will use to stir-fry your rice sticks and vegetables or deep-fry those bean thread noodles or some egg rolls in? Head to the far end section of shelf 1 of the Lins' store to pick from a variety of cooking, flavoring, and seasoning oils. Oils are mainly used for basic cooking—stir-frying, sautéing, and deep-frying, but are also used in marinades to add flavor. Small amounts of aromatic sesame oil and chili-infused oils are used as a seasoning ingredient, table condiment, or added to marinades and dipping sauces. Most oils will keep a long time stored in a cool dry place away from direct sunlight.

PEANUT OIL

Peanuts, or groundnuts, were introduced into China in the 16th century where they were successfully cultivated. The oil pressed from this little legume quickly replaced other vegetable oils, and it is now the preferred oil in China and throughout Asia. It has a pleasant, mild taste and heats to high temperatures without burning, which makes it ideal for deep-frying and stir-frying. You will also find semi-refined cold pressed peanut oil. Some cooks prefer this type for its distinctive flavor and fresh peanut fragrance. Look for Lion & Globe brand cold pressed oil, with a gold and green label, in large pour spout cans or plastic bottles. Another cold pressed brand is Double Happiness,

peanut oil

with Chinese characters on a gold and red label, in metal cans or plastic bottles. For regular oil look for Akita, Knife, Red Lantern, and Panther brands.

CORN OIL

A light, healthy, mostly polyunsaturated oil processed from corn, it is slightly heavier in flavor than peanut oil but good for cooking, having a high burning temperature. It has a distinctive smell and taste, so should not be used in delicate dishes. Look for Husty, Red Lantern, and Lam Soon brands in various sized plastic bottles and jugs.

OTHER VEGETABLE OILS

These may include sunflower, soybean, safflower, cottonseed, and rapeseed (canola) oils. They are light in color and taste and can be used for most cooking, but tend to smoke quickly. Thus they are not as efficient as peanut or corn oil for deep-frying.

PALM OIL

An oil extracted from red kernels of the palm oil tree, produced on huge plantations in Malaysia, it is the most commonly used cooking oil in Southeast Asia. Palm oil has a light golden color and rich mild flavor. It is high in saturated fat, but it is easily digested and contains vitamin E and beta carotene. Palm oil has a variety of uses—besides cooking, it is made into products like margarine, soap, and cosmetics. Look for brands imported from Malaysia.

SESAME OIL

This very aromatic, strong flavored, thick, rich golden or dark brown oil pressed from roasted white sesame seeds has a distinctive nutty taste. It is not normally used for cooking, but added as a final seasoning ingredient, drizzled over dishes at the table, or used in marinades. Sesame oil subtly enriches a dish without overwhelming the basic flavor. It may sometimes be used in cooking, but mixed with a larger amount of other oil. Sesame oil is also used in many cold dishes, as a flavoring ingredient in dressings or dipping sauces. The best quality, purest brands tend to be Japanese with clean and aromatic flavors. Look for Kadoya and Maruhon. Other good brands include Lee Kum Lee, Woh Hup, Seng Oil Factory pure black sesame, and Pagoda Top Grade Sesame Oil. Only buy the brands in dark glass bottles—others tend to be old or rancid. Store away from direct light, preferably in the refrigerator and it will keep a long time.

sesame oil

CHILI OIL

Also called chili-pepper oil, it is made by steeping crushed flakes or whole dried red chilies in oil. The infused oil has a sharp, peppery-hot flavor that enlivens foods. Good added in small doses to jazz-up bland soups or egg dishes. Has a rich tawny color due to the chili pigments. Chili oil is used as a dipping sauce, as a table condiment, and for seasoning, but never for cooking. It varies in strength and flavor depending on where it comes from. Sichuan is milder than the chili oils from Southeast Asia. Thai and Malaysian versions are extremely hot, while Taiwanese and Chinese products are more subtle. Chili oil is sold in small glass bottles and jars, and it should be stored in a cool dark place to prevent turning rancid. Look for Koon Yick Wah Kee, China Bowl Select, Sun Wah Best, Evergreen, and Kodoya chili oils; chili lovers may go for Pepper Tree Red Chili Hot Oil.

chili oil

STOCKING UP

Stock up on peanut oil as your main Asian cooking oil. Include sesame and chili oils for flavoring and seasoning dishes.

7

Vegetables

Chinese for "vegetables"

Asian people love their vegetables. They show great respect for each one's integrity and true flavor: no over-cooked mushy green stuff here. Crispness, bright color, and freshness count. Vegetables are probably the most important ingredient in Asian cooking, appearing in almost every dish. The versatile vegetable stars in the Buddhist's vegetarian dishes and complements other ingredients in simple or complex flavor combinations. Tender hearts of bok choy play off succulent shrimp; rich black bean-chili sauce and crunchy water chestnuts create a delicious whole. Mild, sweet, grilled eggplants are intensified with splashes of fish sauce and rice vinegar along with the bite of chili pepper and garlic.

Asian vegetables are classified by three characteristics. First, there are the roots and underground stems such as taro and radishes. Next there are the leafy vegetables such as bok choy and mustard greens. Finally there are fruits like winter melon, gourds, and peas. Fresh mushrooms are also found in the produce section. When shopping, choose from all the categories. Root vegetables can be stored for several weeks, if kept free of moisture in paper bags and refrigerated. Fruit-type vegetables should be used within a week; they should be refrigerated and stored in open paper or plastic bags (to allow them to "breathe"). Leafy vegetables should be kept dry and unwashed in plastic bags and stored for no more than four days.

Root Vegetables

TARO

Woo tau. This tuber root ranges in size from a small potato to a long fat yam. It has dark shaggy brown skin and a pale speckled or purplish streaked bland-tasting flesh. It is starchy with a sweet nutty flavor and doughy texture. Taro becomes somewhat slimy or gummy when cooked and it is often paired with duck or fatty pork.

Taro can be baked, braised, boiled, steamed, stewed, or deep-fried into chips. It is also ground into flour and made into a paste to

 fill dim sum or for dessert puddings such as Hokkien "or ni" (black earth) which conceals luscious morsels of soft gingko nuts. You must peel it before using. Choose a firm one—press the skin to make sure the root is not soft or dried up. Store in a cool dry place and use within a week.

taro

WHITE RADISH

Loh bak, and luo bo in Chinese and labanos in Tagalog. This is also called icicle radish, Chinese turnip, mooli or daikon (which means "great root"). Some can weigh up to 30 or more pounds. Once in Japan, I came across an elderly lady hauling a giant daikon home, strapped into the seat of a baby stroller! They look like huge smooth-skinned white carrots, and raw daikon has a sweet mild peppery flavor and is juicy but crisp. The Japanese have many uses for it: in salads, shaved into thin threads as a sushi garnish, grated and added to dipping sauces, deep-fried for tempura, braised, or stewed.

daikon radish

It soaks up other flavors and blends well with rich, fatty, or spicy ingredients. In China it is used mainly in slow cooked stews, soups, and braised dishes, much like a potato. In Vietnam it gets carmelized with fish sauce and sugar in slow-cooked fish and pork dishes and is used raw in salads. In Singapore soft grated shreds are fried with garlic and egg—and for some reason called carrot cake. The first time I ordered it, I was expecting a slice of sweet cake with icing, so you can imagine my suprise when a savory dish appeared (but it was very tasty). White radish is also pickled. The root is a good source of vitamin C. Select rock hard roots which feel heavy, and store up to two weeks, refrigerated.

> The small type of taro is a traditional item for the Mid-autumn dinner in Hong Kong. It is boiled in its skin. The cooled taro are peeled, dipped in sugar, and eaten after dinner while the family toasts the full moon.

KOHLRABI

Gai lan tau. This large, pale green, round, bulb-like stem is in the same family as Chinese broccoli. Looks like a giant baseball with cut off stems sprouting from the top and sides. It is about 3 to 4 inches in

kohlrabi

diameter and may have a few shriveled leaves attached on top. The flesh is creamy white and firm with a slight cabbage flavor and crisp texture. Eaten raw or cooked. To use, cut off stems, leaves, and base, and peel. Slice in strips or cut in cubes and use braised, steamed, or stir-fried with meat or poultry. The whole root can be parboiled and sliced or shredded for salads. Keeps a week in a paper bag.

LOTUS ROOT

This resembles a string of hard, pale beige sausages. It is the rhizome of the lotus flower that grows in muddy ponds throughout Asia. To use, cut the segments apart at the narrow sections between the oblong links. Peel and slice crosswise to reveal a flower-patterned Swiss-cheese cross-section of air holes that run the length of the root. Lotus has a mild sweet taste, faintly reminiscent of artichokes, and adds crunch to soups and braised dishes. It is also used raw in salads, and can be pick-led, steamed, stir-fried, candied, or deep-fried to use as a garnish. Buy crisp firm roots which are free of brown bruises. Will keep, uncut and refrigerated, for two to three weeks. Lotus root is often boiled in a soup with pork bones and peanuts, and is

lotus root

said to be good for the lungs. For quick relief from heat rash, mash fresh lotus roots into a pulp and apply to the skin. Use in the lotus root pickle recipe on page 219.

JICAMA

Sa kot. Also known as yam bean, this is a pale tan, medium to large hard round root tuber with leathery skin and sweet, crunchy, white flesh. It originated in South America and is related to the morning glory vine and sweet potato, but now it is grown all over Asia. This root is more fibrous than water chestnuts but makes a good substitute for them. Jicama adds a crisp texture when used raw in salads and mu-shoo pancake fillings. It is delicious cut in thin slices, sprinkled with lime juice, and dipped in salt mixed with chili powder. This versatile vegetable can also be boiled, stir-fried, or deep-fried. You can make a vegetarian spring roll using blanched jicama strips, carrot julienne, bean sprout, and finely sliced Chinese mushrooms. Pick firm ones without mold spots. Keeps one to two weeks, refrigerated and wrapped in plastic.

WATER CHESTNUTS

Fresh water chestnuts are walnut-sized, dark brown skinned corms that are grown in muddy ponds or rice paddy edges. These must be peeled to use and have a mild slightly sweet taste and crunchy texture. They are sliced or chopped and added to stir-fries, soups, and egg roll or dumpling stuffings, and eaten raw in salads or as snacks. Also can be peeled and simmered with rock sugar for a cooling drink. Buy firm ones with tight, unwrinkled skins. Soft ones are old or rotten. Will keep, unpeeled in a paper bag in the refrigerator for two weeks.

water chestnut

TWO-HORNED WATER-CALTROP

A water root or corm, sometimes found in Asian groceries, this has hard shiny black shells that look like bizarre little bats or twin-horned rhino beetles. Must be boiled or steamed before eating, and can be used like water chestnuts, which they resemble in taste. Using a nut cracker, crack the shells after boiling and pry out the small round off-white tubers. Will keep two to three weeks in a bag, refrigerated (in their shells). This is another item which often appears around the mid-autumn Festival and is eaten then.

CHINESE ARROWHEAD

Tsu goo. These pale tubers appear in Asian markets during winter and early spring and are the size of water chestnuts. They look like little eggs with one sprout on the top. The ivory tubers are covered in thin, papery brown peeling skin and have a sweetish, slightly bitter flavor and crunchy texture. To use, peel, rinse, and cut off the sprout. Can be cooked whole, sliced, chopped, braised, or stir-fried in the same way water chestnuts are used. Also are mashed as a bed for grilled or sauteed dishes. Store in a paper bag, refrigerated, for up to a week.

BAMBOO SHOOTS

Chuk sun. There are two main types of fresh bamboo shoots: spring and winter. The winter shoots are best: they are smaller and more tender than spring shoots. Both have a mild sweet taste and add a crunchy texture to the dish. Whole fresh shoots look like pointy cones with an overlapping scale-like pattern of greenish and golden-brown papery leaves. The leaves must be pulled off and the pale, fibrous shoot has to be parboiled to use.

You will also find pale yellow, sliced or shredded bamboo shoots floating in tubs of water, sold by weight. They have been processed, but don't have the tinny taste of canned ones. Use bamboo shoots in stir-fries, hot-and-sour soups, fried rice, curries, and egg roll stuffing. Make sure the

bamboo shoots

shoots in water don't have an off odor or slime coating. Store in water in a plastic container, changing the water daily, and they will keep one week, refrigerated. Unpeeled whole shoots will keep at least a week. Bamboo shoots are often cooked with meats to neutralize the "hot energy" of the meat, thus providing a necessary balance.

Leafy Vegetables

CHINESE BROCCOLI

Also called Chinese kale or gai-lan, it has thin, dusty green smooth stems, wavy oval-shaped dark leaves, and tiny white edible flower clusters in the middle of the plant's center stalk. The leaves taste a bit like slightly bitter swiss chard. The stems are reminiscent of asparagus with a crunchy texture. Kale is very nutritious and rich in iron, calcium, and vitamins A and C, and is frequently stir-fried with meats or just plain with garlic, a dash of sugar, and a splash of rice wine. It can be added to fried noodle dishes or blanched in salted boiling water and served drizzled with oyster sauce.

chinese broccoli

Look for stalks with thin stems as larger ones tend to be older and more fibrous. The tender young stems are a delicacy. There's a version called kai lan sum, or kai lan heart, which is a 7-inch stem, about 1 to 2 inches in diameter with a tiny crown of leaves and flowers. These are best lightly steamed or stir-fried quickly to retain the fresh flavor. The outer skin of large or tough stalks may be peeled before being cut in transverse chunks roughly half an inch thick. Will keep three to four days, refrigerated in a plastic bag.

BOK CHOY

This is also called pak-choy, bai cai, or Chinese white cabbage. It is a versatile vegetable with long, smooth, creamy white stems and large, dark green, crinkled leaves. The stalks have a mild tangy taste and crunchy texture. The leaves are tender with a peppery spinach-like flavor. The smaller the plant, the more tender it will be. Bok choy cooks quickly and is good stir-fried or chopped

bok choy

> Another seasonal use of bamboo comes on July 7th for Tanabata, or Star Festival. It originated in China, where it's known as Maiden's Festival to celebrate an immortal love story between two celestial lovers—the cowherd and weaver lady—the stars Altair and Vega, forever separated by the Milky Way. On the night of the 7th day of the 7th month, they can meet as the birds of heaven form a bridge over which they can cross. In Japan, people write love poems and tie them to decorated trees made from bamboo. Chilled somen noodles are eaten (representing the bridge) and delicate vinegared salads featuring bamboo shoots.

and added to soups. Choose the ones with crisp stalks and no yellow spots on the leaves. Rinse the leaves in several changes of water and drain before cutting and cooking. Store wrapped in paper towels in the refrigerator for up to a week.

FLAT CABBAGE

Called tat soi in Japanese, and tai goo, or tai gu cai. This cousin of bok choy has short stems, thick rounded flat, very dark green leaves, about 5 to 10 inches across. Has a flavor similar to bok choy, with the small tender leaves being more delicate, sweetish, and juicy. Bigger leaves have a stronger flavor. Good stir-fried with soy sauce, garlic, and ginger or added to soup, even raw in salads or lightly steamed. Sold in plastic bags, by weight. Use within a day or two of purchase. Store loosely wrapped in the vegetable bin of your refrigerator. Wash well to remove any grit.

SHANGHAI CABBAGE

Another type of bok choy, it is smaller and jade green with spoon-shaped stalks and curved short leaves. The very small young ones are called baby Shanghai bok choy. The hearts of these are considered a delicacy in China and are often served at banquets. It has a sweeter taste and is less fibrous than regular bok choy. It is sold in bunches of 5 to 6 in plastic bags, or loose by weight. Excellent stir-fried, blanched, and drizzled with oyster sauce or added to soups or other vegetable dishes. Cooks quickly and retains a bright green color and a soft, slightly crunchy texture. Rinse

shanghai bok

and drain before using. Wilts and yellows easily, so best used within a day or so of purchasing. Baby bok choy are added to the vegetable stir-fry recipe on page 212.

MUSTARD GREEN

Also called Chinese mustard cabbage or gai-choy, this has deep green stems extending into broad, oval-shaped, ribbed and ruffled leaves with a distinctive astringent, tangy taste. It is very rich in vitamins and calcium. Older mustard greens are pickled in brine with chilies. Fresh, young tender ones are used stir-fried, seasoned with ginger and garlic, or chopped and added to soup. Look for firm, crisp leaves and stems; avoid limp, yellowed or hole-pocked ones. To use, wash in several changes of water and drain before slicing into pieces. Keeps refrigerated about a week.

mustard green

AMARANTH

A leafy vegetable called een choy, snow cabbage, or red-in-snow. It is a very hardy plant which pokes up through the snow-covered ground

in early spring, thus the name. There are two types you may find. One is green, similar to spinach but with broader leaves and thicker light green stems. The other variety has red stems and green leaves with reddish-purple streaks in the center. Both have an earthy, cress-like, slightly peppery-tart flavor. The leaves are added to soups and stir-fried, braised, or steamed dishes. Amaranth should look fresh with no wilted leaves and is best eaten right away. It will keep one day, stored in the vegetable bin of your refrigerator, wrapped in paper towels and in a plastic bag.

amaranth

STEM LETTUCE

Wo sun. This Chinese lettuce is grown for its thick pale stem and looks like a fat white asparagus spear with a bunch of light green leaves at the top that resemble leaf lettuce. The leaves are mainly added to soups. The crunchy stems are about 10 inches long and 1 to 3 inches thick. The greenish-white stems are grooved with light brown scars from where old leaves fell off. Tastes like mild celery with a crisp texture. Both stem and leaves are pickled. The stems are peeled and cut in chunks or julienned and stir-fried. Good with meats or fish and seasoned with oyster sauce. Can be added to soup or lightly boiled. Young tender stems can be used raw in salads. Store loosely wrapped, refrigerated up to two weeks.

FLOWERING CABBAGE

This is related to bok choy and is also known as choy-sum. The plants have slim, long, bright green stems, broad oval-shaped leaves, and small, edible, yellow flowers. Another very quick-cooking vegetable with a mild mustardy flavor, it is good stir-fried, added to noodle dishes or soups, and used in dumpling fillings. It also can be used as a salad green. Wonderful stir-fried with black mushrooms, lightly seasoned with soy sauce and garlic. Look for firm stalks and make sure there are no brown spots on the leaves. Wash well and shake off water before using. Will keep about one week, wrapped and refrigerated.

flowering cabbage

NAPPA CABBAGE

Also called Peking cabbage, Chinese celery cabbage, and Tientsin, this comes in two shapes. One is squat and football-shaped with a tightly packed head; the other has long stems with less compact leaves. Both have milky white stalks and pale green ruffled leaves. They have a sweet mild taste and can be used raw in salads. It is a versatile vegetable used in soups, braised, or stir-fried with meats and other rich ingredients as its sponge-like quality absorbs flavors easily. The large outer leaves can also be parboiled a few minutes until softened, then stuffed and steamed. Ignore the tiny black spots sometimes found

nappa cabbage

73

near the base—they are normal and result from unpredictable climate conditions. Look for firm cabbages without any shriveled leaves. Keeps about three weeks, refrigerated. Chinese cabbage is said to contain Vitamin U, which is used in the treatment of ulcers. For a vegetarian Buddhist recipe using nappa cabbage see page 209.

The Chinese prefer spinach with the sweet reddish-pink roots attached. This is poetically called "red-mouthed green parrot." Imagine the red tips as a bird's beak and the spinach leaves as feathers. Be sure to clean the roots well, using a small knife or your fingernails.

WATER SPINACH

Also called ong-choy, kangkong, or swamp cabbage, it is a hollow-stemmed aquatic vine with dark green arrow-shaped leaves. It belongs to the sweet potato family and grows in the waterways throughout Southeast Asia. All of the plant is used except the tough lower stem parts and roots. It tastes like spinach and, like spinach, reduces when cooked, so buy a lot. Wash well and drain to remove any mud from the stems, before cutting and cooking. Add this vegetable to soups and curries or stir-fry with garlic, sambal belacan, and small dried shrimp. The soft leaves provide a pleasing contrast to the crunchy stems. Blanched water spinach is used in Asian salads that feature a peanut sauce, such as gado-gado and satay bee hoon (noodles with satay sauce). Store in a plastic bag in the refrigerator for up to four to five days. You can substitute spinach.

water spinach

BEAN SPROUTS

Nga choy. These are made by soaking dried green mung beans until they sprout. The sprouts have pale yellow heads with silvery 2-inch stems trailing a root thread. In Asia, ladies crouch on stools to remove the head and tail of the shoots, leaving only the pale stem. This is not necessary—it just makes a prettier sprout. You can simply toss the whole sprout into any number of dishes to add a light crunchy texture. If you want the sprouts to stay crisp, don't add them to a hot mixture until just before serving. A gourmet dish can be created by stir-frying the sprouts for 1 minute in a touch of oil, then serving them with flaked, crisp-fried salted fish. You can also parboil them for a minute, drain and chill to use in salads. When buying bean sprouts, avoid limp, wilted, or brownish ones—they should be crisp. Only buy what you need, because they won't keep long.

mung bean sprouts

Fruit Vegetables

BITTER MELON

Foo-kwa. Also called bitter gourd. It resembles a wrinkled cucumber with a light green to yellowish-green, bumpy, ridged skin. It has a

sharp, bitter taste. Yellowish ones tend to be slightly milder. The fibrous seed core is usually scooped out, leaving rings of melon skin and flesh. Bitter melon can be stir-fried

bitter melon

or sauteed with rich, salty, and spicy ingredients to mellow the bitterness. It can be cut in half and parboiled in salt to reduce bitterness. You may want to dig out the inner membrane and stuff the shell with seasoned minced pork, then steam it. It can keep up to five days in the vegetable crisper. This "cooling" fruit is said to be a blood purifier and good for the digestion.

FUZZY MELON

Mo-kwa. Also called hairy squash. There are two varieties, both with apple green skin covered with short hairs: one is long and about 2 to 3 inches in diameter, while the other is short and oval shaped. You should peel the skin before cooking. It tastes like a mild squash or cucumber. It can be stewed with pork and dried prawns, added to soups and Indian curries, or sauteed or stir-fried with salty and spicy ingredients to pep up the bland taste. It can keep up to a week in the refrigerator.

fuzzy melon

BOTTLE GOURD

Also called po qwa, woo lo qwa, and hu lu gua or nam tao in Thai. Two shapes are found of this pale green, smooth skinned gourd. One looks like a small baseball bat and is somewhat larger, from 12 to 24 inches long and 3 to 4 inches thick. The other resembles a small bottle or flower vase and is about 7 to 8 inches long and 3 to 5 inches thick. Has white smooth textured flesh and tastes like summer squash. Look for firm gourds, peel, and scoop out the seeds. Can be cut in half lengthwise, hollowed out, stuffed with a meat and vegetable mixture, and baked. Use also in soups and stir-fries. Good with spicy seasonings as it is bland. Keeps up to a month, stored in the refrigerator.

In Japan never call anyone a pumpkin. It is not a term of endearment. Calling someone an old kabocha (pumpkin) is an insult. In fact, it means a cross, ugly old witch of a person! Also, pumpkin is not too popular with older folks in Japan. When food was scarce during the war, people grew and ate an awful lot of it. To this day, the sight of it makes them sick.

WINTER MELON

Tung qua. This pumpkin-shaped wax gourd has a frosted white and pale green skin. It can range from a few pounds up to 100 pounds or more! You will often find it cut in wedges, sold by weight. The interior flesh is white with yellow seeds and if buying by the wedge, check to make

winter melon

75

sure it hasn't dried up or turned yellow. The flesh is soft with a sweet mild flavor. It turns almost transparent when cooked and is popular used in soup with duck, pork, chicken, or crab. The empty melon shell is often carved into decorative soup tureens. Whole winter melons will keep for two to three months in a cool dry place, and wedges should be covered in plastic wrap and used within a week.

SILK SQUASH

Also called Chinese okra and sponge gourd, this is a long, thin, cylindrical squash, tapering at one end with deep narrow grooves running the length of the vegetable. Peel off the ridges and use sliced crosswise. If it is small and young, leave on some of the green skin; if older, it is best to peel away all the skin as it can be bitter. When cooked, the inside turns soft and spongy, and it absorbs the flavors it is cooked with. Tastes a little like zucchini or okra-flavored cucumber. This squash can be fried up, omelet-style, with egg, or used in braised dishes. It can be deep-fried and served with a pungent dipping sauce. Look for firm, small sized squash without dark spots. Keeps refrigerated about one week.

silk squash

Thais are Buddhists and merit making is an important aspect of the religion. One way to make merit (tum boon) is to offer food to monks. Every morning people drop packets of rice with tasty morsels into monks' alms bowls as they make their rounds. July through September is Buddhist Lent season (also called the "rain retreats" as this is the rainy season too) when monks devote themselves to spiritual studies. Wing beans are at their peak then, so this crunchy salad is a favorite tum boon offering.

KABOCHA

Also called fak thong in Thai, this is a small, squat, pumpkin-shaped squash with a hard dark-green mottled shell and sweet, mild flavored interior flesh. The skin is difficult to peel—it sort of chips off. A popular item in Thai cooking, it is often added to curried fried rice and coconut curry soups, stir-fried with basil and tofu, served as a dessert in sweet coconut milk, or filled with custard and steamed. It is also used in Japan for tempura, or grilled with miso, simmered, or stewed. Choose a firm feeling one, and it can be stored in a cool dry place for two to three weeks.

WING BEANS

This legume, called tua proo in Thai, is also known as four-angled bean or asparagus pea. It has four serrated, ruffled ridges resembling wings running the length of the bean—from 4 to 5 inches up to a foot. It can be blanched and added to salads and

wing beans

other cooked dishes or served raw as a crudite for hot chili sauce dips. They have a delicate flavor, reminiscent of asparagus. Look for firm beans without any dark spots and store in loose bags in the refrigerator for up to a week.

CHINESE LONG BEANS

Bak dau gok. Also known as snake bean, long-podded cowpea, and yard-long beans as they grow up to three feet long and are often sold in looped coils or loose knots. These green chopstick-thin beans are really the immature pods of black-eyed peas. They are drier, more dense, and crunchier in texture than regular green beans. The beans' mild flavor blends well with pungent and spicy seasonings. Chopped finely, they can be fried in a soft omelet. They

chinese yard-long beans

can also be deep-fried and mixed with soy sauce, garlic, and chili paste, or blanched and served in salads. Look for fresh, flexible beans without dark spots. Store in the refrigerator in a plastic bag and use in four to five days.

SNOW PEAS

Hoh laan and he lan dou in Chinese and chicharo in Tagalog. The name derives from the fact that they were an early spring crop in ancient China, harvested when snow was still on the ground. The ones grown in the West tend to be larger and available year-round. Snow peas are flat tender pods with a sugary, mild flavor and crisp crunchy texture. They are completely edible, but the stem ends should be snapped off and strings running along the sides removed by pulling. They make delicious additions to stir-fried vegetable dishes, soups, and salads. They go especially well with fresh shrimp. Pick young snow peas that are free of dark patches and look brilliant

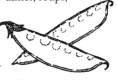

snow peas

green, flat, and crisp. You should use them within a few days.

In Japan, some people believe eating eggplant (nasu) can lower your body temperature and many mothers warn their children not to over-indulge in them, so as not to lose their pulse. It is also used in Japanese folk medicine. A powder is made from the tops of eggplants to cure many ills, especially hang-overs and upset stomachs. Cut-off eggplant tops are applied to warts.

PEA SHOOTS

Dau mui and dou miao. These are the tender tiny leaves, stems, and tendrils from snow or garden pea plants. They have a delicate flavor and are stir-fried quickly with just a touch of oil and a little water or light seasoning or added to soup and noodle dishes. The shoots should be fresh and not look wilted. Use the same day they are bought or at the latest the next day.

77

SUGAR SNAP PEAS

These are green peapods, similar to snow peas, but having thicker skins with small peas inside the pod. The whole pod and peas are eaten so they don't need to be shelled. Just remove stem ends and fibrous strings. These crunchy pods have a sweet taste when cooked and are

good stir-fried with just a touch of garlic. They can also be added to rice and noodle dishes, or steamed and tossed in salads. Buy the young, tender pods as larger ones tend to be tough. Will keep one week refrigerated, in a plastic bag. Sugar snap peas are a sweet, snappy addition to the vegetable stir-fry recipe on page 212.

sugar snap peas

EGGPLANT

The most commonly found Asian eggplants, called ai qwa (in Chinese) and terong (in Malay) are slim and long, or plump and stubby with pale lavender to dark purple skin and black stem tips. They have a delicate mild flavor and soft absorbent texture. They don't have the seeds which make Western eggplants bitter, neither do they require peeling, salting, or rinsing. Use them stir-fried with strong spicy seasonings and meats or eggs. They are also good braised in curries, grilled, and topped with a light tangy sauce, roasted or deep-fried in tempura. If you are feeling adventurous, you might like to halve the eggplant, spread it with one or two cubes of fermented bean curd and steam it. The tiny Thai green pea-sized ones, called mak-hua phuang are added to curries and nam prik, a hot dip for raw vegetables and fried fish. Then there are the round white, pale green, and yellowish or cream striped ones called ma-kheua solanum, which range in size from golf balls to marbles. They are eaten raw with spicy dips or cooked in curries and stews.

asian eggplant

Always choose a firm eggplant which has no soft or brown spots. They can be stored up to two weeks, refrigerated, in loose paper or plastic bags. Eggplants are said to prevent hardening of the blood vessels. Try the grilled Thai eggplant salad recipe on page 206.

Fungi

MUSHROOMS

Fresh varieties include oyster mushrooms with large, wide, fluted greyish-beige caps, a faint oyster aroma, and delicate flavor. Enoki are tiny white mushroom with slender 2- to 3-inch-long stems and small caps with a mild flavor and slippery texture. They are often used raw in salads or added to clear soups. Nameko mushrooms have small reddish-brown caps on pale, short stems and are very slippery— it's best to rinse them before using to remove

oyster mushrooms

some of the clear goop they are covered in. Shitake are dark brown mushrooms with wide flat caps, short hard stems, and a rich meaty flavor. Only the caps are used as the stems are fibrous and tough. They are good in earthy clay-pot stews or added to dumpling stuffing. All varieties of mushrooms have a velvety-smooth texture and can be stir-fried, braised, added to egg, rice, or noodle dishes, and soups. Shitake are good *enoki mushrooms* grilled—remove the stems and cut a cross in the cap. They can also be stuffed with a shrimp paste and deep-fried. Serve with a soy sauce dip and grated daikon radish mixed with red pepper powder. Make sure you choose firm ones and wipe off any moisture before wrapping in kitchen paper and storing in a plastic or paper bag in the coolest part of the refrigerator. Oyster, enoki, and nameko will keep up to one week, and shitake can keep up to two weeks if properly stored.

shitake mushrooms

Adding healthy and nutritious vegetables to your diet is easy and delicious when you cook Asian-style, or Asian-inspired, dishes. With a good stock of veggies, you need only small amounts of meat, seafood, or bean curd to round out a meal with a pot of rice or bowl of noodles. So, get your vitamins and enjoy eating them too!

STOCKING UP

Basic root veggies to stock up on are white radish (daikon), water chestnuts, and bamboo shoots. Then choose several leafy greens such as bok choy, nappa cabbage, and bean sprouts. Round out your shopping with eggplants, snowpeas, and at least one fresh mushroom.

· 8 ·

Herbs & Aromatics

สมุนไพร

Thai for "herbs"

One of the most distinctive aspects of Asian cuisine is the blending of seasonings, from fresh herbs and aromatic rhizomes to pungent chilies and fragrant leaves. Herbs add scent, flavor, and splashes of color. Essential oils in the leaves, stems, or flowers release aromas and flavors when cooked. Certain herbs add character or are crucial components in making, for example, Thai food Thai. The classic combination of lemongrass, chili, lime, and coriander define the flavor of Thai food just as mint, cinnamon, and sweet basil do Vietnamese, or spring onions, chives, and ginger infuse Chinese dishes.

Many herbs are native to Asia while some come from far away. Others were brought with waves of immigration from other regions in Asia and were adopted and incorporated into the indigenous cuisine. What is hard to believe is that the chili pepper, one of the hallmarks of Asian cuisine, only showed up in the 16th century, brought by the Portuguese. Today, dozens of chili varieties can be found throughout Asia and permeate the cooking.

You will find the chilies and fresh herbs in the produce area of the Lins' grocery. These items, arranged in eye pleasing patterns in plastic baskets, are kept fresh with regular spritzes of water. In general, most herbs will keep about a week when stored correctly. After purchasing, wipe off any moisture with a paper towel, then wrap in a cloth to absorb any condensation and keep in an airtight

chili pepper

plastic container in the refrigerator. Other storage tips for specific herbs will be included where appropriate.

Chilies & Chives

FRESH CHILIES

Chilies contain varying degrees of heat depending on size, shape, color, or type. The general rule of thumb is: the smaller and greener the chili, the hotter it will be. Red chilies are riper versions of green chilies, thus slightly less hot. Probably the most common are the finger-length chilies found in red and green or yellow, which are hot but not overwhelming. Next are the medium-length plump chilies, which can be yellow, pale orange, green, or red. The slightly larger, smooth-skinned, round serrano chili is a bit milder than the stubby dark green or red jalapeño, but both are strong flavored and packed with heat. The very hottest is the tiny, ½-inch to 1-inch long "birds eye" or "rat dropping" red or green Thai chili (phrik khee nu). This little 3-alarm chili is used whole as a garnish, added to soups, or nibbled on during meals.

Experiment and find what chili is best to your taste. The heat comes from the whole pepper but the tip end is the mildest and the area where the seeds attach to the membrane is the hottest. Any chili automatically loses its fire when the seeds are removed. Slit the chili lengthwise and rinse under running water, being careful not to let the chili oils irritate your eyes or skin—wearing rubber gloves helps. If you find the chili is too fierce, drinking water or beer only spreads the hot oils around your mouth. You are better off quenching the heat with a mouthful of rice, which soaks up the fire. Sugar on your tongue also helps. Some of the many uses for this versatile gift from the New World to Asia include

"rat dropping" chilies

being pounded into sauces, pastes, and dips, and used sliced or whole in cooking, pickling, and preserving foods. Fresh chilies will keep for several weeks, kept dry in a paper or plastic bag and refrigerated.

CHINESE CHIVES

Gau choy. These are long, thin, flat chives that look like blades of grass. Tastes like a blend of garlic and onion and is a popular Chinese flavoring herb. Good stuffed in summer rolls, added to dumpling fillings, snipped and sprinkled over cooked dishes or in soup as a garnish. They can be used the same way as Western chives but have a stronger flavor and coarser texture. Chinese chives are sold by the bunch. Will keep, refrigerated and wrapped in a plastic bag for up to three days.

CHINESE GARLIC CHIVES

Also called gau choy sum or flowering garlic chives, they have long, flat, green blades with teardrop-shaped, cream-colored edible buds at the tip, and a delicate garlic taste. These are sold by the bunch, and are generally lightly cooked rather than eaten raw. Look for ones with tightly closed buds as they are younger and more tender. Good stir-fried with eggs, bean curd, or prawns, or added to soup and other dishes for an onion-garlic flavor. Try them stir-fried with mussels with garlic, pepper, and oyster sauce. The filling of pot sticker dumplings (wor deep) is made of seasoned minced pork and chopped chives. They also make a pretty garnish.

YELLOW CHIVES

Also called gow wong, yellow chives taste similar to mild or sweet onions and are flat with a pale yellow color as they are grown with no exposure to sunlight. They cost slightly more than other sorts of chives and are sold by weight. They are used in soup and dim sum dishes or as a garnish. Store loosely wrapped, refrigerated.

Onions, Etc.

SPRING ONIONS

Also called tsung or cong (in Chinese), ton horm (in Thai), and scallions, they have hollow round green stalks tapering to a white stem base. Spring onions grow in clusters and are sold in bunches, wrapped with a plastic or rubber band. They are used raw as an herb to add flavor and a touch of bright green color in soups, noodle dishes, or stir-fries and are wrapped in rice paper summer rolls. Try adding half a cup sliced scallions, sliced beef pieces, and chopped watercress to an egg batter and fry into patties, called minari juhn in Korea. Serve with a sesame, soy, and chili dipping sauce. They will keep a week or more if refrigerated with the stem ends in a glass of water. You may also find spring onion flowers called chong far or chang hua. They are about a foot long and have thin round, pale green stems with a long greenish bud, which is hollow on top. Chop and add these to stir-fries.

Scallions are used to garnish pad Thai noodles on page 210, are added to the bean curd cabbage recipe on page 209, and to the sweet sesame-rice noodles on page 215.

SHALLOTS

Called hom daeng (in Thai) and bawang merah (in Malay). The red Asian shallot is the everyday onion of Southeast Asian cooking. They are small, garlic-clove shaped, mild flavored, aromatic members of the onion family with coppery-red skins and light purple interiors. They are used extensively in cooking, pounded seasoning pastes, and salads. They are pickled in acars (mixed vegetable pickles) or sliced and deep-fried to use as a crispy garnish. Store in a cool, dry place but not in the refrigerator.

Greens

CORIANDER

Yuen sai. Known alternatively as cilantro, or Chinese parsley, it is indispensable in Southeast Asian cuisine. It has delicate, flat, green, ruffled leaves with a distinctive aromatic flavor. Roots are ground and used in marinades and

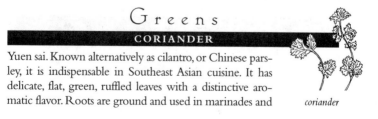

coriander

chinese parsley

curry pastes. Leaves are used for garnish, in dipping sauces, or chopped and sprinkled on to add flavor to many dishes. Choose fresh unwilted bunches with crisp stems. Store by standing in a glass of water in the refrigerator with the tops loosely covered in a plastic bag.

Use to garnish the recipe for green papaya salad, page 205, and Balinese tomato lemongrass broth on page 208. The roots and leaves are used in the grilled eggplant salad recipe on page 206.

CHINESE CELERY

Kun choy. This somewhat straggly, slender plant resembles cilantro. The stems are thin and hollow and very crisp, ranging from almost white to deep green. It grows in bunches of stalks topped with flat cilantro-like leaves. The leaves have a strong celery flavor and are used as an herb. Mainly added to soups (the Malay name, duan sop, means "soup leaf") but sprigs are also added to some fried rice and noodle dishes. Portions of the chopped stems may also be added to stir-fried dishes. It is sold in bunches and will keep several days, wrapped and in the refrigerator. You can substitute the leaves of regular celery.

MITSUBA

Trefoil. A Japanese herb very similiar to Chinese celery or flat leafed parsely. Has thread-like pale stalks topped with three serrated greenish-yellow leaves. Tastes like celery-sorrel. Used raw as a garnish and in cooked dishes, such as chawan-mushi (savory steamed egg custard) and simmered soups. Chopped trefoil is sprinkled over soba and udon noodles. Sold in small plastic baggies of several clumps. Store in a glass of water with a plastic bag encasing the leaf tops, it will keep up to a week.

mitsuba

KINOME

kinome

Sprigs of small oval-shaped green leaves from the Japanese pepper tree. They have a minty-pepper taste and symbolize spring as they are the new leaves that sprout in spring. They are used as a garnish for soups, simmered foods, tofu dishes, and grilled foods. The mature pods of this plant yield sansho, Japanese pepper. Sold in some stores, on plastic wrapped plastic trays. If you can't find it, substitute watercress, cilantro, or celery leaves. Store in refrigerator, up to a week, or dry and use as a less aromatic herb.

SHISO LEAF

Zi su in Chinese. Also called perilla leaf. This is a Japanese herb used for seasoning, coloring, pickling, and garnishing. It has dark green, slightly serrated, heart-shaped leaves with purple specks and a reddish underside. They are used to stain pickled plums, added to soups, rolled into sushi, deep-fried in tempura, and dried to sprinkle over rice. Shiso has a slight gingery taste and cinnamon scent. Sold in neat little leaf stacks of about six, tied together with string, or arranged flat on styrofoam trays wrapped in plastic. Store loosely wrapped in the refrigerator and use within three to four days.

MINT

Bac-ha (in Vietnamese) and bai saranae (in Thai). A variety of Asian spearmint that has red stems and clusters of small, soft, dark green leaves with a refreshing tangy flavor, it is used mainly in Thai, Vietnamese, Lao, and Cambodian cuisine. Sprigs or shreds of mint are liberally added to hot and spicy salads and are used to garnish noodle soups. Platters of salad greens served with Vietnamese spring or summer rolls always include fresh mint. A delicious Thai soup is made with canned sardines in tomato sauce, chicken broth, chili, and lots of mint. In Cambodia, mint, grilled fish pieces, chilies, tamarind, and peanuts are pounded into a thick dip for raw vegetables, called tuk kroung. Refrigerate mint, wrapped in a moist paper towel, in a bag.

BASIL

Three varieties of this fragrant herb are found in Asia—and Asian groceries. The most common one is sweet basil, called lokak (in Chinese), bai horapa (in Thai), and rau que (in Vietnamese), which has pointy, slightly serrated, dark green leaves, tiny purple flowerheads, and reddish-purple stems. It has an intense anise scent and licorice flavor. This is often served raw in Thai and Vietnamese salad platters, wrapped with lettuce around spring rolls, or added to *Thai holy basil* stir-fried beef and chicken dishes and coconut curries. Lemon basil has a citrus scent with smaller, paler green leaves. It is used fried with seafood and in noodle soups. The gummy black seed coats of lemon basil are soaked until they swell, then mixed with coconut milk in Thai desserts. Holy basil (as the plant is sacred to Hindus) has narrow, dark green leaves. Its aromatic flavor is released only when cooked, and it is used in chicken, seafood, and beef dishes and curries.

Holy basil is used in the recipe for shrimp coconut curry on page 211.

Ginger

GINGERROOT

Called khing (in Thai), halia (in Malay), and gung (in Vietnamese). This knobby, golden beige, smooth-skinned rhizome with a yellow-green interior is found in "hands" or broken knobs. Thick peeled slices are bruised or crushed with the side of a cleaver to release the flavor, aroma, and juices, or minced, shredded, or grated before using. Ginger adds a clean, aromatic fragrance and spicy bite to all sorts of dishes including claypot stews, soups, sauces, *ginger root* marinades, and steamed fish. Juice, which is extracted from

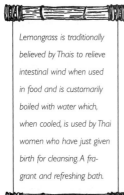

Lemongrass is traditionally believed by Thais to relieve intestinal wind when used in food and is customarily boiled with water which, when cooled, is used by Thai women who have just given birth for cleansing. A fragrant and refreshing bath.

pressed ginger, is used in drinks, sauces, and marinades. You may also find young stem ginger in the spring. It has moist pinkish knobs. It is often pickled to make gari, the Japanese sushi garnish. Choose pieces that are hard and free of wrinkles or mold. It will keep several weeks in a paper bag in the refrigerator. To preserve it longer, peel and slice the roots and cover with rice vinegar in an airtight container.

GALANGAL

Also called kha, ka choy laos, and galanga, this member of the ginger family is native to Java and Malaysia and has a much hotter, sharp, peppery taste. Galangal has translucent golden skin and slightly ridged rings around the root. Pale pink shoots of the tender young rhizomes are even more flavorful than the old ones. Galangal is too hot to eat raw, so it is pounded or ground into curry pastes with other spices or added in peeled chunks to soups. It can keep for several weeks stored in a paper bag.

galangal root

KARACHAI

Often called lesser Siamese ginger, this rhizome is a relative of ginger and has a mildly spicy flavor and is very aromatic. Has light brown skin and a yellow interior. It is used extensively in Thai, Lao, and Cambodian cuisine, mainly in fish curries and soup broths. Store in a paper bag in the refrigerator.

KENCUR

Aromatic ginger, a rhizome of the curcuma plant, is related to, but does not taste like, ginger. It is also called cenkur in Indonesia and saa-jiiang in China. It has a unique camphor flavor and is used in Balinese pounded spice pastes to neutralize strongly flavored duck, lamb, or pork. In Thailand, both the root and leaves are added to fish curries and the young leaves are eaten raw with shrimp paste chili dips. The fresh ginger-like root is pale yellow or off-white. Dried, it is light tan and slightly curled at the edges. Fresh kencur should be washed and peeled. Soak dried pieces in hot water for about 30 minutes to use.

LEMONGRASS

Serai in Malay and takrai in Thai, this fragrant herb with a citronella scent resembles a long woody stalk with coarse leaves and a bulbous stem end. It is essential for Southeast Asian cuisine. Fresh lemongrass is

lemon grass

pale yellow-green. If it is to be eaten raw, peel away the outer layers of the bulb base until you see the pinkish ring of the tender heart inside. This must be finely sliced. When used in cooking, use only up to 6 inches above the stem base, discarding the top and leaves. This part is bruised to release the lemony-floral aroma and flavor. Cut it in pieces and add to hot-sour soups and coconut chicken soup, or pound into spice pastes. Sliced pieces are not eaten; they are just for flavoring and are discarded like a bay leaf from the soup bowl. In Bali and other parts of Indonesia whole trimmed stalks are used as skewers for seafood satay, imparting a subtle flavor. Will keep several weeks in a paper bag in the refrigerator. Use to make the coconut shrimp curry recipe on page 211 and the Balinese tomato and lemongrass soup on page 208.

Limes

KAFFIR LIME LEAF

Magroot in Thai, this is an indigenous, warty-skinned green citrus of Southeast Asia, with dark glossy green double leaves. Its leaves have a unique lemon-lime perfume and are used to impart zing to soups, sauces, curry pastes, and other dishes. They are added for flavoring in the same way that bay leaves are used; the whole ones are not eaten, but discarded from the dish. Fine shreds, cut with kitchen scissors, are left in and also added raw to salads. If the fruit is available fresh, the grated zest can be used too. Use zest in soup, curries, and cooked dishes. Fresh leaves, still attached to tree twigs, are packaged in plastic bags and will keep several weeks in the refrigerator or may be frozen.

kaffir lime leaf

LIME

Two types of limes (besides the kaffir) are used in Southeast Asia. The larger is a bit smaller than a lemon and round. Called limau nipis, it turns from green to yellowish when ripe. The small, round, slightly less acidic, and more fragrant limau ketsuri is also called by its Filipino name, calamansi. In Cambodia it is called musk lime or kalamansi. The juice of either one is essential in spicy sambals and curry pastes. Lime juice adds spark to rich coconut curries (add after cooking to prevent curdling) and salads, and balances sweet and salty flavors in dipping sauces made with fish sauce. Halved limes are served as a table condiment, meant to be squeezed over everything from fried noodles to grilled fish. Store in the refrigerator. Lime is used in grilled eggplant salad, page 206, and in Vietnamese nuoc cham dipping sauce, page 217.

It is well worth seeking out fresh herbs, chilies, and aromatics to keep on hand for adding a pinch of punch or to pack a wallop of flavor in any dish. Herbs and aromatics marry and meld with other ingredients, altering even the simplest recipe into something at once fragrant and deeply delicious.

STOCKING UP

Basics include chilies, spring onions, coriander, lemongrass, and gingerroot. Limes are handy to squeeze into dipping sauces and marinades, and to balance rich coconut curries.

· 9 ·

Fresh Fruit

水果

Chinese for "fruit"

In some Asian cultures, fruits are beautifully sculpted into edible art and in most, fruit forms part of any offering to the spirits or ancestors. You will find a dish of fruit in front of the altar in practically any Chinese temple. Banana leaves and sugarcane stalks are propped against the doorways of Indian temples when a wedding is being celebrated. Bananas figure in Malay folklore with the swishing leaf fronds believed to be the arms of a spirit, which resides in the plant.

Fresh fruit is the principal dessert of Asia—peeled, sliced, and served in eye pleasing arrangements. It is plentiful, inexpensive, and makes a cool soothing end to a hot or spicy meal. Fruit grows in abundance throughout Asia, especially the tropical regions. One fruit that is even an enigma in Asia—with almost cult status—is the giant spiked durian. This monster exudes a peculiar, almost nauseating, odor, but when split open (try a machete!) the inner globs of pale custardy flesh are delicious—almost like caramel-garlic-laced ice cream. You either love or loathe it. Sir Stamford Raffles, the founder of Singapore, loathed it. When given a gift of six prickly beauties, he held his nose and ran off, saying the smell gave him a headache.

A fresh juicy mango or cluster of rambutan may taste best under the shade of a palm while kicking back on a Thai beach, but luckily many Southeast Asian fruits are exported. The next best thing for a taste of the tropics in a bite of fruit is to head to the fruit crates near the front of the Lins' grocery to see what fruits are in season.

ASIAN PEAR-APPLE

Nashi in Japanese. Also called snow or Fugi apple, it is a squat apple-shaped fruit that is juicy like a pear and crisp like an apple. It also tastes like a cross between an apple and pear. Has a sandy texture with the speckled yellow-green or pale brown skin of a pear. In Japanese orchards the apples are coddled until ripe, each one wrapped on the tree in tissue to protect the fruit from

pear-apple

birds, blemishes, or sunburn. This one-on-one care, of course, raises the prices astronomically. Most in U.S. markets are grown domestically. Mr. Lin recommends the smaller, brown skinned ones, which are sweeter and juicier. Big ones tend to be bland.

CUSTARD APPLE

Nawy-naa in Thai, this is also called cinnamon or sugar apple, sweet-sop, annona, srikaya, and cherimoya. Its tough outer skin of dark and light green nodules covers a plump heart-shaped fruit resembling a

tiny hand grenade. You can tell it's ripe when the area around the stem turns blackish and the fruit seems swollen and about to burst. To eat, the skin is peeled off and discarded with the seeds. Scoop out the soft, pulpy, and very sweet flesh and eat. Tastes a bit like a pina colada. Good blended with vanilla ice cream in

custard apple

milkshakes and added to fruit salads.

SOURSOP

Also called guanabana, this is an oval, green skinned, aromatic fruit covered in dark pointy nubs with soft pale fibrous flesh inside. They range from the size of a small mango up to 10 pounds and taste like a slightly acidic combination of mango and pineapple. Peel to eat or make into juice, custard, ice cream, or smoothie drinks.

soursop

GUAVA

Guava shapes vary from round or oval to pear-shaped and range from the size of an egg to the size of a baseball. The skin color is yellow or greenish-yellow and the flesh varies from light yellow to white or pink with numerous tiny edible seeds. They have a crisp texture and tart-sweet taste. In Asia they are eaten fresh—the skin is edible too—sliced and dipped in hot-and-sour sauce, sprinkled with salt, or made into a refreshing juice. You can also make guava jelly, fruit paste, or preserves. They are in season from July to January. Mrs. Lin is a big fan of the green slightly pear shaped guavas, beloved in Thailand as snacks with chili-salt powder and lime juice.

MANGO

A member of the cashew family and one of the most widely cultivated fruits in Southeast Asia, it is also inextricably connected with folklore and religious ceremonies. The Buddha loved mangoes so much he was given a grove to meditate in. The mangoes you'll find in Asian groceries are mainly exported from Thailand, Malaysia, or the Philippines. These tend to be light yellow, pale orange, or green-ish skinned and oval shaped. The fruit's flesh is light to deep yellow with a smooth and creamy texture. The taste is like a cross between a peach and an apricot with pineapple and coconut undertones. They are most abundant in spring through early summer. Hard unripe green mangoes are eaten raw with salt or made into pickles or salads. Ripe mangoes should be soft and fragrant near the stem. They are often eaten as a dessert with sticky rice and coconut cream.

mango

BANANAS

There are over 15 types grown in Southeast Asia, from plump red ones to small yellow hands of banana fingers. There are starchy green ones and the large pisang raja—or king banana—used in desserts or battered and deep-fried into fritters. In Thailand bananas are soaked in coconut milk and grilled over charcoal. In Cambodia banana chunks and sticky rice mixed with coconut milk are wrapped in banana leaves and grilled.

banana hand

GREEN PAPAYA

Muk qwa and mu gua. Usually only the hard, unripe green fruits are stocked in Asian markets. They are shredded to make a salad, eaten with sticky rice and grilled meats, or pickled. When cut open they reveal pale green flesh and tiny white seeds.

green papaya

POMELO

Also called som-o and pummelo, this is a large, pale yellow-green tropical cousin to the grapefruit with a slightly pointy top. Peeled and eaten in sections, it has a crisp snappy citrus texture and tart taste. It is usually found in mid-November through January. Often eaten with a mixture of salt and chili powder as snack in Thailand and Malaysia. Also added to Thai pomelo and shredded chicken salad, seasoned with fish sauce, onions, and fresh herbs, and garnished with roasted peanuts.

pomelo

LOQUAT

This is a small, egg-shaped orange or deep yellow fruit with a slightly tart citrus flavor. The fruits grow in clusters on the loquat tree, a small ornamental evergreen. The fleshy fragrant fruit contains many seeds around a papery core and the skin is edible. They are soft and bruise easily when ripe. Loquats are eaten fresh, cooked, and made into jelly. Sliced and added to flavor beef or poultry dishes. Also made into cough syrup for sore throats and coughing.

KUMQUAT

Also called golden bean fruit and meiwa, this has long been grown in Asia as the "good-luck" plant. Kumquats are eaten as part of Chinese banquets and are popular Lunar New Year gifts. In Japan and Vietnam they are used for holiday decorations. The fruit resembles tiny oranges, but is eaten whole and unpeeled—the spongy rind is the sweet part while the pulp is tangy and not very juicy. It comes into season in late winter—perfect for Chinese New Year. This versatile fruit can be eaten whole, sliced into salads, candied, or made into jams and chutney. Fresh kumquats are said to be good for indigestion. Candied fruit is taken to stimulate the appetite.

kumquat

BUDDHA'S HAND

Also called fingered citron, fo-shouin, and bu-shukan (meaning "Buddha's hand" in Chinese and Japanese), this is a very unusual citron containing no pulp, just rind. It is a close relative of the lemon, and resembles a mutant yellow squid or bunch of gnarled bananas. Finger-like segments splinter from the bottom of the fruit, as if the whole thing is exploding from within. Usually found only in the winter, it is a traditional New Year's gift, temple offering, and symbol of happiness, longevity, and good fortune. Has a strong fragrant citrus scent and a kumquat-tangerine taste. The grated zest is used to add delicate flavor to seafood dishes, soups, and sweets. The dried peel is used in medicinal cooking, said to be good for lungs, liver, and spleen, calming the mind, helping circulation, and strengthening the stomach.

Buddha's hand citrus

In Southeast Asia, mangoes are worshiped and adored. I have great memories of the midsummer mango madness in Thailand, which reaches a peak in April. It is so blistering hot then that a 90 degree day seems cool. Mangoes overflow the markets. People stay up all night in search of the best ones. This culminates with Songkran, the New Year water festival. This began centuries ago as a rain-making ritual to ensure water after the dry season for rice growing. Everyone from Buddhist monks to school kids joins in, throwing water at everyone else.

STARFRUIT

Also called carambola, belimbing, and five-finger fruit, this pale waxy yellowish-green thin skinned fruit has five fused wedge segments that create star shapes when sliced crosswise. The less-than-ripe fruit has a tart, not too sweet, taste, crisp texture, and is very juicy. Very ripe fruit is a rich golden yellow and bruises easily,

starfruit

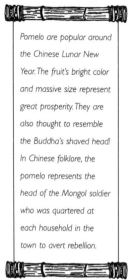

Pomelo are popular around the Chinese Lunar New Year. The fruit's bright color and massive size represent great prosperity. They are also thought to resemble the Buddha's shaved head! In Chinese folklore, the pomelo represents the head of the Mongol soldier who was quartered at each household in the town to avert rebellion.

so has brown patches along the ridges. Often added to hot and sour salads, used as a pretty star-shaped garnish or made into juice. Claimed to be a cure for hangovers.

JAMBU AIR

Water apple. "Jambu" means apple and "air" is water in Malay. It is a pale pink waxy-skinned bell-shaped fruit with watery spongy flesh. It is a thirst quencher and has a slightly sharp taste. The skin is edible too. Can be made into a refreshing drink or sliced and added to rojak, a mixed salad of cooked and raw vegetables, tart fruit, and crunchy fried tofu bits tossed in a sweet dark shrimp paste (petis) sauce. In season from May to October.

RAMBUTAN

This is a Malaysian fruit from a type of soapberry tree. The name is derived from rambut which means hair. Looks like a hairy strawberry-red oval with soft long spines covering an egg sized fruit. Related to the lychee and has translucent pale flesh that tastes like a juicy sweet zinfandel grape. Best way to eat is to pop the flesh out of its spiny shell and bite in, watching for the oval pit. In season May to October.

rambutan

LONGAN

longan

Called lam-yai in Thai (the name means "drag-on's eye"), it looks like a round, yellowish brown grape, but with a shell. Peel to eat the syrupy, pale white fruit inside. Tastes slightly like fresh fig and has a small pit. Often sold in bundles of the branches they grow in clusters on. Some of the tastiest grow in Northern Thailand where fruit festivals are held each year when they are in season from February through April.

LYCHEE

Also called litchee, this is the fruit of an Asian evergreen tree that originated in Southern China. Looks like a big, crimson-pink berry with bumpy, leathery skin. Peel this shell to eat the semi-translucent, juicy white flesh with a single dark brown seed. Sugary sweet with a texture of soft grapes. Usually available from July to September. The peeled fruits are also dried like raisins; they are then called litchi nuts and used in cooked savory or dessert type dishes. They are also added to a sweet soup made of rock sugar simmered with water and white fungus, served chilled.

DURIAN

This is that dull green football-sized monster with spiky thorns that gives off a pungent odor like old cheese laced with garlic. It is the jurassic fruit of a Malaysian tree in the Bombax family. The tough rind spines can be sharp, making it painful to handle without thick gloves. In Southeast Asia durian sellers slash them open with a sharp Malay knife called a parang. Once opened, creamy pale yellow segments of a custard-like fruit are picked out. Dark brown egg-sized seeds are in the clumps of flesh and the seeds can be roasted or boiled and eaten. The taste of the custard is very sweet, almost like rich vanilla ice cream with a hint of sulfur.

durian

Eating durians is said to cure stomach ailments or act as a potent aphrodisiac—if you can stand the smell! Small pieces of durian are added to sticky rice cooked in sweetened coconut milk, used in cakes and ice cream, or preserved into a thick paste, mixed with spices. In season December to February, but newly developed strains make them available almost year round now. Asians never mix alcoholic beverages with the powers of whatever is in durians!

MANGOSTEEN

This is a plump, pincushion-shaped dark purple fruit in a shell with four green leaves on top. To eat, cut shell all the way around horizontally in the middle of the fruit, being careful not to pierce the flesh. Lift off top shell to find creamy snow white segments in the lower section. Has a tart-sweet taste. Large ones have small pits. Be careful not to get any sap on your clothes as mangosteen peel can stain. Often eaten after indulging in durian to counter their "heatiness." In season between December and February.

mangosteen

GREEN DRAGON FRUIT

Known as than long in Vietnamese, it is a very rare find in U.S. markets. This fruit from Nha Trang is the size and shape of a tiny pineapple and has almost smooth magenta colored skin. Its pale bluish flesh is speckled with little black seeds and tastes a bit like kiwi. Green dragon fruit grows on a type of creeping cactus said to look like a dragon. When I was in Vietnam, I tasted it in a refreshing drink made out of crushed fruit pulp, ice, sugar, and sweetened condensed milk. It is also made into jam. Some are exported from New Zealand and Mexico.

Besides the fruits mentioned above, you may also find mandarin oranges, tangerines, sour green oranges, limes, watermelon, stalks of sugarcane, fresh pineapples, or ripe papaya which are yellow-orange and very soft with black seeds inside. It is worth exploring some of the fruits you are not familiar with. Also try some types unripe—green papaya and mango make tart and tangy salads, can be eaten raw dipped into spicy sauces, or cooked as a vegetable. Under-ripe pineapple can be stewed to make the filling for delicious tarts.

10

Soybean Products

Korean for "soy products"

This little bean is the source of an amazing number of soy products important to Asian cooking. Soybeans have been a staple of the Asian diet for over two thousand years, having been first cultivated in China. This legume forms the base for products as diverse as soy sauce, beancurd, soy, and bean sprouts. Soybeans grow in clusters of fuzzy pods, each containing two or three pea-sized beans. They are highly nutritious, rich in protein, cholesterol-free, easy to digest, and used to replace meat in vegetarian diets. As ingredients go, not even rice is as diverse as the soybean, making soy products a mainstay of Asian cuisine—and on the shelves of Asian groceries.

Soy products are scattered throughout the Lins' grocery, as they will be in most Asian markets. Soy sauce, bean sauce, funky smelling fermented curds, and soy oil are found with the salty flavorings and cooking oils. Natto (Japanese fermented soybeans) are in the refrig-

black bean sauce

erator case and soy flour is with starches and flour. Plain and sweetened soy powders for drinks are in the aisle with beverage and dessert mixes. Dried sheets of beancurd skin as well as dried soybeans are stocked with the dried goods. In this chapter we start with the beans themselves followed by soy products—tofu in various forms (pressed, baked, fried, dried skim, etc.), then black bean sauces, fermented curds, and so on, ending with sprouts.

Whole Beans

DRIED SOYBEANS

These are the hard, small round beige beans harvested from soybean pods. To use, soak for six hours or overnight in water (place in the refrigerator), drain and drop into a pot of boiling water. Simmer about 30 minutes or until tender. They now can be used fried in hot oil and sprinkled with salt to make soy nuts—great for snack food—or made into bean soup and simmered dishes or liqufied to make soy milk. The milk can then be used to make tofu and other soy products. Look for Oriental Mascot brand in 12-ounce bags. A black type of soybean, called kuromame in Japanese, is used boiled in syrup as a sweet, or steamed with rice. Look for CTR Thai brand in 14-ounce bags.

TEMPEH

This chewy mixture of whole cooked soybeans infused with a yeast culture and mixed with grains such as millet or rice into dense chewy cakes originated in Indonesia. It is available plain or seasoned with spices. It looks knobby and is light brown with a slight whitish film on the surface. Tempeh is often used as a meat substitute. Good in vegetable burgers and, when deep-fried, makes a crispy addition to salads. It can be added to soups, stews, chili, and vegetable stir-fries. Tempeh is found in thin flat blocks in vacuum-sealed plastic packages in the refrigerator case. Keeps about one week unopened and should be kept no more than three to four days after opening.

Beancurd

Known as tau hu or doufu in Chinese and tofu in Japanese, this white, custard-like product is made from soaked and pureed soybeans mixed with water, then strained through a cloth. The resulting liquid "milk" is brought to a boil and the coagulant gypsum is added to set it into a curd. The curd is then put into boxes, weighted to squeeze out any remaining whey, and packaged. Beancurd is found in either small firm blocks or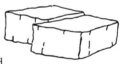

fresh (silk) tofu

soft pillows—depending on the amount of solidifier added to the soy liquid to mold it. These textures range from silken, semi-soft, and firm to extra firm. Choose according to what you are cooking and to your taste. Buy firm for stuffing and deep-frying, semi-soft for stir-fries and braising, and silken for soups, steaming, desserts, and drinks.

To use, cut carefully and cook gently to prevent the fragile beancurd from breaking up too much. Deep-frying gives it a "thick skin" which contrasts well with the soft interior, and it is often served with seafood, vegetables, and a sauce in a claypot, or as in the Malay tau hu goreng, where it is served with a peanut sauce. Tao hou tod is Thai-style deep-fried cubes of beancurd in sweet chili and ground roast peanut sauce. Some stores sell cubes or triangle-shapes of tan-colored deep-fried beancurd. These are found in plastic bags in the refrigerator case. Check that there are no mold spots.

Fresh beancurd will be found in the refrigerated cases at the back of the store, often packed in water in sealed plastic containers. Check the date for freshness. Once opened, store the beancurd in the refrigerator, covered in water, for up to five days and change the water daily. Best used in two or three days. Some brands to look for (along with locally-made ones in your area) are Vitasoy, Orifood, The Soy Shop, Hinoichi, and Fully.

PRESSED BEANCURD

Tau kwa. These are hard flat blocks of compressed beancurd. Whey is extracted from the fresh beancurd cake by pressing with weights until it becomes firm and compact. Next the cake is simmered in water, becoming smooth and resilient in texture. Plain pressed beancurd looks yellow and the seasoned type, which is simmered with soy sauce,

star anise, and sugar, is pinkish or dark red. Cut it into small pieces and add to stir-fried meat and vegetable dishes, stews, and soups. You can also slice it into strips and deep-fry them. Eat the strips with your favorite dip as an alternative to potato chips. You will find pressed beancurd in vacuum-sealed plastic packages of three to six in the refrigerator case. Keeps two or three days after opening. Brands to look for are AFC pressed curd, Wen Hsin aromatic curd, Tung Woo, and Orifood.

pressed seasoned bean curd

DEEP-FRIED BEANCURD

These are often called tau pok or fu pea. They are cubes of deep-fried beancurd, which puff up into light and airy golden pillows. They are often stuffed and put in soups or added to sauces and braising dishes, as they absorb flavors and juices. They can be sliced and used in stir-fries and vegetarian dishes. They are found in the refrigerator case in plastic bags of about six. Best used within two to three days of purchase. Look for Orifood puffs. You may also find abura-age, a Japanese product made by frying very thin slices of tofu in oil. It resembles deep golden sheets of rubber and is used to form the casing for stuffed sushi called inarizushi. Sold in sealed plastic

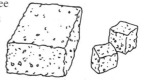

fresh (firm) tofu

bags, this should be used within two to three days. Look for JFC brand in the refrigerated case. You may also find small cans of abura-age for inarazushi in the Japanese aisle. Look for Hime brand.

SAVORY GRILLED BEANCURD

Also called yaki-tofu, these firm cakes of tofu are marinated in soy sauce and baked, broiled, or grilled to develop a rich savory brown coating that contrasts with the white interior. This process reduces the moisture content allowing it to keep longer. Used sliced into chunks or thin matchsticks and added to stir-fries or one-pot stews. It can also be heated and served with mushroom soy sauce as "steak." Sold in plastic packages in the refrigerator case. Use within four days of purchase.

FREEZE-DRIED BEANCURD

Called koyadofu in Japanese, or "ice tofu." It is made by freezing thin slices of beancurd, then evaporating the moisture content in a high vacuum. The end result is a light, spongy dried product that can be kept a long time. To use, soak until softened in warm water. It will swell in size. Squeeze it almost dry and add to simmered dishes or stews or cut into strips and use in stir-fries or salad. Good simmered in dashi stock with soy sauce until the liquid is absorbed and sprinkled with seven-spice or sansho pepper. Sold in plastic bags, often of three pieces tied together with straw or loose cakes.

The 4th day of the 4th month of the lunar calendar honors the birth, enlightenment, and death of Buddha. Called Vesak day or Bathing of the Buddha, festivals are held in temples throughout Asia. Statues of the Buddha are washed with aromatic water and candles are lit for departed loved ones and to offer blessings. Vegetarian food is eaten, such as "Buddha's robe." This is made from stacked layers of beancurd skins, yam slices, and mushrooms wrapped and rolled up in another skin and steamed. The rolls are served in a thick sauce made of preserved red beancurd, stock, and soy sauce.

BEAN CURD SHEETS

Called fu pei in Chinese and yuba in Japanese, these are dried creamy, off-white, very delicate sheets of wrinkly bean curd skin—a by-product of the tofu making process. The thin film that forms on the surface of heated soybean milk is carefully removed and dried on bamboo mats or hung on poles like laundry to dry! To use, soak 5 to 6 minutes in warm water until softened. Tears easily, but can be patched with other soaked pieces. Use as wrappers for dim sum dumplings or cut into squares and stuffed with rice, meat or vegetable fillings, rolled-up, then steamed, sauteed or deep-fried and served with a dipping sauce. Bean curd skin has a pleasant chewy texture and mild bland taste. You can also add torn soaked pieces to stir-fries, soup, or stews.

Fu jook are rolled-up, long rumpled cream-colored sticks of bean curd skin, bent in two. These are used in desserts, boiled with rock sugar, fresh ginger, and quail eggs, and also in red-braised savory dishes. For flat sheets and bent sticks of dried skin look for Goldensail, AMY products from Hong Kong, Ding Hao, Golden Food, and Gui Lin Scene brands.

You will also find tim jook, small won-ton wrapper size dried flat pieces or rolls of bean curd skin with soy sauce or bran added that look like creamy brown cardboard. Delicious deep-fried (it will turn dark brown). Can also be soaked until soft (cut if in rolls), stuffed with fillings, and steamed or pan-fried.

dried beancurd skin

Look for Mount Elephant brand flat squares and Goldensail brand in bags of fifteen small rolls.

Fermented Beans

PRESERVED BLACK BEANS

Also called salted or fermented black beans or "tau see," this is made by steaming small black soybeans, then fermenting them with salt and spices. Used in a variety of dishes to add a pleasant rich aroma and salty taste. They are good in braised, steamed, and stir-fried dishes. Crush or mash beans slightly to release more flavor or mix with garlic, fresh ginger, or chilies. Available in small glass jars, cans, and plastic bags. They should feel soft and not be dried out. Transfer to a clean, tightly closed jar and store in the refrigerator after opening. Look for Pearl River Bridge brand labeled "Yang Jiang Preserved Beans" in a 1-pound yellow canister, and Koon Chun Sauce Factory, Double Parrot, and Zu Miao Trademark brand all in 8-ounce bags.

BEAN SAUCE

Varieties of this Asian staple include yellow bean sauce, brown bean sauce, bean paste (tau jeong), or sweet bean condiment. All are made from yellow or black soybeans, fermented with salt and in the sweet Northern Chinese type, with sugar-sweetened crushed yellow beans. Two forms are found: whole beans in a thick sauce and bean paste, which is mashed ground or pureed beans. The whole bean type has a rounder flavor and adds texture while the pastes are very salty and should be used sparingly. Both are used to add a distinctive salty and aromatic flavor to many dishes and are combined with hoi-sin or chili paste to make sauces. Or fry with seasoned minced pork and minced garlic and place on (or stuff into) firm tofu, then steam it. Lee Kum Kee has this already mixed with garlic, very salty—you need a touch of sugar to tone down the taste. The yellow bean paste is tau cheo and it is added to mee siam (hot and sour rice vermicelli noodles), among other things. Sold in glass jars and cans. Look for Koon Chun Sauce Factory, Koon Yick Wah Kee bean sauce, Amoy, or Yeo's.

TOEN-JANG

Korean reddish colored fermented soybean paste, similiar to Japanese red miso. It is used to make soup broth, sauces, and dips, and is smeared on foods for grilling or steaming. Look for Assi brand in glass jars or plastic tubs.

CHILI BEAN SAUCE

Or hot bean sauce. This is a popular Sichuan cooking sauce and condiment, made from fermented brown bean sauce infused with mashed chili peppers, vinegar, and other seasonings. Adds an intense fiery flavor and vivid red color to dishes. Used in claypot stews, meat marinades, stir-fries, and sauces. Sold in cans or small glass jars. Look for Kim Lan brand in squat 7-ounce jars, Pearl River Bridge brand, and Koon Yick Wah Kee with garlic added.

hot bean sauce

FERMENTED BEANCURD

fermented beancurd

Also called lam yee, fu yee, and beancurd cheese. A very rich, pungent flavoring agent made from fermented creamy beancurd cubes with a smooth thick custard-like texture and wine-like aroma (less enthusiastic people would say "stinky"). There are two varieties, white and red. White are ivory colored 1-inch cakes fermented with rice wine, sugar, chili flakes, and salt. White curd is used mainly to season vegetables and at the table as a condiment. Red curd (nom yee) is cured in a brine with red rice, rice wine, and crushed dried chili peppers, and is used in braised meat or poultry dishes. Once the curd begins to cook, it releases a fragrant aroma and enriches the flavor of vegetables or meats, and blends well in sauces. It can also be made into a dip, mashed up with chili and lime, or crushed and mixed with sugar and soy sauce and added to simmered dishes or sukiyaki broth. Some people eat it "neat" with their rice. Red curd is also added to fried rice, turning the rice pink. Sold in glass jars, cans, or ceramic crocks, this will keep indefinitely if resealed and refrigerated after opening. Look for Chan Moon Kee, Fu-Chung, and Pearl River Bridge brands for red and white types. Red curd is found in brown crocks in pink nets by Zhejiang South "Golden Smell" brand. And you may see jars of lurid magenta-red paste made by Foodex Co. This is yen taofu, a creamed substance made from fermented red curds, used as a soup noodle flavoring sauce.

Bean Products

OKARA

A valuable nutritious by-product of the beancurd making process, this is the refuse or lees left over when the soybean milk is squeezed out of ground soybeans. The lees contain all the fibers of the beans and have even more protein than tofu. It is sold in plastic bags and resembles off-white crumbled cheese. It can be used to enrich soup and added to stir-fries, or made into breaded and fried croquettes. It is sold in plastic bags which can be found in the refrigerator case.

EDAMAME

"Eda" means "branch of" in Japanese and "mame" means bean. These are fresh sweet soybeans, found seasonally in the produce section or, most likely, frozen in the freezer case. They are the young green pods of soybeans, harvested while still tender. Usually steamed and lightly salted, the beans are popped out of the pods and eaten as a snack or added to rice dishes. The frozen ones have already been steamed, so you need only to plunge them into boiling water for a few minutes and then refresh them in cold water. Look for Shirakiku and Oriental Mascot brands. They come frozen and in 1-pound bags.

edamame

SOYBEAN SPROUTS

soy bean sprouts

Daai dau or ng choy. Soybean sprouts have larger, pale greenish-yellow heads and are crunchier than mung bean sprouts. The sprouts are slender and about two inches long with a slightly raw taste so are usually cooked and added to stir-fries and other dishes for texture. You will find them in the produce bin in a large plastic bag to scoop out the amount you want. Best used the day of purchase, but will keep a few days if refrigerated.

SOY MILK

Called tau fa sui or dou-nai this creamy, milk-like liquid is made from crushed, finely ground soybeans mixed with water. An ideal protein source for dairy sensitive or allergic people, it is available in cans, like soda, in the refrigerator case, and in shelf-stable cartons, either plain, sweetened, or flavored in the beverage section of aisle 7. There is also dehydrated soymilk powder, sold in plastic bags. Reconstitute with water to make soybean milk. Look for Bing Quan brand soymilk powder in beadlike granules.

Asian people have been feasting on this bean and using soy products like tofu, tempeh, miso, soy milk, and soy sauce for thousands of years. Its many health-giving aspects and delicious flavors are just now being "discovered" in the West. So, be sure to add some to your shopping cart and discover the joys of soy!

STOCKING UP

You should pick a carton of beancurd of whichever texture you prefer to use in any number of dishes—plain, stir-fried, stuffed, or added to soup. Choose pressed curd to keep in stock, as in the sealed package it will keep a long time. Add a jar of at least one type of preserved bean sauce for an all-purpose seasoning and flavoring ingredient. Dried bean-curd skin sheets are handy wrappers for stuffed rolls and will keep well in your pantry.

11

Eggs & Preserved Meats

Trứng

Vietnamese for "egg"

Eggs often appear on Asian festival days and special occasions as offerings to the spirits or as gifts. In many Asian myths eggs, or "dragon seeds," are the origin of the universe and as an egg contains potential for life, it represents life and birth of the cosmos. Eggs also represent hope and immortality. The yolk and white symbolize yin and yang—the dual life forces.

Eggs

Since eggs are perishable, methods were developed to preserve them. Chicken and duck eggs were smoked, braised in soy sauce, simmered in brewed tea, pickled in salt brine, or buried and "cooked" in lime and ash. These techniques are still in use, even with refrigeration, because the resulting flavors and textures are relished.

SALTED DUCK EGGS

salted eggs

Salted duck eggs are called harm dan and xian dan (in Cantonese and Mandarin), telor masin (in Malay), and khai khem (in Thai). These are a popular accompaniment to rice dishes and used in Chinese mooncakes and other sweet or savory pastries and steamed dishes. They are made by soaking fresh duck eggs in a salt brine for a month or so. The

brine mixture seeps into the shell tinting them bluish. The whites become firm and opaque and the yolks become semi-soft and bright orange in color with a rich flavor.

To use, boil ten minutes, then cut in half while still in the shell. Alternatively, wash shell and put in rice pot when cooking rice. Scoop out with a spoon and mix into rice as a salty condiment. Also eaten as a side dish with hot and spicy curries, rice congee, or soup. In Thailand quartered salty eggs are always part of a raw vegetable platter served with spicy nam phrik sauce for dipping. They are sold individually from the brine-filled barrel in front of the produce section and in styrofoam packs of four or six on end shelves opposite the back wall refrigerator cases. Look for Hu Bei, Shigu Mountain, Auspicious, and Duck Farm Co. brands in the styrofoam packs. On Foo Co. is in clear plastic packs of four salted eggs. They will keep for months, refrigerated.

THOUSAND-YEAR EGGS

As a kid, a friend of mine dropped a century egg, or pei dan as they are also called, on the floor of an Asian market and fled, fearing that anything a thousand years old must be really expensive. He had nothing to fear. The ancient-looking eggs are really only 100 days old and each one costs about a dollar. Duck eggs are coated with a mixture of clay, powdered lime, salt, and rice husks and buried in ash for three months. This cures the egg, turning the whites to an aspic-like black jelly surrounding a greenish yolk. The egg has a very rich flavor and pungent odor similar to strong cheese. It is used in cold appetizer platters, sliced and eaten with preserved gingerroot, dressed in a rice vinegar sauce, or eaten with rice as a condiment.

Dim sum restaurants also serve a rice congee containing bits of this, together with finely diced Chinese ham, chicken, salted egg, and chopped scallions. Leng pan is a simple Chinese summer salad made by topping sliced sugar-sprinkled tomatoes with wedges of hard-boiled hen and thousand year eggs. Sold by the egg or in styrofoam cartons of four stacked on the end shelves opposite the back wall refrigerator cases. Look for Caravelle, Chin Tsan, and Peony Mark brands. Unopened, they will keep for many months.

RED EGGS

Dyed a bright scarlet, these are hard-boiled eggs; Asian families give them away as birth announcements (8–10 for a girl, 9–11 for a boy). The Lins make theirs and usually have them in stock for Asian families in the community. Red eggs are also popular as offerings to the spirit world and at family altars. Sold by the egg, or in sets depending on which gender the newborn is. Mrs. Lin keeps hers in the refrigerator case next to the deli counter in old egg cartons.

Meat

Pork is to Asia what beef is to the U.S., by far the most popular meat. In fact pork is so dominant that to the Chinese, the pig symbolizes wealth, and when they say meat, they mean pork. No birthday banquet is complete without a pork dish. In early times pork was preserved by drying, pickling, and fermenting. All parts of the pig were used: ground pork was made into sausages, the intestines and solidified blood were made into soup, and whole hind legs cured into hams. These are still made today and found in Asian groceries. Tins of Chinese ham will be in aisle 8 with canned goods.

CHINESE SAUSAGE

Called lap cheung, lop chiang, lap xuong, lap suong, and lachang, they are air-dried savory-sweet red or brownish skinny sausage links, about 6 inches long, with a mottled texture and salami-like density. Made from cured pork, pork fat, beef, pork, or duck liver seasoned with salt, sugar or honey, spices, and strong rice wine, they were traditionally available only during the

chinese sausage

winter months. Pork sausages are red colored with a sweet pungent flavor. Duck or pork liver sausages are brown with a sweeter taste and smoother texture. Blanch before using to remove some of the fattiness, then slice thinly. Add to stir-fried rice, scrambled eggs, or mix into dumpling fillings. An easy way to cook this sausage is to place it directly on top of rice as it steams in the pot. This gives the rice a fragrant and rich feel. Usually sold in strings of two and in 1-pound vacuum-sealed packages in the refrigerator case. Keeps for weeks refrigerated, longer if frozen. Look for Wing Wing brand and Jimmy's "jan gon cheong" sausages both made in Vancouver, Kam Yen Jan brand from Seattle, Formosa brand from California, and Hsin-Chih brand from College Point, NY.

THAI STYLE SAUSAGE

Called boun sou nam sausage, this is made from fermented sour pork, pork skins, garlic, chili peppers, sugar, and salt. In order to pass U. S. agricultural inspection, it is manufactured following a Thai recipe in several American plants. It tastes similar to salami but spicier, with a slight tang, and must be thoroughly cooked before using. Steam and add to rice dishes and stir-fries or eat as a snack. Found in the

A famous Thai dish that uses fresh or salted eggs is kai look koei, or "son-in-law eggs." The story goes that a new son-in-law wants to impress his mother-in-law, but all he knows how to cook are boiled eggs. He hits on the idea of deep-frying them until golden brown. Still not satisfied, he halves them and makes a sauce from fish sauce, sugar, and chili powder. He serves the eggs with the sauce poured over them and adds crispy fried onion. Other friends in Thailand told me the name is really a euphemism for the son-in-law's "eggs" or "family jewels."

Onsens are Japanese spas built on natural hot springs. The waters of each are therapeutic for various ailments and all are relaxing and feature beautiful surroundings. Special onsen foods are served in your private room, but the actual steaming onsen waters are used to cook "onsen eggs." The boiled eggs take on the mineral flavor of the water and are eaten in the water with flasks of sake floated to you on trays.

refrigerated cases, it is sold in vacuum-sealed plastic packs of a single sausage stick or up to six, with tiny green chilies included.

VIETNAMESE PORK SAUSAGE

Called gio, this is a savory boiled sausage made from ground pork, cooked rice, garlic, fish sauce, and spices. It is sold wrapped in banana leaves and aluminum foil in the freezer case. It is used to flavor rice and noodle dishes, and is cooked with eggs or added to dumpling fillings. Look for Huong Duyen brand in 1-pound rolls. There is also Phu Huong brand fried pork patties, a round 15-ounce cake made from anchovy flavored pork paste from Rosemead California. Cut in slices and add to soup or stir-fries, or grill and serve with chili sauce and lettuce leaves for wrapping.

PORK SKIN

Called bi heo kho in Vietnamese, this is dried whole sheets or shreds of pale tan pigs' skin. It has a bland taste and is eaten mainly for its chewy, gelatinous texture. The stiff skin has to be boiled until softened. Pork skin is cut into fine strips and made into salads, added to soups or simmered dishes. Naem sot is a Thai salad made from fried ground pork and finely sliced boiled pork skin seasoned with garlic, lemon juice, and chili peppers, served in lettuce cups. Sold in plastic bags in the dried foods section. Look for Golden Dragon and Viet My brands. Also look for dried shredded skin "Ta Ho" produced by Westlake Food Co.

CHINESE HAM

Called Yunan or Jinhua ham depending on the province it's made in, the Chinese name "huo tui" means "fire legs." The hind legs of the pig are preserved by curing with salt and seasoning, dried, then smoked, creating a sweet flavor and smoky aroma. It is used to season soups and added in small bits to seafood, poultry, and vegetable dishes. Minced ham is also added to dumpling fillings or used as a garnish. Unfortunately, these hams are not allowed into American groceries except in tins. You will find these in the canned goods aisle. Substitute Smithfield ham, which is cured in a similar way, or use Italian prosciutto. You will also find cured ham pieces and pork belly strips in the preserved meat section of the refrigerator case. These can be substituted for Chinese ham and used in the same way. Look for Jimmy's brand from Vancouver and Hsin Tung Yang made in San Francisco. They will be in vacuum-sealed plastic packs and will keep several months, refrigerated.

CHAR SIU

Chinese-style barbecued pork ribs and strips, steamed, then marinated in a sauce made of honey, black bean sauce, garlic, and spices that gives the meat a sweet rich taste and deep reddish-black sheen after roasting. Found at the deli counter, hanging from metal hooks and sold by weight, cut into chunks with the deft strokes of Mrs. Lin's cleaver. Eat as is with rice and pickled mustard cabbage or slice into matchsticks and add to sweet-and-sour soup, stir-fries or fried rice. Use within a day or so of purchase.

You will also find "siu yoke," slabs of barbecued pork with a crusty skin and a layer of fat under it. It is usually sold by weight, chopped off the big slab in strips so that each piece has a bit of the crunchy skin on it. It is eaten like char siu, and often with char siu on rice smothered in a gravy made from the drippings from the meats roasting. It is also good with garlic chili sauce and pickles. You can also add it to whatever dish you like—stir-fried rice, noodle soup, or claypot with tofu and vegetables. If you have any leftovers, you might like to refry the strips with some dark soy sauce, grill it in a toaster oven (so the crunch is restored), or add leftovers to a curry.

FLAT SMOKED DUCK OR GOOSE

This is produced by removing bones, steaming and pressing the duck flat, then smoking it and hanging it out to dry in the cool, crisp winter air. The result has a sweet, lacquered, glazed skin and dark chewy meat. Use sparingly in pieces or strips to flavor soups and claypot stews. "Lap mei" is a deliciously fragrant rice prepared by placing strips of duck, Chinese sausage, and other smoked, air-dried meats over the rice as it is steaming. The oil seeps out from the meats and flavors the rice. Eat with a salad or braised vegetables. These are found in congealed fat-smeared plastic bags in the refrigerated cases. Look for Kam Yen Jan cured and dried ducks from Seattle or Hsin Tung Yang brand from San Francisco. Will keep for months unopened in the bag, in your refrigerator.

Most of the preserved meats and eggs are pungent, spicy, rich, and salty, and, to the first-time consumer, a little overpowering. Try using small bits with large amounts of bland rice to absorb the flavors and mellow the intensity. Be willing to dabble in new and unusual taste sensations such as strong-flavored, melting-textured century eggs partnered with sharp rice vinegar, ginger root, and green peppers or salted duck eggs mixed into soft steamed rice with chopped bits of pickled cabbage. Remember, most of these ingredients are kept on hand for seasoning and flavoring dishes, not to be used as the main event—except the irresistible char sui pork dangling above the deli!

barbecued meats

· 12 ·

Pickled Items & Preserves

ผักดอง

Thai for "pickles"

Pickled vegetables are as popular now as they were in ancient times. In those days, vegetables were salted and dried to preserve them. Later, vinegar-based brines were developed: rice, fruit, and wheat were fermented into vinegar solutions with herbs added to enhance the flavor. Mustard greens, bamboo shoots, water chestnuts, and radishes were some of the early pickles made in these brines. Salt and rice wine were used to ferment cabbage—creating an early form of sauerkraut—and people often subsisted on diets of rice and pickled vegetables during harsh winters. Today pickles are relished for their piquant flavors and the zip they add to plain rice and congee, and they are valued as a pungent seasoning ingredient in cooked dishes.

On the upper and mid-level shelves of our grocery you will find lots of glass jars and cans filled with whole, shredded, and sliced pickled roots, shoots, vegetables, fruit, leafy greens, garlic, fish, wheat gluten, and even tiny whole chilies. Under these is a selection of salt-preserved "dry" pack items in plastic bags and "wet" pack ones in vacuum-sealed brine-filled plastic pouches. A large crock containing the extremely strong-smelling preserved Sichuan vegetables is on the floor, mid aisle. Mustard type pickles—popular on their own or as part of other dishes—are listed first. The least popular—pickled fish and hot chilis—are mentioned last. Once you get your pickles home, remove from can, crock, or bag and store in a glass jar. They will keep indefinitely, refrigerated.

Mustard Pickles

CHINESE MUSTARD CABBAGE

Harm choy in Chinese and hua pak kad dong in Thai. This is also called mustard greens or "green hearts" as only the main stem, or heart, buds, and young leaves are pickled with salt, vinegar, and sugar to create an intense sweet-sour product. "Cabbage" on the label means mustard greens, and Chinese mustard greens are totally different and unrelated to the type grown in the American South. The large whole stems with leaves are used in making soups,

mustard pickle

such as seafood or duck and salted vegetable soup. Good braised with pork or dried tofu and dark soy sauce and eaten with rice. You can buy shredded or chopped mustard greens in small cans and glass jars labeled "salted mustard stems." Chong choy are small jars of a pickle condiment made of a mix of cured bits of Chinese cabbage and seasonings. As it is very pungent, use small amounts to flavor soups or noodle dishes.

You may also find Tianjin preserved cabbage in dry packs or small earthenware crocks. This is Chinese preserved cabbage with garlic shoots, and gives flavor to soups, congee, fried rice, noodles, meat, or bland vegetable dishes. Dried mustard cabbage, sold in foil packs, is called mei gan tsai and is best added to soup or steamed dishes to soften it. There is also bottled, preserved cai xin "vegetable hearts," which are sweet pickled cabbage stems. They are dark olive-green, ½-inch cubes in a sweetish brine fluid. These are delicious rolled

mustard green pickle in brine

inside rice balls to eat as a snack. Look for Companion, Ma Ling, First World, and Queens brand mustard pickle in cans and Yin Fa, Chao Sheng, and Umeko in glass jars. Tianjin pickles are in earthenware crocks, made by Greatwall brand.

Whole stems are found in wet packs of brine in sealed bags, labeled "sour mustard." Lotus, CTF Thai sour mustard, and Rolin brands are good. In dry pack look

for Wings, Wansheng, and Yuh Ming Enterprises. When you find them sold by weight from crocks in some Chinatown stores, they will usually be locally made.

Pickled Vegetables, Etc.

PICKLED RADISH

Also called tang chi and tong choy (similar, but sweeter and available in fine strips or bits) or sweetened radish, this is made from the large white root grown in Asia, known locally as Chinese radish. The pale ochre or tan colored pickle is found whole or in strips in vacuum-sealed dry-pack plastic bags or jars, sometimes flavored with chili. It is eaten with rice or slivered and added to dishes for its crunchy texture and slightly sweet, salty-sour flavor. It can be chopped into seasoned minced pork and steamed to be eaten with rice. Look for Thai Family Elephant brand, Qin Gquing shredded radish in dry-pack bags, and Oriental Mascot chili radish in soy sauce in a glass jar.

PRESERVED TURNIP

Also called chi po, this is similar to pickled radish, except that it is made from turnip shreds or slivers cured in salt then dried in the sun. The result is orangish-brown in color and is often sold, coarsely chopped, in sealed plastic bags. Chi po is added to Thai fried noodles, scrambled eggs, and other dishes in small amounts. It can also be mixed with chopped garlic and steamed with rice cakes to make chee kuey. Look for Thai Family Elephant brand and Wings in dry-pack 14-ounce bags. Also Siamese Coin brand sweetened turnip, whole or in strips, in 8-ounce bags. Pickled turnip or radish is used in the pad Thai noodle recipe, page 210.

radish pickle

SALTED TURNIP

Here the large white Asian turnip root is sliced crosswise and preserved with the stems and leaves by salting. The dark green stem dyes the white slices pale green. This is used as a condiment or garnish for rice dishes and soups and it is added to stir-fries or slow cooked stews, giving a pungent, salty, and tangy flavor. Choong toy are rolled up bundles of salted, semi-moist turnips with tops. To use, unroll bundles, rinse well, and chop, then add to soups, fried rice, or stir-fries. Salted turnip comes in dry-pack bags: look for Man Chong Loong Fisherman brand in slices or rolled bundles. There is also Wings brand sliced turnip.

salted turnip

SNOW CABBAGE

Amaranth. Also called red-in-snow because its red leaves and roots often sprout in early spring through the snow. This leafy vegetable has a distinctive earthy, pungent taste and crisp texture when salt pickled. The pickle is used as a condiment and flavoring in soups, in braised or stir-fried dishes with pork, or a filling ingredient of dumplings. Pickled snow cabbage is found in cans. Companion and Ma Ling brands from China are good.

SICHUAN PRESERVED VEGETABLE

This hot, spicy, pickled radish, or kohlrabi, is called jah choy. This type of preserve can be made from other vegetables, such as mustard greens, nappa cabbage, and turnips. These pickles have a dark olive-green color and a spicy-salty flavor due to their chili paste and ground Sichuan peppercorn covering. To reduce the strength, soak them in fresh water or rinse off some of the seasonings. They are used in a variety of Sichuan and other Chinese dishes and added to Northern Thai and Laotian noodle soups. They can also be chopped finely and sprinkled over rice congee. Delicious chopped and mixed with chili bean sauce and poured over a block of drained beancurd, garnished with a drizzle of sesame oil and sliced scallions.

In the Lins' grocery these pungent pickled vegetables are in an earthenware crock on the floor. You use the tongs to pluck out the amount you want and take the bag to the check-out counter for weighing. In many stores you can find Sichuan preserved vegetables in cans or vacuum-sealed plastic bags. Look for Bright Pearl, May Ling, and Tang Meng brands.

Kimjiang, or pickle making takes place every November in Korea when mountains of fat cabbages fill the markets. Whole families work to complete this monumental task. Hundreds of pounds of kim chee are prepared and stored to ferment in large earthenware jugs, which by age old tradition are buried in the ground with only the mouths of the jugs above the surface. During this month a friend will ask not about your health but whether you have finished your pickle making.

PICKLED WHEAT GLUTEN

Wheat gluten is made from wheat dough with all the starch washed out. These small globs are then boiled, braised, or fried and pickled in seasoned brine. They are added to vegetarian stews and soups as mock meat or used in stir-fries and other cooked dishes. They have a rich, meaty, salty taste with a chewy texture. Pickled gluten is sold in glass jars. Look for Kimlan pickled wheat or peanut gluten (made in the same way), Queens, Master Sauce Co., and Wen Hsin brands.

KIM CHEE

This mainstay of Korean cuisine is a hot, pickled, and fermented Chinese cabbage with a lot of garlic and red chili. Some varieties

kim chee

include layers of pickled carrot, radish, or red bell pepper. It is very spicy and pungent. Kim chee accompanies rice as a condiment and is added to cooked dishes. It is also used to make a soup, which really starts a fire in your belly! In most stores kim chee is packed in glass jars and found in the refrigerated cases. Look for the Assi or Kikkokin brands.

PICKLED BAMBOO SHOOTS

Also called mang cha, these are small shoots or strips of bamboo fermented in a chili-laced vinegar brine with a very sour-hot taste. Soak the pickle in water to remove some of the sourness before adding to stocks, soups, or Thai curries. You can stir-fry it with meat, especially duck or pork. This is sold in glass jars and vacuum-sealed plastic bags. Look for Caravelle, New Horizon, Wei-Chuan, and TAS Thai brand spiced sour sliced bamboo shoots, all in glass jars. Grand

Western brand has boiled whole shoots or strips vacuum-sealed in brine-filled pouches.

PICKLED LOTUS ROOTLETS

These are the pale, long, slim (¼ inch across) stems of the lotus plant, cut in 3- to 4-inch lengths and sold in a brine solution in glass jars. They have a crisp texture, taste like white asparagus, and are good added to hot-and-sour soups. Cambodian somlah machou is made with tamarind juice, broth, fish chunks, lotus rootlets, tomato, and pineapple, spiced with chili pepper slices. Look for TAS brand in 15-ounce jars.

PICKLED SHALLOTS

Also labeled as pickled leeks, they are the tender bulbs of small onions packed in a brine solution made with vinegar, sugar, and salt. They are used as a condiment to accompany grilled foods and fried noodles or to season sweet-sour dishes. These come in glass jars or cans and you should drain off the brine. Good brands are Mee Chun, Blooming, and Champion.

PICKLED FISH

You will find small, sliced fish steaks, 3-inch headless white fish, or tiny anchovies pickled in salt brine with seasoning in glass jars. Some are fried first before pickling. The silvery anchovies are used to garnish rice, noodles, and soup, while the larger pieces are added to flavor stock or stir-fried with leafy greens. Look for Imperial Marine Products pickled salted Spanish croaker steaks and Battleship brand preserved white fish in soybean sauce. Amofood has anchovies in spices, called sambal ikan bilis.

PICKLED CHILI PEPPERS

Tiny whole red or green chilies are pickled in a vinegar brine and used to add fire to soups or as a condiment at the table. The brine, chopped chilies, sugar, and fish or soy sauce are mixed together to make a dipping sauce for fried or grilled fish and meats and is spooned into rice noodle soup. Try them stir-fried (slit and de-seeded for less fire) with thin slices of pork, chili powder, garlic, ginger, and scallions in peanut oil with a splash of rice wine, soy sauce, and pinch of sugar. Pickled chilies are very hot, so use with caution! Look for Jo-Na brand tiny whole hot peppers, papaya shreds from the Philippines called siling labuyo, and the Thai pickled hot chili P. Pra Teep Thong brand called cot chua.

Mrs. Lin suggests using pickled chilies (if you like really hot food) in a main dish Thai omelete. Stuff the omelete with ground pork mixed with chili paste and pour over a sauce made from coconut milk, curry paste, pickled chilies, and palm sugar. Garnish with cilantro. Enjoy the fiery flavors!

The pickle section also has many more items than mentioned above, some of which are more of an acquired taste. You may also find small pickled

chili

eggplants from Thailand, papaya pickle from the Philippines, and Malaysian achar—salted, sun-dried carrots and cucumbers pickled with vinegar, ginger, garlic, and sugar. You can also find jars of pickled bean sprouts, lotus root pickles, sour green mango pickle, pickled ginger, and peeled pickled garlic heads. Choose whatever looks good to you, then try as a condiment or addition to rice and noodle dishes. Bland ingredients contrast best with the sharp, hot, salty, and sour flavors of pickled or preserved things.

STOCKING UP

Sour mustard, handy as a quick side dish, appetizer, or soup addition, sweet turnip for authentic pad Thai, and sichuan preserves if you are a hot food fan. A jar or two of pickled fish stretches a simple vegetable stir-fry or adds depth to a soup.

13

Dried Goods & Spices

매운것

Korean for "spice"

Dried products run the gamut from crinkled black mushrooms, spices, chili peppers, peels, pods, beans, nuts, and seeds to strips of seaweed gelatin, dried fish, oysters, and shrimp, plus other marine life specimens in stiff and wizened forms. Shelves are stocked with heaps of plastic bags and clear boxed goods in stacks. The better quality and more expensive grades of fungi and dried seafoods are in the boxes, usually shrink-wrapped in cellophane. There are whole shriveled fish with dark glazed eyes, slabs of pale fish, and bags of dried shrimp in sizes ranging from miniscule to several inches long, dried flower buds, curled cinnamon bark, yellow curry powder, and lotus seeds. You will also find salt, pepper, and dried onion and garlic flakes.

cinnamon sticks

Dried products play a significant role in Asian cuisine. Drying was developed to preserve foods before the invention of canning, freezing, and refrigeration. Even though most of these products can now be found fresh or frozen, dried items are still very popular and prized, despite a sometimes higher price tag. This is because the preserving process concentrates flavors and aromas, thus creating a much more intense form of the original. Seafood products become richer in taste while lending an unusual texture. Dried mushrooms, white fungus, lily buds, and other products absorb flavors while adding slippery or chewy texture. Sesame seeds, nuts, spices, and citrus peel add subtle flavors or perk up plain dishes.

While impossible to list all of the hundreds of dried products made, our little grocery has a pretty good cross section, from Korean sweet potato stems to Thai sweet basil seeds and cinnamon bark from Vietnam. Again, following the logic of shelf order and use, dried goods are organized from fungi, nuts, and seeds to powdered and whole spices to dry seafood.

Fungus

DRIED MUSHROOMS

Also called Chinese mushrooms or shitake, they have brownish-black caps, light tan undersides and, when cooked, a rich meaty texture and robust, smoky wild-mushroom flavor. The more expensive "winter black" variety have wider cracked caps and are a darker brown color with a superior texture and richer flavor. These are reserved for fancy banquet dishes or recipes needing whole caps. The other grades are used as a seasoning, chopped and combined with other ingredients, and

dried black mushrooms

in stir-fried vegetable and meat dishes. You need to soak the mushrooms in a bowl of warm water for 20 minutes or until pliable. Squeeze out excess water and discard woody stems, as only the caps are eaten. You can strain the soaking water and save it to add a rich flavor to soups or the water for cooking rice. Once

opened, the dried mushrooms should be stored in an airtight container in a cool dry place, with a dried chili pepper added to prevent worms. Sold in plastic bags and cellophane wrapped boxes. Look for Dynasty, Tai Wing Hong, and Golden Lion brands for whole black mushrooms. STR brand sells sliced ones. Dried black mushroom and wood ear fungus are added to the vegetable stir-fry recipe on page 212.

CHINESE TREE FUNGUS

This tiny black fungus, also called cloud ears, grows on trees and is dried after picking. These fungi are used for their crunchy texture, slightly smoky flavor, and ability to soak up the flavors of what they are cooked with. When soaked they puff up and look like little clouds. They should be soaked in hot water for 20 to 30 minutes until soft. Rinse and cut away any hard portions before using them in spring or egg roll stuffings, soups, stews, and stir-fries. Will keep indefinitely if stored in a cool dry place in an airtight container. Cloud ears are usually sold in cellophane bags, and may also be found in pre-cut or shredded pieces, which are convenient for egg roll stuffings. Look for Caravelle, Swallow, and Happiness brands.

WOOD EAR FUNGUS

A larger variety of cloud ear fungi, it is prepared and used in the same manner. After soaking, they swell to four or five times the dry size.

WHITE FUNGUS

Tremella. Also called snow flake fungi or silver fungus, this dried, crunchy tree fungus looks like a golden crinkled sponge and turns silvery-white after being soaked. It is often confusingly labeled as "sea vegetable" because it so resembles something harvested from the ocean and it is rinsed in vinegar and dried, thus giving it a faint brine

white fungus

smell. It adds texture more than flavor to savory dishes or sweet dessert soups and absorbs the flavors of other ingredients. Believed by the Chinese to be good for the health. A soup of fungus and rock sugar is supposed to brighten the eyes and refresh the palate. To use, wash and soak in warm water for 1 hour. It will expand greatly. Remove any hard stem parts and cut into bite-sized pieces. It is sold in cellophane bags or flat boxes. Look for Golden Dragon and Shiu Cheong Co. in bags. Peony Mark is found in boxes.

Nuts, Seeds, & Blossoms

LOTUS SEEDS

Mooncakes are exchanged as gifts among families and friends during the Mid-Autumn Festival, a celebration of harvest time and the full moon. According to legend, messages or weapons were hidden in large mooncakes prior to the successful Han revolt against the Mongols. Around this time of year (mid-September to October) mooncakes will be found in Asian groceries. Look for individually wrapped single cakes at the front counter or tins with decorative pictures, often of beautiful Asian ladies.

Shi lian zi, also known as lotus nut, is the dried seed from the large lotus pod left after the flower has bloomed. This dried seed resembles a small beige olive with a hard black tip and core. It must be soaked in boiling water for 1 hour, then peeled and the central core poked out with a thin skewer or a toothpick. Lotus seeds are used in savory and sweet soups and stews, and can be ground into a sweet paste filling for pastry, mooncakes, and buns. They are sold in plastic bags. Look for Peony Mark and Tai Hing Foodstuffs Factory brands.

lotus seeds

DRIED CHESTNUTS

The nuts of the chestnut tree which are encased in a prickly burr that pops open when they are ready to harvest in the autumn. The pale cream-colored wrinkled nuts have been shelled, dried, and halved. The ones in Asian groceries come from China and Japan. Dried chestnuts must be soaked in warm water several hours until soft or parboiled about 15 minutes before using. The nuts have a mild slightly sweet flavor and crumbly texture. The Chinese add them to braised chicken dishes, steam them with rice, or use them in dumpling stuffings. They are called kuri in Japan and are eaten roasted, steamed with rice and red beans, boiled, or mashed with sweet potatoes. Look for Peony Mark and Oriental Mascot brands in 12-ounce bags.

CANDLENUTS

The Malay name is buah keras: they are called candlenuts because they have such a high oil content that tribal people used to grind them up and use them as candles with a palm leaf wick! They are small, round, waxy, and cream-colored and resemble a large macadamia nut. The plant is native to Indonesia and Malaysia and the nut is pounded and added to spice pastes, sambals, and curries to give richness, body, and a nutty flavor. You will find shelled, roasted, and dried candlenuts in small jars or plastic bags. You can substitute raw cashews, macadamia nuts, or brazil nuts.

PINE NUTS

The seed or nut comes from cones of the pinion pine tree. They have been cultivated in China for thousands of years and are added to numerous dishes for buttery flavor and crunchy texture. Toasted or fried until golden brown, these pale ivory kernels garnish sweet and sour fish, pork, and crispy fried cabbage, or stir-fried spinach. In Korea they are added to sinsollo, a casserole of vegetables, eggs, strips of meat, and fish mixed with pine and gingko nuts. Look for Assi, Red Flower, and Oriental Mascot brands in 6-ounce bags.

LILY BUDS

Also called jin zhen (golden needles) and tiger lily buds, they are the dried, long, thin, unopened flowers, not buds, of the day lily. They are about 2 to 3 inches in length and have a slight velvety texture with a sweet earthy fragrance. Must be soaked in cold water for 30 minutes. Any hard stem parts should be cut off. Use them shredded in mu shu dishes or add to hot-and-sour soups and vegetable dishes. You may also like to put a few, together with some soaked mushrooms, slices of ginger, and maybe half a tomato, on a fresh fish to be steamed. Store the buds in a jar in a cool place after opening. They are sold in cellophane bags, often in knots. Look for Peony Mark, Golden Lion, and Tang Tai Marine Products brands.

dried golden needles

DRIED SWEET POTATO STEMS

The dried stem removed from the vines sweet potatoes grow from. Cut in pieces, they look like little twisted dark brown twigs. Used to make the Korean dish known as bokkum, stems are stir-fried with red pepper flakes, soy oil, sesame seeds, garlic, and scallions. To use, boil stem 30 minutes, rinse, drain, then stir-fry with meats, vegetables, or beancurd. Adds a chewy texture, woodsy fragrance, and smoky flavor. Look for Assi brand in plastic bags. Assi also offers dried taro stems, very similiar but must be soaked overnight in salted water, kneaded, boiled, then cooked. Use in stir-fries.

S p i c e s

JUK SONG

This spongy, dried interior pulp from bamboo stalks resembles lacey off-white tubes. They are tied with strings and packed in thin plastic

boxes or bags. Immerse in warm salt water about 15 minutes, wash and soak another 5 minutes, then drain and use as a vegetable in stir-fries, soups, and stews. It has a bland taste and chewy texture, and absorbs the flavor of other seasonings. Look for Crown, Panda, and Golden Lion brands.

juk song

FIVE-SPICE POWDER

Called ng heong fan in Cantonese. This all-purpose pale chocolate colored Chinese seasoning is made from a blend of ground spices—usually star anise, cloves, cinnamon, fennel, and Sichuan peppercorns. According to ancient folklore, the spices represent the five elements of the cosmos—earth, fire, metal, water, and wood. The powder is used in Cantonese barbecue marinades, braised and simmered dishes, and for roasted meats, giving a hot, pungent, mild, fragrant and slightly sweet taste—all in one mouthful. It is also used liberally in "ngo hiang"—fried meat rolls of minced pork, crumbled crackers, chopped onions, and egg wrapped in a soy skin, and to season fried peanuts as a snack. Five-spice powder is also mixed with salt and rubbed into the skin of chicken before deep-frying. Found in small plastic bags or spice jars. Look for Wah Loong Co., Oriental Mascot, Sinbo, and Peony Mark brands in small bags.

STAR ANISE

Ba-jiao. This spice is the 1-inch, hard, dried, six-to eight-pointed star-shaped flower head of a Chinese magnolia tree. Each point of the star encases a shiny dark brown seed. It is added to flavor and scent rich braising and poaching liquids, soups, and stews and has a distinct spicy, licorice taste. Wonderful with Sichuan peppercorns and soy sauce for roasted and barbecued meats. Remove from the sauce or finished dish before eating. The Chinese believe anise aids digestion and freshens the breath. Star anise is sold in small plastic bags or spice jars. Be sure to buy whole pods, and not broken pieces, as these will lose their flavor sooner. Ground star anise is one of the spices in five-spice powder.

star anise

CLOVES

This nail-shaped spice was originally found only in the Moluccas islands, east of Bali—the famed Spice Islands. It is the dried, unopened flower bud of an Indonesian evergreen tree with a pungent fragrance.

Cloves are used whole to scent and flavor stock and braised dishes, and ground into spice pastes for grilled meats. They are also used to make clove-scented cigarettes popular throughout Southeast Asia. You will find them in small bags and jars.

CINNAMON

Also called rou gui and cassia, it is harvested in China, Vietnam, India, and Indonesia from the bark of a type of laurel tree. The dried, rolled sticks and curled bark have a strong concentrated spiciness. One stick may be added to impart an aromatic flavor in braised, roasted, and claypot dishes, and it is used to flavor Vietnamese beef noodle soup stock. It should be stored in a tightly sealed jar to preserve flavor. Sold in plastic bags. Ground cinnamon powder can be substituted but will not have the special taste and aroma.

SICHUAN PEPPERCORNS

Also called hua-jiao, wild pepper, or flower pepper, it is not really a pepper but a small berry that resembles an opening flower bud from a shrub related to the prickly ash tree. The seeds are reddish-brown with

sichuan peppercorns

a sharp tingling taste and lemony-spicy fragrance. Widely used in Sichuan cuisine, it is toasted, ground, and mixed with black pepper, dried chili, and salt as a dry marinade for meats and fish. Mixed with salt only, it makes a dip for fried foods. It is one of the ingredients in five-spice powder and is called sansho pepper powder in Japan. You need to dry toast the seeds in a clean hot wok or heavy pan before grinding in a pepper or spice mill. Store seeds in a tightly closed glass jar. The seeds are sold in cellophane or vacuum-sealed plastic bags to retain freshness. Look for Wah Loong Co. and Peony Mark brands.

PEPPER

The dried, whole berries of a vine native to the Malaber coast of India. The pepper vine is now grown throughout tropical Asia, particularly in Sarawak, the Eastern state of Malaysia. The black variety, which are whole berries picked unripe and sun-dried until shriveled, is the most widely used form in Southeast Asia. Sold as whole peppercorns or coarsely ground in spice jars. Before the arrival of red chilies, peppercorns were the main source of heat in Asian food. For whole black peppercorns look for Peony Mark. White pepper is made by removing the reddish skins of ripe berries, then drying and bleaching them in the sun. Sold in powdered form and used sprinkled on many dishes. Look for Bright, Ho-Wai, and Oriental Mascot brands, or the 1-inch wide blue tube cans of "Thumbs Up" Hand brand No.1 white pepper.

LIME STONE PASTE

Calcium oxide. This is a white powder mixed with water into a paste and used in the making of some Thai desserts to prevent the flour from becoming mushy. It is also the lime used in preserving century eggs—not to be confused with citrus lime juice! Look for small 3.5-ounce containers of Combine Thai Foods brand.

CURRY POWDER

The word comes from the Indian word for sauce—kari. It is a mild to hot aromatic yellow spice powder, originally from South India, blended and fresh ground to suit a number of regional recipes. Its ingredients include six or more powdered spices, including cardamom, cinnamon, cumin, cloves, black peppercorns, and turmeric—which gives it its characteristic yellow hue. Cooks in Asia do not use just one blend of curry powder for all dishes, but change the mixture depending on what is being cooked. For example, spice blends used in cooking fish are different from those used for a meat dish. Generally meat mixes have cinnamon, cumin, and cardamom while fish do not, using fenugreek and curry leaf.

Curry powder is used to make curries, in coconut-based soups, and as a seasoning for fried fish and meat. It can be made into a paste and added to mashed potatoes and minced meat or vegetables to make samosa filling. It should be mixed into a thick paste with a little water, then fried with oil and onions in a pan to release the fragrance when making a curry or a sauce. If you find the result too spicy, temper it with either milk or tomatoes (depending on whether you want a rich watery curry or a thicker sauce).

When you need curry in a hurry, use the premixed powder type, sold in plastic bags or shakers. Malaysian and Thai brands are the mildest. Look for Javin, Siamese Coins, and CTF Thai brands in glass spice jars and D & D curry powder in 4-ounce packets.

GARAM MASALA

This is a mixture of ground spices, used in Southeast Asian dishes, and often mistaken for curry powder. Curry powder seasons food at the beginning of cooking. Garam masala, however, is added as an additional seasoning, sprinkled over many dishes after cooking to give extra fragrance and flavor. The overall taste is slightly sweet. A basic combination might include corriander, cumin, cardamom, black pepper, cloves, cinnamon, and nutmeg. You can make your own by lightly roasting the whole spices in a dry pan and grinding them. Look for pre-made blends in paper wrapped round packets and spice jars.

DRIED TANGERINE PEEL

Known as chen pi in Mandarin, it is the brown or rusty orange dried brittle and gnarled peel of tangerines. The older and browner the peel, the more it is prized. It adds a light citrus zest to sauces, herbal soups, braised meat, fish, and poultry dishes. It is also added to the dessert soups made with red (adzuki) beans or green mung beans. Soak the peel before using in warm water and scrape the underside with a knife to remove the bitter white portion of the peel. Chen pi is sold in clear plastic boxes and plastic bags. Look for Oriental Mascot or Wing-Shing brands in small bags. You can make your own by air or sun drying cut strips of peel a few days until they're stiff, very dry but still flexible. Store all peel in an air-tight glass jar in a cool dry place.

DRIED BAEL FRUIT

Matoom in Thai. Thin, dried, and round light rusty-orange slices of a bright orange Thai fruit with seeds arranged in a circle around the core. This creates a circular hole pattern in the dried slightly curled slices. To use, roast them and steep in hot water to make a fragrant tea or sour sauce base. Look for Kwang Yak Joo brand.

SESAME SEEDS

These tiny dried seeds can be either white or black. White sesame seeds, unhulled or hulled, have a sweet nutty flavor while the black seeds are slightly bitter. The white seeds should be toasted prior to use: this intensifies their flavor and fragrance. Whole sesame seeds are used as a coating for fried foods and sprinkled over noodles, rice, pickles, and salads.

In Japan, sesame seeds (goma) are lightly roasted, then ground in a mortar until flaky and aromatic. This paste is used to season blanched vegetables (spinach is especially good), make salad dressings and dipping sauces, and is mixed with miso (soybean paste) to make grilling sauces. Crushed, toasted sesame seeds are used liberally in Korean cuisine in everything from rib soup to namul, marinated briefly cooked vegetables tossed in a soy-sesame dressing.

To toast sesame seeds, heat a skillet until hot, add seeds and stir a few minutes. Watch closely and keep stirring. Remove from heat as they crackle and turn light brown, and pour onto a plate to cool. Store sesame seeds in a glass jar in a cool dark place. They are sold in plastic packets or small shaker jars.

Peanuts, Mustards, Etc.

PEANUTS

Raw peanuts are used to add flavor and a crunchy texture and should be boiled or dry-roasted in a hot pan before being chopped and added to dishes. They are good in vegetable and meat stir-fries or added to pan-fried or steamed noodles. The Chinese like to leave the skins on the peanuts and either braise them or cook them in soup. You can remove the thin red skins by immersing the nuts into a pot of boiling water for a few minutes. Drain and cool: the skins will then rub off easily. Raw peanuts are sold in plastic bags. Look for Oriental Mascot, Red Flower, and Lucky Farmer brands.

peanuts

ROASTED PEANUTS

Unsalted or salted, these are already roasted before packaging. They are often chopped and added to noodle dishes such as pad Thai or used to garnish salads, rice, or noodles. They can be mixed with crisp fried anchovies or silver fish, sugar, salt, and chili sambal to go with rice.

Peanuts may be ground into a paste for dressings and satay sauce. You can even find packets of ground peanut powder, to use in pastes, sprinkle over dishes as a garnish, or make sweets from. Look for Red Flower peanut powder and salted, roasted skin-on nuts in 6-ounce plastic tubs; Golden Boy, Farmers, and Yang Tze roasted, salted nuts in 14- to 16-ounce bags. Use roasted peanuts with skins to make chili peanuts with anchovies, a savory snack or side dish recipe found on page 207.

FRIED SHALLOTS & RED ONIONS

These crispy bits of deep-fried shallot or red onion are used mainly as a garnish in soups, salads, and vegetable dishes or on noodles and fried rice. They can also be sprinkled on omelets or a slice of bread and are used in some Thai sweets—folded taco-style inside thin crispy cookie shells with dried shrimp and dabs of thick coconut cream. Maesri Thai brand makes a delicious blend of fried red onions, dried chili flakes, and shrimp seasoned with tamarind, sugar, and salt called nam prik klang dong, sold in small glass jars. This is good on noodles and plain rice or sprinkled over soup and stir-fries. The fried shallots and onions are available in sealed plastic tubs of varying sizes. Once

fried red onion flakes

opened, use up soon as they can turn rancid, or store in the refrigerator, tightly sealed in a glass jar. Look for Thai P. Pra Teep Thong, Asian Boy, and Grand Western brands. You will also find fried garlic bits and flakes in plastic tubs. Look for Oriental Mascot and Mount Tai brands.

CHINESE HOT MUSTARD

This fiery hot, pungent condiment is made from the ground seeds of the mustard plant. It gives food a pleasant hot kick, but use sparingly as it can clear your nostrils! Added to various sauces and dressings and served as a dip with deep fried appetizers. Sold powdered in tiny cans or plastic containers or prepared in glass jars. The powder is mixed with water to form a creamy, pale yellow paste. Look for Oriental Mascot brand prepared mustard in tall skinny jars. S & B and Hana brands of powder are in tins and Assi brand prepared hot mustard is found in small tubes.

MUSTARD SEEDS

These are black or pale yellowish tiny round seeds from the mustard plant. You should fry them in hot oil until they pop. Then remove from heat and use to flavor curries, Indian dahls, and vegetable dishes. They add an olive-like, nutty taste. The ground, toasted seeds are also added to spice pastes, pickles, and chutneys. They are sold in little packets or glass containers.

CURRY LEAVES

Also called kari patta, it is the small leaf of a Southeast Asian plant that smells like curry when crushed, but it is not related to any of the spices in curry powder. The leaf has a mild sweetness and faint lemony fragrance. To release the leaves' aromatic essence, crush them before adding to curry, spicy soups, stews, and Indian dahls. The leaves are especially good with lentil dishes and added to fish curries. They are sold in plastic bags.

CORIANDER SEEDS

These are the small, round, off-white, aromatic "seeds," or more specifically the ripe dried fruits, of the cilantro (Chinese parsley) plant. They smell like a blend of caraway, citrus, and onion and are used whole or ground to flavor curries, pickles, and meat or fish marinades. It is best to roast and grind the seeds just before using. Sold in small bags or spice jars. You can find powdered seeds, but the flavor will not be as good as freshly ground ones. Look for Sing Kung Corp. whole seeds in a bag with a logo of two dancing elephants and Thai Hand Up No. 1 brand powdered coriander.

coriander seeds

Mrs. Lin shared her secret for seasoning chicken to grill: crush together dried coriander seeds with some fresh coriander roots, garlic, and black pepper and smear the paste all over the chicken pieces. Let sit about one hour and grill over coals—or under a broiler. Delicious accompanied with jasmine rice, green papaya salad, and a squeeze of lime.

SWEET BASIL SEEDS

These are the tiny dried black oval seeds from lemon basil (bai manglak). When soaked (about 20 minutes) they swell and become encased in a translucent mucus-like jelly. These are used in Thai desserts. Med manglak nam ka-ti is made of soaked seeds in sweet coconut cream. Look for Erawon Thai brand in 1.9-ounce packets.

TURMERIC POWDER

Made from the ground root stem of a member of the ginger family, it has a bright, deep yellow color. Bitter and pungent, turmeric is blended with other spices into curry powder and tandoori pastes. It is also added to pickled vegetables, used to season flour for deep-fried foods, and to color festival rice and Indian bryani rice. You can rub some turmeric over fresh fish steaks before pan-frying them, but be careful, the color leaves a long-lasting stain. You should dry roast the powder before adding to sauces or curries to release the aroma and temper its bitterness. Turmeric is sold in small plastic bags or glass spice jars. Look for Caravelle, Foodex, and Thai Hand Up No.1 brands.

DRIED CHILIES

Drying chili peppers concentrates their power and makes them fiercely hot. Look for the ones that are bright red and have a pungent aroma.

dried chilies

Large chilies tend to be slightly milder than the small ones. Chilies can be used whole or broken into pieces in soups, curries, and stir-fried dishes, or pound them to make sauces or dips. You should soak dried chilies before using, unless you are adding them to a Sichuan-style stir-fried dish. For less heat, you can remove the seeds before cooking. Using a small pair of scissors, snip off the stem and cut the chili open on one side. Scrape up and down the inside with the scissor blade and the dry seeds will fall out. Discard them and use the pod. Wear rubber gloves and wash your hands thoroughly after handling chilies, as the oils in them can burn or irritate your eyes and skin. They are sold in plastic bags, either whole or in crushed flakes. Korean silgochu are thread-fine chili strips sold by Assi brand. Look for Mount Tai and Oriental Mascot chili flakes and powder; Wings, Vasinee, and Oriental Mascot ground and whole chilies.

Use whole or flaked chilies to make the chili peanuts with anchovies snack on page 207. Chili powder adds punch to pad Thai noodles on page 210, jazzes up vegetable stir-fry on page 212, and is added to Vietnamese nuoc cham sauce on page 217.

Dried Beans

MUNG BEANS

These small, dried, olive green beans are from the mung bean plant. Two types are available: dried whole mung beans, with green husks, and dried yellow split beans, which have the husk removed. They are boiled to make savory or sweet dessert soups. The large white bean sprouts in the produce section are sprouted from soaked ones and cellophane noodles are made from the starch of mung beans. They are sold in plastic bags. Look for Golden Chef, Mon Chong Loong, and Caravelle brands in 12- to 16-ounce bags.

RED BEANS

Also called adzuki, they are small, dried, dark red, high-protein beans, about half the size of kidney beans. They are mainly used in dessert soups and coconut milk drinks or are ground and made into a sweetened paste to stuff buns, pastries, and pancakes. Soak and boil until soft to use. The colors red and white are considered lucky in Japan so adzuki beans with sweet rice are customarily served on happy occasions such as birthdays and weddings. The cooked beans and rice are steamed together with sugar. Bags of red beans are sold by Oriental Mascot and Selected Food brands.

Dried Seafood

AGAR-AGAR

Also called kanten, it is a colorless gelatin made from seaweed and sets without chilling. It is available in powdered and solid forms, and also feather-light, sometimes multi-colored strips resembling crumpled scotch tape or thick green easter grass. Powdered or solid agar-agar needs to be dissolved in hot water before being used as a jelling agent in cakes, dessert puddings, and molded jellies. The strips must be soaked and are used in salads, often with wakame seaweed. Malaysian cakes are made with agar-agar and have a thick, chewy gelatinous texture. Look for Florence brand agar in two long clear sticks; Peony Mark, Oriental King, and Horn Dean brands in strips.

agar-agar strip

IKAN BILIS

Also called ikan teri and kung yue. Sometimes labeled as silver fish, these are tiny, salted, sun-dried anchovies from Malaysia or Indonesia. The best way to appreciate them is to fry them crisp, then mix with roasted peanuts, sugar, finely chopped fried garlic, and chili powder. This can be eaten as a snack or sprinkled over fried rice. They are also used to season vegetable dishes, and boiled to make soup stock. Found in plastic bags. Look for Shiu Cheong Co. Anchovies, Hang Loong Marine Products, or Sea Star in 4-ounce bags.

anchovies

DRIED FISH

These are the salted, sun-dried whole, chunks, fillets, or thin strips of a variety of Asian fish. You might want to soak the hard, dried fillets in several changes of water for a few hours or up to overnight before using in soups and stews or adding to vegetable dishes. A small cube of (unsoaked) dried fish is one of the ingredients of the fragrant clay-pot rice and small pieces are added to homestyle beancurd, chicken, and salt fish casserole. Some types are in a semi-moist state; these can be cut up and fried or steamed, and used to accompany rice. They have a flaky, slightly chewy texture. Sold in plastic bags often with plastic twine handles. Look for Wings brand (big fillet chunks), Yacht brand small fillets, Sea Star, Assi, and Hang Loong Marine Products whole fish, and SSH Shenzhen dried pieces of grouper.

DRIED SHRIMP

Hay bee in Cantonese and kung haeng in Thai. These are miniature peeled shrimp preserved in brine and dehydrated in the sun. They are

dried shrimp

hard and should look plump and be a bright pink-orange, not brown or gray, which means they are too old. The pungent odor disappears when they are cooked. Very small ones are fried and sprinkled over foods as a garnish and have an almost bacon-like flavor. Larger ones need to be soaked or steamed for 10 to 15 minutes to soften before using to add a delicate taste to sauces, soups, noodles and stir-fried dishes. Sold in air-tight plastic bags and sometimes on styrofoam plastic wrapped trays in the refrigerated case. To keep their flavor, store in a tightly sealed jar in the refrigerator. Look for Sea Emperor, Wings, and Caravelle brands. Recipes that call for dried shrimp are green papaya salad on page 205, grilled eggplant salad on page 206, both the Thai fried noodles on page 210, and sweet sesame noodles on page 215.

SHRIMP POWDER

This is not really a powder, but small dried shrimp that have been shredded into fine flakes. It is used to flavor and garnish salads, soups, and rice or noodle dishes. Looks like sawdust. Sold in small plastic

packets or glass jars. Look for Tom Cha Bong and Maesri brands.

DRIED SQUID

Forms of sun-dried, salted squid range from whole, flattened, almost transparent creatures to thick pale lavender strips and whole baby ones seasoned with soy sauce. Whole squid need to be soaked for up to 24 hours, then are cut up and added to seafood and vegetable stir-fries, or used (unsoaked) to make soups. It is valued for its unique chewy texture and slightly brine-infused taste. Small octopus and cuttlefish will also be found and used in the same way as squid. Cuttlefish, like squid is sold in shredded, flaked, flattened, and seasoned form. All types are sold in cellophane packages. Look for Shiu Cheong, So Sing Hing Trading Co., Peony Mark whole squid, and Eastern Oceanic (also for small dried octopus) brands among the many, some with only Chinese characters.

DRIED OYSTERS

They resemble shriveled dark brownish-green or black olives and are sold in many grades and sizes. Preserved in the sun which concentrates the flavor, dried oysters are used to add a rich dimension to other dishes, or are finely minced and used in stuffings and added to soups, stews, and stir-fries. Use sparingly as their pungent, smoky flavor can overwhelm a dish. Soak in warm water at least one hour or up to overnight before using. Dried oysters are sold in plastic bags. Avoid any very shriveled and dark ones; they are too old. Look for Peony Mark and So Sing Hing Trading Co. (also for razor clams and mussels) in 1-pound bags.

dried oyster

DRIED SCALLOPS

Canpoy. They look like small hard tawny brown discs with cracked tops. Preserved in brine and sun dried, they have a concentrated flavor so should be used sparingly to add a sweet richness to soups and vegetable dishes. Soak in warm water or steam 20 minutes before using whole or shredded. Sold in plastic boxes (the highest quality) and bags. Look for So Sing Hing Trading Co. in boxes and Peony Mark in bags.

dried scallops

DRIED ABALONE

Found in fancy cellophane sealed boxes, in slices that are pale yellow and translucent, or whole, which are shriveled and black. An expensive luxury item. Used in special dishes, soups, and salads. Whole ones must be soaked for up to 24 hours before using. Adds texture and status more than flavor. Look for Peony Mark and Selected Japanese Yu-Bi for abalone slices in boxes, and Shiu Cheong Co. or EOE brand dried chips in 16-ounce bags.

dried abalone

DRIED JELLYFISH

Sold shredded and in salt encrusted dried sheets, this is used for its unique refreshing crunchy texture. It is often marinated in rice vinegar, soy sauce, and sesame seeds and served as an appetizer, and it turns translucent pale gray after soaking. You may also find convenient, prepared and seasoned "instant pack" jellyfish distributed by AUSNA Trading PTY of Australia. Just cut open the plastic pouch and serve. Good with barbecued pork or roast duck as a side dish. For dried, look for Sea Whale, Hang Loong Marine Products, or Summit Import brand in 16-ounce bags labeled "medusa sea nettle."

STOCKING UP

Now that you have browsed through the abundant cornucopia of dried products, no doubt some have been added to your shopping basket. And that's good. You should stock up. With lots of dried goods in your cupboard, you have the resources for endless meal possibilities. By adding just a few fresh ingredients to some of your dried supplies

and cooking a pot of rice, supper is ready. And most dried products keep indefinitely if stored in air-tight containers. Take advantage of this and lay in a supply of dried seafoods—they add an intense gourmet flavor to simple ingredients. Think of dried scallops, shrimp, and oysters as Asian proscuitto or bacon. A little goes a long way while adding subtle smoky undertones. And with a stash of seductive spices, sesame seeds, fragrant leaves, fried shallots, peanuts, cloud ears, and curry powder you can instantly add zip, crunch, and texture interest to any recipe. Essentials include black mushrooms, white pepper, sesame seeds, a spice or two, curry powder, chilies (whole or flakes), dried shrimp, and one other dried seafood product of your choice.

dried whole squid

14

Canned Goods

Korean for "canned goods"

Canning is, of course, a method of preserving foods for export, long shelf life, and availability when fresh is not.

Moving along through the Lins' grocery, let's ease over to shelf 8. Long rows of stacked cans run the length of the right side and oppo-

wheat gluten

site are the housewares. Small- and medium-sized cans share space with squat oval cans and jumbo tins packed with everything from Asian fruit cocktail to quail eggs. The cans are wrapped in colorful paper labels with pictures or photos of each can's contents— use these in helping identify what you want. The dizzy array of canned goods will have you pondering everything from moon snails, sugarcane, coconut jam, and straw mushrooms to banana buds and a fruit resembling hairy red golf balls. You will find Asian sta-

ples like soup stock, bamboo shoots, water chestnuts, coconut milk, and baby corn, and those strange "whazzis" like grass jelly, ginkgo nuts, yanang leaves, and mock duck. Let's check out what they are.

In exploring the canned goods, you will find items arranged as they are usually found on Asian grocery store shelves: from popular water chestnuts, baby corn, and straw mushrooms, to wheat gluten (very important to vegetarian cooking and always in a prominent place), lots of canned seafoods, seeds, nuts and eggs (always together), and the vast array of coconut/coconut milk products. The more exotic, less used items—vegetables, fruits, and so on—are arranged by contents at the end of the canned goods section. Find the category you want and select from many varieties and brands. Can sizes range from 8-, 12-, and 16- to 28-ounces.

Canned Vegetables

BAMBOO SHOOTS

These are preserved in brine and they are pale yellow, with a crunchy texture and slightly sweet taste. There are several forms available, including whole tips, young tips, and sliced or chopped. They taste the same but the texture varies, depending on the fiber content. Tips are tender while sliced shoots are the most fibrous. All are added for texture to a variety of dishes and used in hot-and-sour soups. Rinse and blanch a few minutes in boiling water before using any type to get rid of any slight metallic taste. Store leftovers in fresh water in the refrigerator. Look for Eagle Coin, Globe, and Ma Ling brands.

WATER CHESTNUTS

When peeled, this is a pale white, slightly sweet corm the size of a small walnut. They add texture but little taste. Rinse in cold water before using and store leftovers in fresh water in the refrigerator. Used in stir-fries, salads, and diced in soups. Also used in some Asian desserts and in dumpling stuffings. Sold whole and sliced. Look for Ma Ling, Oriental Mascot, and Wei-Chuan brands. Water chestnuts are added to the vegetable stir-fry recipe on page 212.

BABY CORN

These are pale yellow tiny ears of very young corn with a sweet taste and crunchy texture. Sold whole or sliced crosswise in small coins or "flowers." Drain, rinse, and use in stir-fries, salads, and soups or stews to add subtle textural interest. Look for Mount Tai, New Lamthong, and Family Elephant brands.

Mrs. Lin makes a delicious Thai dish using baby corn stir-fried with shrimp in chili-tamarind paste (nam phrik pao) with crushed garlic blended with a

baby corn

little chicken stock and pinch of sugar for balance, making a lucious smoky-sweet and spicy sauce which contrasts the fresh shrimp and mild corn. Garnish with sprigs of cilantro.

GRASS OR STRAW MUSHROOMS

These cute little mushrooms have big dark brown, oval caps and short straw-colored stems. They are cultivated on rice straw in paddy fields and have a mild sweet flavor, chewy meaty texture, and leave a velvety smooth feeling in the mouth. Most varieties are peeled but you may find the unpeeled type with cap and stem encased in a brown film, resembling little eggs with flat bottoms.

straw mushroom

Either variety should be drained, rinsed, and added to

soups, stews, and stir-fries. Look for Oriental Mascot large peeled straw mushrooms. Also Rolin, Red Rose, and Golden Summit brands.

WHEAT GLUTEN

This is also called mock duck, and goes by various other mock meat names. It is made by washing out the starch from wheat dough until only the gluten—an adhesive, sticky substance—remains. The result is boiled or deep-fried and may be found in cans with pictures of the mock meat implied on the labels. In Asia wheat gluten is a staple of vegetarians and in Buddhist temple cooking. It is usually cooked with other vegetables in sauces or stir-fries and stews. It has a chewy texture and mild, bland taste and absorbs the flavors of what it is cooked with. Look for Mong Lee Shang, Companion, and Caravelle brands in flavors like curry, "lo han chai" mixed vegetables, and Mandarin jah-jan in kung pao sauce. Wu Chung brand offers mock pork, mock abalone, and vegetarian fish balls. All are in 9- or 10-ounce cans.

Canned Seafood

This section of the aisle will be large, stocked with all types of fish and seafood. The most common ones include sardines in various sauces, mackerel, oysters, scallops, flaked or whole claw crabmeat, minced or whole tiny clams, green mussels, long razor clams, cockles in brine—also labeled "ark shell"—and grilled or sauteed eel, often in little rolls. Brands to look for include Pan

prawns in spices

Sea, Pan Asia, Wei-Chuan, Smiling Fish, and Shirakiku. Other fish you will find are carp and catfish. Look for Eagle Coin brand grass carp with black bean sauce in large oval cans. This is a good all-purpose fish to add to hot-and-sour soups, stir-fries, and claypot dishes. For spicier fare try Yeo's and Por Kwan brand minced prawns or crabs in spices, delicious for curries and noodle sauces. If you're a fan of escargot, check out the snails—in the shell in a soy brine, or removed from the shells and packed in water. For an even more exotic variation look for moon snails canned by Yoo-Dong Korean brand or South Sea's top shells in soy sauce.

red clams

The ultimate and most expensive canned seafood is abalone, prized more for its texture and status than flavor. The ivory mollusk slices are cooked and canned in their juice. Use in cold platters or heat very gently and briefly or you will have a $15 slice of rubber! The packing liquid can be used in soup stock or sauces. Look for New World and Wing Tai brands.

SQUID-IN-INK

This is whole squid, cooked and canned in the dark purple ink that the squid ejects at its predators. To use, slice the squid, reheat in the ink brine, and serve over steamed rice. The idea is to make use of the ink, which has a rich earthy flavor. Look for Old Fisherman brand.

SHARKSFIN SOUP

Expensive and exotic, this saves you the lengthy soaking and shredding process in making the status symbol soup and banquet staple relished for the gelatinous texture (and expense) of sharksfin. With canned soup, the work and seasoning has been done for you, just heat and serve. May contain fin shreds or whole braised fin, usually in chicken broth. Additions include crab, ginger, white pepper, vinegar, soy sauce, soy oil, and tapioca starch as a thickener. They average in price from $10 (shreds) to over $20 for whole fin. Look for Oceanmex refined sharksfin soup and H & N Fish Co. braised whole fin in chicken broth.

Moving along, you'll find some other, non-fish, canned things . . .

Canned Delicacies

GINKGO NUTS

These are the small, yellow or ivory colored nuts from the ginkgo tree. They have been shelled from their hard white cases and parboiled with salt. They have a unique bittersweet taste and, in Asia, are considered an excellent food for cleansing one's system. They are also regarded as a symbol of good luck. Drain and blanch briefly in boiling water before using. Traditionally used in Buddhist vegetarian stews and served during the lunar New Year, they are good in soups and slow-cooked stews or roasted with salt as a snack. They are also added to syrupy desserts, sometimes with a combination of grains (sweet corn, barley), lotus seeds, fruit, and jelly cubes. Look for Pagoda and Chining brand labeled "boiled white nuts."

ginko nuts

LOTUS SEEDS

The canned seeds or nuts from lotus pads are soft, peeled, and normally have had the hard center core poked out, so they are ready to use. Used in savory dishes or mashed into a sweetened paste for bun and pastry fillings. Look for Sailing Boat brand.

QUAIL EGGS

The tiny eggs of the quail are hard boiled, peeled, and packed in a preservative brine. They are found in small- to medium-sized cans and used in soups and stews, or added to salads. They can also be breaded, deep-fried, and eaten as a snack with hot mustard. Look for Hua Peng Peace Canning, Lucky Man, and Golden Summit brands.

quail eggs

Coconut

COCONUT MILK

Called ka-thi (in Thai), santan (in Malay), and nuac dua (in Vietnamese). This is the unsweetened processed liquid made from grated coconuts. It is an essential ingredient for Southeast Asian curries, soups, and sweets, adding flavor and creaminess. Canned coconut milk has a thick cream at the top and under this will be a clearish liquid, the coconut water. In soup and curry both parts are added but some desserts and

sauces just use the layer of "cream." If you are using a recipe that calls for the cream alone, open a can without shaking it up and skim off the thick cream on top; you can also refrigerate the can for a few hours and spoon the hardened cream off the top. Many good Thai brands are available, including Chao Kroong Mae Ploy, Chef's Choice, Thai Chao, and Chao Koh. Canned coconut milk is used in the shrimp coconut curry recipe on page 211 and in Singapore chicken curry, on page 214.

coconut milk

COCONUT JAM

Called kaya in Southeast Asia, it is a thick yellow jam made from eggs, coconut extract, wheat flour, and sugar. It has a sweet, rich flavor and is most commonly used as a spread for toast or as a filling for pastries and pancakes. There's a coffeeshop in Singapore on Killiney Road which is famous for its homemade kaya. People flock to the shop for coffee and the charcoal-toasted bread spread with kaya. Look for Yeo's brand from Singapore in 6-ounce cans.

kaya

COCONUT MILK DESSERTS

These are pour and serve coconut milk based desserts with various combinations of fruit chunks, taro, tapioca, sweet corn kernels, and palm seeds added. You can chill the cans to serve cold over crushed ice, or heat in a pan for a warm dessert soup. Look for TAS, CTF Thai, and Sung Dragon brands.

Jellies & Sweets

GRASS JELLY

Also called chinchow, qing cao, and ling fen (in Chinese), thach-den (in Vietnamese), or agar jelly, these canned cubes of a blackish-brown gelatinous product are made from the extract of a grassy seaweed and cornstarch. It looks like black jello, smells faintly of iodine and tastes like vanilla soda. It is most commonly used, diced or shredded finely, in sweet beverages made with flavored syrups, coconut milk and crushed ice, coconut cream, or soybean milk. It is said to be cooling and makes a most refreshing drink. Look for Wu Chung, Eagle Coin, and Heaven Temple brands in 8- to 19-ounce cans.

grass jelly

AI-YU JELLY

Similiar to grass jelly, this pale green substance is made from gelatin, sugar and water and is flavored with mugwort extract. Mugwort is used by the Chinese as a bitter to increase the appetite and to promote digestion. It has a sweet slightly herbaceous flavor and is used diced and shredded in coconut milk desserts or served with crushed ice and soybean milk. Look for Golden Sound and Mong Lee Shang brands.

SUGARCANE

Mia (in Vietnamese) and oie (in Thai). This is a tall tropical grass with thick, jointed bamboo-like stalks. The juicy yellow flesh is spongy and fibrous. Throughout Southeast Asia, the pressed juice from the canes is made into a cooling summer drink. In winter, it is mulled with ginger as a warming beverage. Canned sugarcane is available when fresh is not. The peeled pieces are used to make chao tom, Vietnamese barbecued shrimp paste on sugar cane. Try it also with fish paste or grilled chicken—it imparts a subtle sweet flavor. In Bali, it is added to soto babat, clear tripe soup, to help soften the tripe rather than to add sweetness. Look for Chaokoh and Lucky Man brands in 1-pound cans.

Ratna, the mountain god's beautiful daughter, fell in love with Rahim, a Malaysian prince who was given the task of moving a mountain in order to marry her. After accomplishing this feat, Rahim was tricked by the god and turned into stone. This broke Ratna's heart, transforming her into a palm tree. The leafy fronds represent her hair, the coconuts her head, and the slender trunk is her body forever dancing in the wind. Next time you are lying prone on a beach under a coconut palm, imagine that a princess is shading you with her hair. But watch out for falling coconuts.

C a n n e d   F r u i t s

BANANA BUDS

banana blossoms

These brine-packed buds are the unopened flowers of banana plants. The large reddish-purple petals have been peeled off, leaving the tender, pale hearts of the buds. The taste is similar to artichokes and it is cooked as a vegetable. To use, rinse off and sprinkle with a little salt and lemon juice to prevent discoloring. Cut in half lengthwise, then cut crosswise in coarse slices. Banana buds are mainly used in spicy salads or added to hot-and-sour or coconut soups. Look for Caravelle and Chaokoh brands.

YANANG LEAVES

These are the fragrant leaves of the tree from which comes the yellowish-green ylang-ylang flower. The leaves and extract are used in scenting Thai desserts. Look for Singing Bird and CTF Thai brand.

SA-DOU

This is an astringent bitter herb plant used in Cambodian, Thai, and Vietnamese cuisine. It resembles green twigs and tastes like asprin. Canned sa-dou should be drained and is served with a crushed garlic, tamarind, and fish sauce dip with grilled or roasted fish and poultry. The plant's bitterness contrasts with the rich succulent roasted foods and cleanses the palate between servings. Look for Chaokoh brand.

GREEN JACKFRUIT

This is young, unripe jackfruit, cut in slices and canned in brine. Used cooked as a vegetable in coconut curries and soups or sauteed with other greens. Tastes a little like chayote squash with a slight sour fruity flavor. A popular vegetable in Malaysia and Indonesia, it is added to lodeh, vegetable curry made from eggplant, green papaya, long beans, and fried beancurd in coconut milk. The canned type has been cooked in processing and is softer than fresh would be, so don't boil too long or it will turn to mush. Look for First World, Jack Hua Company, and New Lamthong brands.

CANNED FRUIT

A large segment of the canned goods shelf is filled with a variety of tropical fruits. Some are difficult or impossible to find fresh, so take advantage of the exotic selection here. Most of them can be eaten straight from the can, or served with chunks of ice or ice shavings. There are rambutans (which look like red hairy golf balls), lychees, and the smaller longan, all translucent, pale, white-fleshed fruits with a soft succulent texture and mild sweet taste. A refreshing drink is often made using longan or lychee, together with the syrup, diluted with water and ice; and they can be served with almond jelly as a dessert. Look for Chaokoh, Golden Deer, and Tong Ling brands. Pigeon brand has fruit cocktail made with chunked papaya, pineapple, guava, palm seeds, and grapes. You will find canned pineapple, mango slices, mandarin orange segments, white peaches, guava, soursop, sweet chunks of papaya, small red bananas, and syrup-packed pumpkin chunks. Many are also found, when in season, fresh in the produce section.

One that is almost never found in fresh form is the gigantic jackfruit. This is a relative to the durian and breadfruit and grows to enormous sizes—up to one hundred pounds! The rind is light green and covered with little spikes. Canned Jackfruit is peeled and packed in syrup in chunks. The yellow-orange flesh is juicy and smells a bit like fermented pineapple but tastes like a cross between banana, mango, and pineapple with a sweet mild flavor. Look for Malee and CTF Thai brands. Have a quick meal and an instant dessert ready with fruit.

STOCKING UP

The fan of Asian food would usually have a can or two of bamboo shoots, coconut milk, water chestnuts, and mushrooms on hand. Having some tins of longan, jackfruit, or rambutans will ensure an unusual yet welcome dessert.

15

Snacks & Sweets

อาหารว่าง

Thai for "snack"

B y now your shopping cart is probably just about full with all the makings of an Asian feast. But save room for a few more sweet and savory nibbles to crunch and munch before or after meals, take on picnics, or snack on anytime. Head to the aisle with tins of biscuits, bags and boxes of candy and cookies, bags of seeds and nuts, dried fruits, bean and fruit pastes, fish and meat jerky, and syrup-packed jars of coconut gel. You will find coffee powders, big green tins of Milo and other chocolate malt drink mixes, and cans of sweetened condensed milk used to whiten and sweeten hot drinks in Asia. There are also some unfamiliar looking boxes of instant beverage powders and flavored gelatin and custard powders to make jelly and pudding desserts. Take a look and try some; most of these are non-dairy versions of familiar Western products.

almond soybean milk

Sweet Mixes

INSTANT POWDER & PASTE MIXES

These are soluble protein beverage or soup powders in boxes of packets, with one packet making a serving when reconstituted with boiling water. After pouring in the water, stir well, and drink warm or chill for later. Gets slightly thicker when refrigerated. The mixes are based on dehydrated soybeans and other powdered flavorings with sweeteners. For a different dessert, look for instant cream of black sesame, green bean, red bean, almond, and peanut paste powders. You might like to try Torto instant sesame or peanut paste powder, Sunways almond paste, and Altimix cream of green bean,

almond, black sesame, peanut, and red bean flavor with three 1-serving sachets to a box. Drinks include Cup-A sesame and green bean paste drink mix, Chia-Chia instant cream of red beans, and Cointree brand almond health drink powder. Other variations include almond soybean "cheese" drink or soup mix made by Mount Elephant and Ice Fountain brands with eight sachets to a box.

CEREAL DRINK POWDER

This features a mix of powdered grains, including soy, wheat, millet, and rice with malt extract, sucrose, and non-dairy creamer, fortified with minerals and vitamins. Since most Asians lack the necessary enzyme to break down dairy proteins, substitutes like soy milk and sweetened grain powders fill the need for an easily digested "milk." They are also a delicious breakfast or snack drink for anyone. Look for Goldroast, Shui Heung, Pine, and Crane brands.

PURE POWDERS

These plastic bags contain the whole ground powders needed to make your own drinks or dessert soups by adding sweeteners and flavorings. Look for pale tan-colored soybean powder and pearl barley, bran, and sesame seasoned millet mush made by Lin Yuan brand, or Sunlight brand soybean mix powder. To use, mix a few spoonfuls of powder in a cup or bowl with your choice of sugar or honey and flavoring extract, then pour in hot water and stir well.

AGAR DESSERT GELATIN POWDER

These are pudding-type dessert mixes made from soybean powder, agar-agar—a dried seaweed gelatin—and flavorings. Hot water is added to the mix, stirred until dissolved,then chilled to set in molds or plastic containers. Look for Jen Yi Co., Dofu Delight in almond, mango,

agar gelatin powder

and strawberry flavors, and Golden Coins Instant Agar-Agar powder for gelatin desserts. You may also find ready-made agar jellies packaged in tiny clear plastic cups. You can eat them popped directly from cup to mouth. Look for Cosmic and Eishido brands.

Concentrated Syrups

FRUIT SYRUPS

These are large bottles of concentrated syrup diluted with water to make fruit-flavored drinks. Some are fortified with vitamins, minerals, and glucose to replenish salts lost through sweating (much like gatorade). A few also have herbal extracts added. Some to look for are Hales "Blue Boy Brand" pineapple syrup, Ribena currant and glucose syrup, and Lucozade—a glucose sports-type drink syrup. Plum Syrup (suan mei) juice has hawthorn and licorice extract added.

COFFEE CONCENTRATE

These are bottles of sterilized liquid coffee concentrate which is poured over ice and sweetened condensed milk to make Thai iced coffee. Thick, sweet, and time saving as you don't have to brew fresh coffee. Look for O-Lieng "Cofe" instant coffee drink in 26-ounce bottles and Ho-Kee brand instant iced coffee liquid. Family Elephant Thai brand makes small 8-ounce bottles of already mixed (with milk) ice coffee and ice tea.

Thai ice coffee

Seeds, Nuts, & Sweets

You will find a staggering variety of snack seeds, sweet nut brittles, cakes, cookies, and candies in any Asian grocery. Some of the more popular and unusual ones follow. You are sure to find something you like in the mix, even if it's a familiar hard candy, chew, or taffy, but made from purple yam, papaya milk, or tamarind.

WATERMELON SEEDS

These are the dried, processed seeds from the large Chinese watermelon. They can be either red or black and are munched as snacks.

They are frequently served with drinks before meals and are a necessary tid-bit offered during the lunar New Year festivities. They are found in large plastic bags. Look for Oriental Mascot, Sheng Hsiang Jen,

watermelon seeds and Da Wang Ji brands.

KACHANG PARANG

Salted, brown broad beans roasted in palm oil, these crunchy snack beans are sold in plastic bags. Some may be salted or spiked with spices or garlic powder. Look for Tong Garden, Wong Chai Chi Foods, and New Horizon brands, all in 6- to 7-ounce bags.

SICHUAN WALNUTS

These are whole, shelled walnuts which have been glazed with honey or sugar. They are used chopped or ground as coatings for fried foods, added to mooncake and dumpling fillings, or eaten as a snack. They can be added to sweet-and-sour pork and spicy stir-fried chicken with spinach. Found in boxes with clear windows and in bags.

POPPED RICE CANDY

These are caramel colored squares of what look like rice krispies embedded in hardened sugar syrup. They are made from popped grains of rice stuck together with a sugar-honey syrup, which are cut into pieces while soft. Some have sesame seeds or peanut bits as well. Very hard. Sold in plastic bags or boxes.

SWEET PRUNE CANDY

Also found in sour sop flavor. A dark tangy, soft pulp-like confection made from Chinese plums and sold in small boxes. Chewy, but melts in the mouth. Look for Cawaii Trading Co. brand.

PRESERVED TAMARIND CANDY

In Vietnam this is called mut me, a must for the Tet festivities, often labeled "Vietnamese New Year's candy." It is preserved, tangy-sweet, and chewy nuggets or balls of tamarind pulp rolled in salt and sugar. Watch for seeds. Sold in 3- to 4-ounce plastic boxes. Look for Asian Sun World, Dana Rose, and Caravelle brands.

Vietnamese New Year's candy

PRESERVED STAR GOOSEBERRIES

Ma-yome in Thai and mut chum ruot in Vietnamese, these are Asian gooseberries that look like bumpy little Chinese lanterns and are pale greenish-yellow fresh, but dark red when preserved. The preserved fruits are rolled in sugar and salt and have a tart-sweet taste. Look for Cawaii brand tiny skewers of about five berries per stick in a sealed plastic tray and Chun Lee "mut chum ruot" candy in a small tub with a photo of a twig of fresh berries on the label.

SOFT CANDY DROPS

Small drops of chewy, soft candies in bags of six individually wrapped pieces. The variety of flavors include honey-lemon, licorice-salt, licorice-ginger, orange peel, and lemon juice-ginger. Look for Mui Yick Yuen Co. brand in 4-ounce plastic bags. Good for soothing a sore throat.

COCONUT TAFFY

Creamy coconut-fruit flavored taffy logs, each piece individually wrapped in a rainbow of different colored waxed paper. Look for Yan's "super creamy" candies in a 6-ounce, multicolored bag.

PAPAYA MILK CANDY

A taffy like candy made from condensed sweetened milk, powdered milk, emulsifers, and natural papaya extract. Sold in individually wrapped logs in bags. Look for Liuh Der Foods from Taiwan.

THAI COCKTAIL CANDY

Worth buying just for the funky graphics on the wrappers. Little rolls of five candy drops stuck together and twisted in colorful wrappers. Flavors include peppermint, lemon, strawberry, and orange. Tastes more like cough drops than candy. Made by Caravelle and sold in 8.8-ounce bags.

Thai cocktail candy

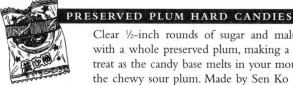

PRESERVED PLUM HARD CANDIES

Clear ½-inch rounds of sugar and maltose candy with a whole preserved plum, making a sweet-sour treat as the candy base melts in your mouth leaving the chewy sour plum. Made by Sen Ko Foods sold individually in 3.5-ounce plastic bags.

plum hard candy

LANGKA & UBE "PURPLE YAM" CANDY

Jackfruit (langka) and purple yam (ube) flavored candies made from fruit sugar, powdered milk, and fish sauce. Crumbly, with an unusual flavor. Made in the Philippines by Annie's brand, each piece is individually wrapped in vivid yellow or purple 4-ounce bags.

BUCAYO

Coconut pastille, a Filipino dense and sweet cake made from boiled shredded coconut, sugar, and spices. This thick, golden cake is sandwiched between pieces of dried banana leaves and wrapped in plastic. Look for Lucia brand in small 2- by 3-inch slabs.

DATE WALNUT SOFT CANDY

Made with chopped black dates, sesame seeds, sugar glucose, ground walnuts, and flour. Soft and chewy, not too sweet. Sold in six square pieces set in compartments in a flat tray, sealed in a small bag. Look for Hui Zhou Hui Jia Food Products from Hong Kong.

date walnut candy

SESAME CANDY

This is similar to peanut brittle, but made with white or black sesame seeds in a hard, slightly burnt sugar candy base. Some have cashew bits

added. Sold in individually wrapped pieces in bags or boxes. It has a delicious nutty flavor, rich in sesame. Hon Fu Food Co., Peacock, and Tong-San brands are all good.

sesame peanut candy

HONEY BAKED COOKIES

Long pale, slim crisp cookies made from flour, sugar, milk powder, and coconut oil with a dark brown crystalized lump of honey and maltose baked in the center. Made by Hsih Tung Yang Co. and sold in orange bags with a cartoon cow on the front.

CHIN HWA COOKIES

Small crisp-baked pinwheel swirl cookies made from light and medium brown doughs with sesame seeds. Nutty, not-too-sweet flavor and very hard. Look for Cho Fu and Seven Strong Co. brands in plastic bags.

chin hwa cookies

PEANUT ROLL

Also called groundnut roll, this pale flaky confection is made from tissue thin rolled up layers of sweetened peanut paste cut into 2- to 3-inch pieces. It sort of splinters and dissolves in your mouth.

Dry, crumbly, and salty-sweet. Look for Tong San brand with four pieces to a bag.

NUT CANDY CAKES

This is a brittle candy made with chopped peanuts or cashew pieces in a hard sugar or butter-sugar base. Very hard and nutty-and-toffee flavored. Sold in scored bars, so you can break little bars off, in a clear plastic wrapper. Look for Hon Fu Food Co. and Asain Boy; also Keo Hat Dieu cashew nut cookies.

SESAME SEED & PEANUT COOKIES

sesame cookie

These are not really cookies, but thin, flat, 4- to 5-inch-wide pancakes of melted sugar and sesame seeds with crushed peanuts. Soft, chewy, and flexible, but not too sweet. Use kitchen scissors to cut these into bite-sized pieces, or roll up and chew off bits. Sold individually or boxed, each pancake wrapped in cellophane. Look for the brand with a red bridge in a square labeled "keo: me xung hue sesame cookies."

BEAN JELLY CAKE

Yokan ogura. Soft, dark brown, square slabs of Japanese cake made from red bean paste mixed with agar gelatin and sugar. Looks like chocolate. Sold in individually wrapped single cakes or in plastic bags of four pieces. Look for ANA brand in 7-ounce boxes or single pieces and Shirakiku brand in bags.

MUSHI-YOKAN

A Japanese cake made by mixing bean paste with wheat flour and steaming the dough, studded with chestnuts in a mold. It is very dense and chewy. Sold wrapped in plastic on a cardboard tray of several individually wrapped cakes. Made by Hana brand.

DODOL

Also called jenang dodol, this is a Malaysian coconut cake made from glutinous rice flour boiled with fresh coconut milk, palm sugar, and salt. Sometimes found flavored with cloves. Very sticky and intensely flavored. Dodol is sold in flat cakes or bars, wrapped in plastic. Look for Tan Kim Hock brand in paper-wrapped 8.8-ounce tubes. Slice in thin pieces for a snack or dessert.

Philippine Preserves

In the next section of sweet products are seeds, gels, balls, preserves from coconut meat, yam paste, and fruits, tapioca pearls, and beans in sweet syrups. Most are imported from the Philippines and are used extensively in sweet drinks, fruit salads, and desserts with the syrup poured over shaved ice and mixed with coconut milk. For a new taste sensation try the vivid purple yam jam on your morning toast. It's sure to jolt you awake, even before that first cup of java!

PALM SEEDS

Also called sugar palm nuts and kaong, these are the chewy translucent white embryo seeds that grow in young green coconuts. They are very nutritious. Some are dyed green or red. Good mixed with coconut milk and fresh fruits for a soup-like dessert. Palm seeds are popular in the Malaysian and Indonesian drink called es teler, *palm nuts in syrup* which is a hodgepodge of fresh fruit juice, pink sugar syrup, condensed milk, tapioca bits, sweet corn, red beans, and possibly some chunks of avocado or mango. It is served with a long spoon and a straw. Found in 12-ounce jars packed in syrup. Look for Florence, Manila, Jo-Na's, and Lucia brands.

COCONUT GEL BALLS & YAM JAM BALLS

These are also available in shredded versions that look like tiny noodle pieces. The balls and shreds are a sweet pale white pulp-jelly made from soft coconut flesh and tropic yams packed in syrup. These are added to drinks and desserts. Yam balls are also served with other ingredients such as diced gelatin, candied beans, and caramel custard topped with shaved ice. Sold in jars. Look for Islands Best small cubes of coco gel and coconut sports balls or Florence brand coconut sports strings.

MACAPUNO PRESERVES

Called nata de coco in Thailand. These are shredded meat from very soft coconuts cooked with a sweetener (cane or palm sugar) and water into a sweet thick preserve. It is used in making coconut custard, cakes, and fillings for tarts. Look for Jo-Na's and Asian Boy Thai brand.

PINEAPPLE GEL

Also called nata de piña, it is a translucent, delicately flavored syrupy gel made from boiled pineapple and sugar, resembling pale gelatin. Used in desserts, drinks, and fruit salads. Delicious served with ice on a hot day. Or combine the syrup from a can of lychees with coconut milk and sugar and chill. Pour sauce over the lychees and some pineapple gel. Look for Jo-Na's, Florence, and Islands Best brands in glass jars.

SWEET CHICK PEAS

Whole garbanzo beans boiled until soft and sweet in a sugar syrup. Sold in glass jars, packed in syrup, and used in sweet drinks, dessert soups, and added to fruit salads. Look for Florence, Oriente, and Jo-Na's brands.

SWEET JACKFRUIT

Chunks of golden cooked jackfruit (langka) packed in syrup in glass jars. Used in sweet drinks, desserts, or fruit salads tossed with coconut cream. Look for Global brand. You will also find jars of Florence brand jackfruit and bananas in syrup.

Gong pancakes are a popular snack sold by street vendors in Japan. One cold night, I stopped at a little stand outside the entrance to a subway station. I watched as a man oiled his portable griddle, poured batter into small rounds and flipped them as they cooked. He then smeared some dark paste between two, making a sandwich. It looked just like a mini gong, and that is why they are called yaki dora, or gong pancakes.

HALO-HALO

Means "mixed." This is a sweet fruit mix made of mung beans, white beans, coconut gel, palm nuts, jackfruit, and sugar syrup. A sort of Filipino fruit cocktail, it is used in sweet drinks, with coconut milk over ice, or poured over ice cream. Look for Sarap and Florence brands.

SWEET YAM JAM

Also called ube halaya, this shocking purple or dull lavender paste is made from mashed Filipino purple yams boiled into a thick jam with cane sugar. Used in pastry fillings, cakes, as a spread, in ice cream, or whirled in a blender with sweetened condensed milk and ice as a drink. Look for Tasty Joy, Insta Pack Co., and Manila brands.

TAPIOCA IN SYRUP

Also called ang tunay, this has large pearls of cooked tapioca in a sweet syrup. Used in desserts and sweet drinks mixed with coconut milk or fruit juice. Look for Insta Pack Co.

TODDY PALM PASTE

A Thai product made from toddy palm extract, water, a preservative, and coloring dye. The paste is made from unfermented sap, which is sweet, thin, and tinted bright orange and mainly used in Thai sweets and steamed custards. It can be mixed with coconut cream and tapioca pearls to make a sweet soup or steamed with sticky rice in banana leaves to make a kind of cake. Look for Por Kwan brand in 15.5-ounce jars.

toddy palm paste

Pastes

SWEET RED BEAN PASTE

A thick, brick red paste made from sweetened red beans (adzuki) and used as a steamed dumpling, pastry, or pancake filling, or mooncake stuffing. Also used to make sweet red bean soup with lotus seeds. You may also find lotus, sweet black bean, and mung bean paste to use in stuffings or soups. Mung bean paste makes a delicious soup, thinned with coconut milk, and simmered with sugar. All are sold in cans or jars. Red bean paste is made by Shirakiku brand. Look for Wu-Chung lotus seed paste in 20-ounce cans with a red and yellow label. Companion brand offers green and sweet black bean paste in 18-ounce cans.

POMELO PEEL PASTE

A thick brown jam made from pomelo—a giant grapefruit-like Asian citrus—boiled to a thick paste with soy sauce and sugar. Has a sweet-tart-salty flavor and is used in meat and poultry glazes, sweet-sour dishes, on steamed fish, or as a spread on bread or in summer rolls. Look for Mee Chun brand in glass jars.

Savory Snacks

KRUPEK

Indonesian Shrimp crackers or kroepeck. Also called banh phong tom in Vietnamese. These are puffed wafers made from tapioca starch and shrimp, fish, or an Indonesian bitter nut called melingo. Ready made crackers are sold in plastic or foil bags, plain and in a variety of flavors—onion, garlic, wasabi, and barbeque

krupeck

to name a few. Enjoy as a snack or use to garnish the boiled vegetable salad topped with spicy peanut sauce, gado-gado. Look for Brilliant and Marco Polo brands. You will also find dried pinkish or buff colored dried thin chips in boxes or bags. To use, deep-fry in hot oil—they puff up to triple their size the second they hit the oil. Look for Pigeon and Komodo brands.

JACKFRUIT CHIPS

Thick curled crisp and crunchy chips made from jackfruit slices fried in vegetable oil. They have the unusual smell and taste of jackfruit, sort of a blend of banana, mango, and pineapple. Sold in small snack size foil bags. Look for Niki brand.

jackfruit chips

RICE CRACKERS

Senbei in Japanese. Sweet or savory and found in many sizes and shapes, usually a pale gold to deep orange or mahogany color with a shiny glaze. Some are spicy hot, flavored with wasabi, curry, or chili pepper, some are salty-sweet with a peanut or dried sweet green pea within a ball shaped cracker, and others are flat and wrapped in shiny black bits of nori seaweed. All are made of rice flour and roasted. They are light and crunchy with a nutty toasted flavor. Some crackers may be sprinkled with black sesame seeds or coated in a sweet sugar glaze. They range from small tid-bit size to very large crackled puffy squares. Sold in plastic bags and fancy tin containers. Look for Kameda and Kasugi brands (for a variety of types),

Originally rice crackers were a midday snack for farmers working in the rice fields. They were toasted on the spot over fires and dipped in soy sauce. Gradually, they became more and more refined and were baked in city shops.

rice crackers Imoto Toko snack

hot green peas, and Kaki-No-Tane tiny mahogany glazed tid-bits and nori-wrapped little log rolls.

SIZZLING RICE CRUSTS

These are commercial versions of the layer of crusty cooked rice stuck to the bottoms of large rice pots, which is carefully removed and roasted to use in soups. The kind you will find are dried cakes of glutinous rice, used deep-fried in guoba, sizzling rice soup. To use, drop the cakes in hot oil until they turn golden and puff up. Sold in plastic bags. Look for Oriental Mascot brand with 26 small cakes to a package and Hanh Shyuan Food Factory in small green and yellow bags.

rice cakes

CRYSTALIZED MELON

Chunks of pale icy green colored Chinese winter melon cooked in sugar water and rolled in sugar. Slightly crunchy on the outside with a melting soft inside as you bite in. So sugary sweet you'd never guess it was made from a vegetable! Look for Golden Lion brand in 5-ounce bags.

CRYSTALIZED GINGER

This is gingerroot that has been slow-cooked in sugared water then rolled in granulated sugar. It has a mellow but sweet-spicy bite and is one of the world's oldest candies. Chinese believe ginger stimulates the appetite and helps cure coughs and stomach disorders. Eaten as a candy or digestive. Found in boxes and small jars. Look for the six-sided plastic container sealed with lime green tape made by Kei-Mei brand from Singapore with a gold sticker label and Oriental Mascot "hua mei" crystalized ginger candy lumps in 6-ounce bags.

crystalized ginger

PRESERVED GINGER

Made from fresh gingerroot mellowed in sugar syrup with a spicy-sweet flavor and golden color. Sold in jars packed in a ginger syrup that can be used as a flavoring ingredient. Delicious as a condiment for roast meats or added to ice cream and other desserts. Another soft dried variety is dyed brillant red and flavored with salt and licorice. Look for plastic boxes of Golden Lion or Twin Fish brand bright orange shreds and slices.

RED PICKLED GINGER

These are ginger shreds or slices that have been cured in a salt brine then soaked in a sugar and vinegar solution. Red pickled ginger has a tangy sharp-sweet taste. Used mainly in sauces or dips and marinades. Can be found in small slender glass jars filled with bright red ginger shreds.

GINGER BON-BONS

Labeled Ting-Ting ginger bon-bons, they are hot, sweet chewy candies made from stem ginger and sugar. Look for bags or cigarette-shaped cartons of individually wrapped pieces with a blue-and-white checked border and picture of a ginger stem on white paper.

ginger bon-bons

DRIED PERSIMMONS

Also known as the Chinese date palm and kaki in Japanese, the fruit comes from a flowering tree in the ebony family. The dried fruits are rusty colored, flattened, and slightly shriveled, with a faint white dusting on the skins. Has a tart-sweet flavor and is slightly moist, not rock hard. In Korea they are steeped with ginger to make soo jeung kwa tea. In Japan they are thinly sliced and rolled up in slices of pickled turnip—a popular lunch box (obento) treat and new year's side dish. Look for Sun Wing Hong foods on plastic wrapped trays of six pieces of fruit. Found in the produce section or refrigerator case.

PRESERVED PLUMS

Collectively called "kanna" in Malaysia. You can also find preserved prunes, apricots, peaches, dates, and mango slices. The various fruits are preserved with salt and dried and have a sweet, salty, sour, and puckering taste. The plums are called mui and are sucked or chewed as a snack, eaten to settle upset stomachs and aid digestion, or steeped to make a plum tea. Can be steamed with fish. Found in small plastic bags on wire

preserved plums

racks. Some brands to look for are Golden Lion, Ka-Po, Mei Yuan, and Hua Bee Foods. You will also find Chan Pui Mui, 1-pound bags of large, individually paper-wrapped dried plums and apricots from Muda Jaya Enterprises in Malaysia.

CHINESE OLIVES

Two types are found. One is preserved with salt and has a tangy tart flavor, green color, and hard chewy texture. Golden colored honey olives—preserved with salt, licorice root, honey, and sugar—are juicy with a tart-sweet spicy flavor, delicious for snacking on. Both have pits. Look for Peony Mark salt or licorice olives, STR brand preserved green olives, and Ka Po honey olives.

Dried Snacks

"Jerky with a twist" describes the next group of snacks: spicy hot or fruit flavored beef jerky, seasoned shredded dried pork fu, and lots of fish, squid, and cuttlefish floss. All are made by preserving the meat or fish with salt and seasonings such as soy sauce, chili, sugar, vinegar, and fruit concentrate, then sun drying it.

BEEF JERKY

The kind you will find in Asian groceries is softer and much more seasoned or flavored than normal jerky. It is seasoned, cooked, and sun-dried strips or slices of beef. It is eaten as a snack, and goes well with cold drinks. It is sold in small snack-size packets of U.S. inspected beef. Look for hot chili spiced or sweet fruit-flavored beef jerky made by Formosa brand and China Meat Products of California.

PORK FU

It is also called pork si, sung, or floss, as it resembles cottony fiber or silk threads. It is made by deep-frying finely shredded, dried, cooked, and seasoned pork, then drying it again before packing in plastic tubs or bags. It has a spicy-sweet taste and is often used to garnish cooked dishes like rice porridge, Thai pineapple steamed rice, and green papaya or mango salad, spicy coconut curries, or soups. Also eaten as a snack folded in a slice of bread or out of the bag. Sold in various sized plastic tubs and bags. Look for Formosa, Hsin Tung Yang, and Jin Wei Hsiang brands.

SQUID & CUTTLEFISH FLOSS

Squid and cuttlefish are both in the cephalopod family, but cuttlefish have a hard internal shell that looks like a long, white, oval seed. The translucent white bodies and tentacles of both are used to make a variety of snacks. They are dried, seasoned, and pressed, then cut or shredded. The result is very chewy and salty-sweet or slightly spicy and creamy to tawny gold in color. Seasonings include chili,

squid jerky

spices, soy sauce, sugar, and salt. Large squid and cuttlefish are pressed into flat sheets, seasoned, and dried, then cut into ribbons, shredded, or rolled. Small ones are pressed, dried, and sold whole. Some Japanese types are cut in thick, long, smooth strips or wide flat ribbons and flavored with a sweet vinegar solution. Dried squid and cuttlefish is available in snack-sized and larger plastic or foil bags. Flat, scored, rolled sheets are sold in sealed plastic trays. Eat as is, or roast in a flame or hot pan and serve with dipping sauce or mayonnaise. Look for Ka Po, Jane-Jane, and Yaki-Co brands. Ones from Japan include JFC Wel-Pac cuttlefish and ITO shredded or sweet-sour thick-cut squid strips.

FISH FLOSS

This is prepared the same way as squid (but tastes less salty or spicy), or the fish may be fried or ground very fine, almost into a powder. Mainly sold in pale prepared ribbons or lightly seasoned shreds made from a variety of white fish, marlin, or salmon. Eat as a snack or use the fried shreds and powders to garnish rice dishes and soups. Look for North Sea brand pale, flat fish strips; ITO brand long, thin ribbons; Wei-Chuan brand fried fish shreds; and Kuang Ta Hsiang Foodstuffs Co. brand ground fried fish in cannisters.

143

Other treats you may discover in the snack section include candied citrus peels, dried coconut and banana chips, chicken essence candy, crème filled koala and panda shaped cookies in cartoon splashed boxes, chocolate or lemon puff biscuits, White Rabbit brand vanilla taffy, Botan millet jelly candy, corn or green pea crispy curls, plus more.

botan rice-millet candy

Grab something new and give it a try. You might soon be munching roasted green peas or salad flavored pretzels; chewing spiced fish floss or tossing a jar of coconut gel over a bowl of ice cream. Have fun as you explore the sweet and savory realm of Asian snacks. New ones appear each visit to keep your taste buds happy in anticipation.

16

Teas, Healing Tea, & Herb Tea

Trà

Vietnamese for "tea"

Boxes, bags, ornate canisters, and paper-wrapped blocks fill a large section of any Asian grocery. With a willingness to learn and try new types, you'll be able to navigate your way through the vast sea of tea. Just where does tea come from? My favorite story is the legend of an Indian Bodhidharma who brought Zen Buddhism to China. The monk had pledged to sit in meditation for nine years. However, he fell asleep. Very angry about this, he cut off his eyelids and flung them to the ground. A plant grew from that spot with leaves shaped like eyelids, called cha. The brewed leaves from this plant helped keep him— and all who drank it—awake and alert. The plant is what we now know as tea. In reality, tea did originally come from China, whether or not from a monk's eyelids, over 3,000 years ago. The way of tea also came from China, becoming a ritualized art form in Japan and Korea as the plant became cultivated throughout Asia.

The tea shelf contains a mix of many varieties and grades, arranged loosely in caterories of three main types. These are fermented black teas, semi-fermented oolongs, and unfermented green teas. You will also find white steamed teas and fruit or flower scented tea. A section of the row will also contain brewing utensils—small china cups, teapots, whisks, water ladles, tea scoops, infusing balls, and strainers made of bamboo, metal, and cloth.

All types of tea come from the same tea plant (camellia sinensis). This one species produces thousands of complex flavors and varieties.

Each growing region yields its own distinctive teas with taste determined by local climate, altitude, soil, and time of year the tea was picked along with the care and handling of leaves and method of processing.

How Teas Are Made

The three main teas—green, black, and oolong—all begin their journey from tea bush to teacup in the same way. Distinct manipulation processes applied to the same leaves produce the differing categories. Freshly plucked leaves are dried or withered to soften them. Then they are rolled by hand or machine to crush the cells, releasing enzymes in the leaves which give teas their character and flavor. For green tea, the leaves are next quickly steamed to prevent fermentation. To produce black teas, the fermentation process is allowed to continue, darkening and developing flavor in the leaves. This is called firing or drying. Oolong teas are only partially fermented after withering and they have a color and taste in between green and black. Oolongs are less astringent than black teas with a slight natural smokiness resulting from the processing. Once fired, cut, and sifted, teas are graded in sorting machines by the size of the leaf.

Choosing a Tea

Teas come under a variety of tea labels. It's best to decide first on a type, such as oolong, then take a look at all of those to make your selection. Tea may be sold boxed just by name (black, oolong, or green) or sold with the name and brand. To help in your discovery of fine teas, I've listed the specific tea names in broad groups of the type, often named by the province they are grown in.

Black Teas

These are also known as red tea (hong cha) because the fully fermented leaves produce a beautiful reddish-orange color when brewed. They are like fine wine, leaving a lingering taste on your palette. Although there may be different types of black tea, you might sometimes have only the box and the brand name to go by. For instance, there's Sunflower black, Sprouting brand Fujian black, Rickshaw Finest Brooke Bond black tea, Goldensail black tea, Temple of Heaven black, and Tin Mend brand "China Choicest" black in 10-ounce orange canisters. Others are named by province including Guangdong black, Hainan black, Hunan black (Yihong), Sichuan black (Chanhong), and Yunnan black (Dianhong).

black tea

These are some famed black teas by name, with brands to look for that produce them:

KEEMUN

Chi-men. This comes from Qimen County in the southern Anhui Province of North China. It is a famous black tea with a delicate light smoky taste and flowery aftertaste. Keemun, or "the king of black tea," is amber colored with an aroma of rose or orchid blossoms. Look for Spring Harvest, Dragon, and China Fujian brands.

LAPSANG SOUCHONG

Zengshan Xiazhong. A black, wood-roasted tea from the Wuyi mountains in Fujian Province with a rich deep orange liquor (see glossary), pleasant full-bodied taste, and scent of smoky pine. An old legend claims that the smoking process was discovered by accident. A tea factory full of green leaves awaiting processing was occupied by an army unit in the Qing dynasty. When the soldiers left, the workers realized they couldn't dry the leaves in time to get them to market on schedule. Open fires were lit from pine and cypress wood to quicken the drying. The tea got to market on time and became a huge hit. The tea made today is withered over pine fires, then pan-fried, rolled, and fermented in wooden barrels. The leaves are then fried again, rolled into tight strips, and smoked in bamboo baskets over pine fires to dry and absorb the smoke flavor. The result is a dark red tea with a unique aroma. This is the tea often used to make jang cha yazi—duck boiled in tea and smoked over camphor wood and hard-boiled tea eggs. Meats and poultry are also often cured in the smoke from this tea, giving them a rich reddish-brown color and appetizing fragrance. Look for Twinnings, Sprouting, and China Fujian brands.

YUNNAN

Dianhong. Also called Heavenly black, this is a pleasant-tasting black tea from China's highlands in the Yunnan Province. It is made from thick soft leaves and fat golden buds. It has a full-bodied and rich, almost creamy, flavor that combines a hint of sweet citrus and pepper with a woodsy aroma. Good with meals and made into iced tea. Look for Foojoy Yunnan Bo Nay Tea brand and Dim Sum Herb tea, which is made from Yunnan tea with chrysanthemum and excellent for drinking after a rich meal.

PU-ERH

This is another tea type from Yunnan, with a distinctive earthy flavor from the fermenting process. It tastes slightly bitter but leaves a lingering fragrance in the mouth. In Cantonese, this bitter taste with lingering sweet aftertaste is called "kum" and it makes a good tea. It is somewhere between a true black and a semi-fermented oolong. This tea is made from old leaves but the girls who pick them know that tender young leaves taste better, so as they pick, they stash some in the seats of their baggy pants. They sell this privately and the tea made from it is called "Pants seat Pu-erh." Pu-erh is considered to be a medicinal tea drunk as a remedy for various ills from colds and sore throats to heat stroke, indigestion, and diarrhea, and is believed to reduce cholesterol. It is available in bags, loose leaf, and bricks. Yunnan Tuo

pu-erh tea

Cha is made in bowl-shaped cakes, pressed into tea bowls, and dried. This is found in a pale yellow box with a brown teapot. There's also Sprouting brand from Kwangchow Tea Factory in a box of 20 sachets. You may also find compressed rounds of Pu-Erh Beeng Cha (China Black) and Choice brand Pu-erh in green canisters. Gupu cha, a combination of Pu-erh and chrysanthemum, is considered good for cooling internal heat.

LITCHEE BLACK

Lizhi Hongcha. This refreshing tea from Guangdong Province in China is made by treating black tea with the juices of the lychee fruit. This process produces a mellow tea with a rose-amber color, light sweet aroma, and nutty flavor. This fruit and tea combination is sometimes called Feizi's smile after

lychee

one of the most beautiful concubines in Chinese history, who loved lychee fruits. The Tang dynasty emperor Ming Huang lost his throne by paying Lady Yang Yuhuan (Feizi) too much attention—even having shipments of the perishable lychee brought from the far south by night-and-day relay riders. Look for Goldensail brand in ½-pound tins or 7-ounce peach-and-white boxes, Sunflower brand in canisters, and Spring Harvest brand in a red box of twenty-five bags.

ROSE CONGOU

Meigui Hongcha. This black tea is made by mixing unbroken, or congou, tea leaves with pounded, powdered rose petals. It has a rich, dark flavor and scent of roses and is made in Guangdong and other provinces of China. Look for tins of Spring Harvest and Goldensail Rose.

ORANGE PEKOE

This is a fermented tea from China, Sri Lanka, and Indonesia, made from the smallest top leaves of Yunnan black tea plants. It has a slightly smoky aroma, a delicate but deep flavor, and dark sherry color. The name comes from a size grading term, pekoe, which means a small leaf size, and because at one time it was scented with orange blossoms. It can be mixed with spices and sweetened condensed milk to make "chai." Look for Twinings, Goldensail, and Sunflower brands.

Oolong Teas

Also called lightly fermented, or bohea, and semi-fermented tea. Bohea is the Anglicized version of Wu-I, the name of the mountains in Fujian, China. In general, any tea labeled "oolong" is partially fermented, whether or not it is from the Wu-I mountain region. Basic oolong brands include Fujian Butterfly, Goldensail, Egret River, Four Apollo, Mong Lee Shang, Ten-Ren, and Whole Dragon Choicest China Oolong.

oolong tea

TI-KUAN

Tieguanyin. Iron Goddess of Mercy Tea is a semi-fermented tea from the Wu-I mountains of China. An amber-hued infusion with a floral fragrance, it tastes bitter at first sip, then leaves a sweetly roasted flavor with a lingering orchid aftertaste. Also grown in Guangdong and Taiwan with the best grades being the more expensive. The name comes from a temple dedicated to Kuan-Yin, the goddess of compassion. The first tea shoot of this type was found by a poor farmer who prayed near there and became wealthy growing and selling the tea. Look for Four Apollo, Zibei Tiankui, and Sea Dyke Tikuanyin brands. A related oolong is Ti Lohan (Tielohan or Iron Arhat), named for when a monk gives up all worldly passions.

ti-kuan tea

WU YI

A heavier oolong tea from the Wu-I mountains of China, it has a deep earthy flavor and fragrance of lush ripe fruit with a bright golden color. The flavor remains pure and strong even after several additions of water to the pot. Look for China Fujian Oolong "Wu-I Tan-Chung Chi-Chong" tea in an octagonal silver metal canister, and Golden Dragon brand.

JASMINE

Moli Huacha. A lightly fermented tea enriched with the fragrance of night blooming jasmine petals, it is also known as "silver tip" tea. To

jasmine tea

flavor and scent the tea, jasmine petals, picked at their aromatic peak, are nestled among lightly fermented tea leaves nightly, then removed the following morning, for up to a week. The leaves absorb the flavor and scent of the flowers and are then dried again to remove any moisture. Jasmine teas are delicate and refreshing with a rich flowery aroma and pale greenish-yellow liquor. The finest is produced in the Fuzhou area of Fujian Province, but many others make it as well. Look for Sprouting, Ten-Ren, and Dynasty in boxes of sachets, and Truong Tho Jasmine in a big red canister with a bearded sage on it.

Green Teas

These unfermented teas have a fresh earthy flavor and are believed to be a cancer-preventive. Green teas brew into a lovely pale emerald liquor, are refreshing to drink in hot weather, and soul soothing on a cold day. An important point to remember: green teas are more delicate than the other sorts, they need to be brewed gently. Use water that has just reached boiling point to brew it, and do not steep it too long. Green tea brands to look for are Goldensail, Butterfly, Mong Lee Shang, Foojoy, PCT, and Evergreen in round tin canisters. Green tea can also be used to make Ochazuke—salmon with tea rice (recipe given on page 216).

DRAGON WELL

Long Jing or Lung Ching. This is a celebrated, delicious green tea named for a well outside Hangzhou China. Tea leaves are pan-fried lightly in processing, producing a liquid jade color, gentle aroma, and mellow, slightly sweet herbaceous taste. Considered to have a cooling effect on the body. The best are still made by hand and are the most  expensive. One of the most famous dishes from Hangzhou's Lake district is shrimp in Dragon Well tea. Fresh water shrimp are stir-fried in very strong tea. After removing the shrimp, boiling water and rice wine are added to the tea and reduced to a thick sauce to pour over the shrimp. Any green tea can be used. Look for Whole Dragon brand, Zhejiang Long Jing, and Goldfish Lung Ching in a blue canister with goldfish on it. Also Sprouting brand in a tin

Japanese green tea with pictures of Hangzhou's famous West Lake.

HIDDEN PEAK

Mengding. This tea is named after the central peak of Mount Meng, often shrouded in mists, where it is grown. The name Mengding means "misty peak." It is also often called Immortal's tea or Thunderclap, after an old legend of a sick man who was cured after drinking this tea following the first thunderstorm of spring. This green tea from Sichuan Province was prized for both its former scarcity— originally it was made from seven tea trees planted by a monk in a temple garden—and medicinal properties. Tea from these trees was believed to cure illness and prolong life. It is picked in late spring and early summer and has flowery fragrance, pale jade color, and slightly bitter-sweet taste. Look for Sprouting, Qing, Everlasting Spring Leaf, and Stoneflower (Shihua) brands.

TIANMU QINGDING

Green Summit or Qingding Tea. This green tea comes from the two main peaks of Mt. Tianmu (eyes looking up to Heaven), each one topped by pools (the eyes) that never dry up. The mountain is near the western part of Zhejiang Province and is famed for its beautiful water-fall scenery and natural resources, including tea, bamboo, and walnuts— the "three treasures of Tianmu." The processed leaves are tightly rolled, dark green strips with soft hairs and lots of bud-leaf sets. The brew is a bright yellow-green with a fresh fragrant aroma and mellow taste. Qingding tea is often used for scenting jasmine or Yulan (Magnolia blossom) teas. Look for Spring Harvest, Sprouting, or Sunflower brands.

ZHUCHA

Gunpowder or Pingshui Pearl Tea. It was given the name gunpowder by a British clerk in the East India Company. Each leaf is tightly rolled into pellets that "explode" when infused in boiling water. The

Chinese call it Pingshui Pearl after the town of the same name, southwest of Shanghai, where the tea is produced. When the tea is made, the hand-rolled pellets tinkle as they fall into the pot or cup. Boiling water makes them open like flowers and float or sink in the cup—fun to watch as the dark green, strong, slightly bitter tea brews. It has a pleasant long-lasting aftertaste and can be used

Chinese green tea

to make iced tea with lemon, or boiled with mint and sweetened with sugar. The Chinese, however, always drink it plain and hot. Look for Temple of Heaven China Gunpowder Green brand.

PAI MU TAN

This white tea is also known as White Down Silver Needles, China White, and Fujian White. White teas are really a type of very light green tea and are said to combat heat by lowering the body's temperature and helping aid digestion. They are made from only the fresh tender buds, plucked just before opening when they are covered in whitish hairs. The leaves are then steamed and dried; rolling and fermenting are not a part of the processing. When infused, the buds stand upright in a cup. The flowery scented, pale yellow brew has a sweet, mellow flavor. The smallest buds and leaves make Pai Mu Tan (White Peony, also spelled "pai mao tan") and Show-Mee (Shoumei or eyebrow). Pai Mu Tan is made of dried clusters of tiny round flowers attached to greyish-silver leaves, which make a mild, sweet tasting clear yellow-orange tea. Show-Mee is made from silvery leaves and you get a light brownish-orange tea with a sweet flavor. Look for Sunflower brand Pai Mu Tan in white tins with a watercolor mountain scene and Golden Dragon brand Show-Mee China White.

The first time I took part in a tea ceremony was at the San-ko-ji Temple in Kanazawa. It was a cold February afternoon following a memorial prayer for my friend's ancestors entombed there. We had assembled with the temple priest, his wife, and my friend's sister in a small tatami (mat)-floored room. A single camellia was in the alcove in front of a calligraphy scroll. Tea was whisked and served in ancient bowls, turned three times in the drinkers' hands before sipping. Small sweet cakes were presented on a lacquer tray. We spoke in hushed tones, breathing in the hay-like scent of the tea.

SEN-CHA

The national beverage of Japan, it is sipped with meals, at tea time, on work breaks, and when a guest calls. This green tea is made from tender young leaves, picked in May or June, which are steamed after harvesting, rolled and cut into shreds, then dried. The tea is a pale greenish-yellow color, has a delicate fragrance and slight astringent flavor. The best quality is grown in Uji, just south of Kyoto. Look for Shirakiku Japan green tea in boxes of ten bags (with a picture of a woman picking tea on it), Yamamotoyama brand, Dynasty Green Tea, and Waka-Matsu Sencha.

MAT-CHA

This top quality tea is made by covering the young leaves that unfold in May with straw to protect them from sunlight. The dried leaves are then ground into powdered green tea, which is drunk on special occasions and is indispensable to the tea ceremony. This is called cha-noyu, or "the way of tea," and is a stylized ritual to create a sense of spiritual serenity with nature. Water is poured over the powder and whisked until a fine foam forms in a special bowl called a chawan. It has a bright green color, is strong, thick, and very pungent, and may create a "caffeine buzz" after more than two cups. Mat-cha is always served with special sweet cakes or confections to counter the tea's bitterness. Sold in fancy canisters.

Other Japanese Teas

BAN-CHA

This is a roasted tea made from the large leaves and bits of stem picked in August, after the young sen-cha leaves have been plucked. Has a pleasant earthy aroma, a mild, refreshing flavor, and is light brown. It makes a good everyday tea, being much milder than mat-cha or sen-cha. Hoji-cha is made by roasting a blend of ban-cha and sen-cha over a flame, giving it a smoky aroma. Look for Waka-Matsu and Yamamotoyama brands in boxes of sachets.

GENMAI-CHA

This tea is made from ban-cha and has bits of popped brown rice in it. Sometimes labeled "popcorn tea," it has a delicious nutty flavor. Sold loose in large bags or boxes of sachets. Look for Yamamotoyama (16 bags) brand or Waka-Matsu (12 bags) brand.

MUGI-CHA

This tea is made of roasted unpolished barley. It is the thing to drink in the muggy heat of summer and is considered a sort of health drink. Sold roasted and unroasted in large bags. If you buy the unroasted kind, burn it in a dry pan until it is toasty brown, then add the barley to boiling water and steep, strain, and refrigerate if you want cold tea. Also good warm.

You will also find lots of other teas on the shelf including stop smoking herb blends, Lotus, Gingko, and "slimming" teas. There will also be powdered black Thai-style tea. This is flavored with star anise, cinnamon, and vanilla, which makes a fragrant deep orange tea. Mrs. Lin recommends it brewed strong and mixed with sweetened condensed milk for a drink that tastes like a cup of candy. Look for Caravelle Thai Tea powder or Foodex brand Mixed Cha.

Healing Drinks

Here are some of the healing and curative herbal beverages and instant mixes. Look for cellophane-wrapped boxes. Inside are individually wrapped smaller boxes with dried cubes made from herbal extracts mixed with a sweetener. You drop the cube in a mug or glass, add hot water, and stir until dissolved. Some are in packets of powder, used mixed with hot water. Others are in packets of Chinese herbs with other dried curative ingredients and teas. You will also find boxes of liquid extracts in small vials or jars, soda cans of healing drinks made from vegetables, and cans of congee.

CHRYSANTHEMUM

Ye Ju Hua. This is a dried instant beverage made of powdered extract of chrysanthemum flowers and sugar in packets. You dissolve the yellowish white crystals in hot water to make a drink that is good for cleansing the liver, lungs, and eyes. Also said to soothe sore throats. Look for a 7-ounce yellow box with 20 packets from Shanghai, China. Other instant brands include Ten Fu, Gold Kili, and Prince of Peace Instant Honeysuckle Chrysanthemum beverage in a box of 12 plastic packets of granules. You will also find boxes of dried unsweetened chrysanthemum petals, which are to be steeped and strained to make tea. This tea can also be added to chicken, seafood, and beancurd soup stocks to impart a delicate flavor and aroma. Look for a white box with a dark red middle panel with a white teapot on it and gold Chinese characters. Also Crown brand in 6-ounce plastic bags.

chrysanthemum tea

JU-PU TEA

This is made of dried chrysanthemum, Yunnan pu-erh tea, lou han guo (a dried fruit pod), and cane sugar with vitamins, minerals, and salts. It is an aromatic, sweet tasting, therapeutic, cooling drink for heat exhaustion; also said to soothe the liver and brighten the eyes. Look for Egret River brand in green and blue boxes with silver wavy lines.

LONGAN TEA

Long Yan Rou. This is made from dried concentrate of the longan fruit compressed into sweetened cubes that are dissolved in hot water to make a pale brown drink which has a mild sweet flavor. Good for heart and spleen, it also nourishes blood and liver, helps calm the mind, and benefits memory. Dried longan can also be added to soups, cooked with duck, pork, or chicken, and flavored with garlic, ginger, and pepper. Look for Yang Cheng brand in boxes of cubes. Or you can buy clear plastic boxes of the whole dried fruit and steep them in hot water to make a tea or slice up to add to herbal cooking recipes.

INSTANT LYCHEE BEVERAGE

This pleasant fruity, floral scented drink mix is made from dried extract of lychee fruit mixed with cane sugar and malt extract. It can be dissolved in hot or cold water and is taken as an all-purpose "strong and healthy" drink. Good for heat exhaustion. Look for the yellow box with a photo of a lychee cocktail in an oval on it, made by Shanghai Dong Yang Food Co. You get 10 sachets to a box.

FRUCTUS LYCII TEA

This tea is made from pure powdered lycium berries (Chinese wolfberry), a small oval dried fruit used in herbal cooking. It is good for blood, liver, kidneys, and the eyes. The tea is taken as a medicinal drink to help poor eyesight. Look for Egret River brand in a box of 20 bags. The box has a full teacup on a background photo of dried berries.

fructus lycii tea

ESSENCE OF TIENCHI FLOWERS

These white crystals in one-serving packets are made from pure extract of tienchi flowers and cane sugar. The flowers come from a ginseng-like plant that grows in Yunnan, China. Mixed with hot water, it makes a fragrant therapeutic and refreshing beverage used to prevent or cure cold sores, pimples, boils, dizziness, nausea, vomiting, headache, insomnia, and night sweats. Look for Camellia brand in a blue and white box with a silhouette of a tienchi plant (root, leaves, and flower

ball). There are 10 packets in the box. The root (notoginseng) is used in a famed pill called Yunnan Pai Yao, which stops traumatic bleeding, relieves pain, and promotes rapid healing of wounds. In Vietnam, soldiers carried this little red pill with them in case of gunshot injuries.

essence of tienchi flowers

KAMWOTEA

This blend of 30 herbs is good for cooling an over-heated body and fever, stopping thirst, soothing a sore throat, helping indigestion after eating too much, and for a mouth refresher. Look for a small, lime green and bright orange box with packets of tea bags or a larger box of 10 small individual boxes of loose tea made by Chu Kiang Brand. Brew like tea in hot water and add sugar if it tastes too bitter.

SHEN CHU CHA

This Chinese medicated tea, called fermented leaven tea as it is made into molded blocks, contains 14 herbs, roots, rhizomes, barks, and dried medicinal fruits in a base of flour and bran. It is used as a remedy for digestive problems, hangovers, constipation,

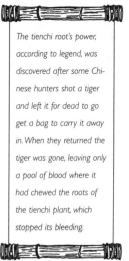

The tienchi root's power, according to legend, was discovered after some Chinese hunters shot a tiger and left it for dead to go get a bag to carry it away in. When they returned the tiger was gone, leaving only a pool of blood where it had chewed the roots of the tienchi plant, which stopped its bleeding.

joint pain, poor appetite, and to eliminate excess phlegm. To use, mix the whole block in a pan of boiling water and drink the strained liquid. Also good mixed with ginger slices to help a cold and fever. Look for green and red boxes of Yang Cheng brand from Guangzhou, China.

shen chu cha

BOJENMI TEA

Bao Jian Mei Jian Fei Cha. Also called "Nature's instant health tea," this Chinese tea is made with Fujian tea leaves plus a blend of 12 herbs, dried medicinal fruit, seeds, rhizomes, and citrus peel. Use brewed and take to maintain energy (chi), reduce fats, lower cholesterol, maximize nutrient absorption, prevent bad breath, and reduce high blood pres-

jian mei tea

sure. It is good for the stomach and spleen. Sold loose in canisters and in boxes of teabags. Look for Egret River brand, Liang's Jianbo royal tea in boxes of 10 bags, and Butterfly brand Jian Mei Tea in a white and orange box with a princess playing a stringed instrument on it.

XIAO ER QUXING CHA

xiao er quxing cha

An herbal powder made of coix (a barley-like seed) and hawthorn extract. Look for the yellow and white checkerboard box with a boy's cartoon face, made by Lap Lau Factory in China. Inside are 12 little red plastic cat-shaped capsules filled with granules that are mixed in hot water or juice. Used as a children's remedy for diarrhea and indigestion. The funny cat-capsules help the medicine go down.

EXTRACTUM ASTRAGALI

Huang Qi. This tea is made from the dried, powdered extract of the astragalus root. It is good for the lungs, spleen, blood, and

astragalus healing drink

overall vital energy (chi). It also helps to increase appetite and aids digestion. Look for packet-filled boxes made by Superior Sunflower brand and brew like tea. Also Astragali Crystals, made by Forest brand in round white canisters; these are used dissolved in hot water as a blood tonic and to improve digestion and clear the skin. Astragali crystals in sachets (12 to a box) are packed by Hsiang Yang brand in a yellow-orange box with a picture of the root on it.

ARTICHOKE TEA

A tea made from artichoke stems, roots, and flowers with a stringent, slightly bitter taste. Good for the liver, is a diuretic, increases bile secretion, and is believed to lower cholesterol and uremia—blood and compounds formed by protein metabolism in the urine. Look for the Ngoc Duy Vietnamese brand in red boxes with 20 tea bags. Brew as any tea and sweeten to taste.

GINSENG TEA

Various types will be found, all made from the extract of a pale brown root that grows on the floor of hardwood forests. Ginseng is believed to help regulate blood pressure, lower stress, slow the effects of aging, and cure sore throats, sleeplessness, and loss of appetite. Generally considered one of the best overall tonics for the human system. Look for Kings brand Korean Ginseng in flat red boxes of 10 or 100 bags, Triple Leaf American ginseng tea in gold boxes of 20 bags, and China National Red Panax.

ginseng tea

LI ZHONG TANG

A ginseng and gingerroot combination in powdered tea form, this is believed to be an anti-aging stimulant, a blood purifier, and good for the throat, stomach ailments, and nausea. Sold in boxes of sachets.

GINSENG & GANODERMA TEA

A tea made from ginseng root and dried, ground ganoderma (ling zhi or reishi), a giant mushroom that grows on tree stumps. It acts as a general tonic for the liver, spleen, and heart; also replenishes the blood and has recently been found to be good for the immune system. Many HIV patients are now trying ganoderma. The dried fungus can be added to cooked dishes or teas and has a sedative effect. Look for Beauti-Leaf brand Relaxing Ginseng-Ganoderma , Z.T. Universal Inc. Natural Herb Ginseng-Ganoderma, and Butterfly brand Reishi Tea.

GINGER TEA

This slightly spicy, sweet beverage is made from ginger, honey, or sugar in packets of crystals or granules. Ginger tea is believed to cleanse the body's systems, help cure a cold, be warming in cold weather, settle the stomach, help relieve nausea, and prevent motion sickness. Look for Gold Kili Instant Ginger Tea from Singapore and Extra Gold Instant Ginger made of honey and ginger crystals. Lizhong Tang tea is a ginseng and ginger combination.

ANGELICA ROOT RED JUJUBE TEA

lo han kuo

A medicinal tea made from ground dried angelica root (dang gui) and Chinese red dates (jujubes). Brewed like tea and taken to enrich the blood, maintain energy, fortify the spleen, and help menstrual cramps, fatigue, and weakness. Look for boxes with a blue flying duck logo from Lanzhou, China.

LO-HAN-KUO

This Chinese product is made from the lo han fruit (momordica fruit) and it is packaged in a flat, rectangular box with a drawing of the round golf ball sized greenish-black fruit on it. The extract of the slightly furry (like a kiwi), hollow, thin-skinned fruit is blended with cane sugar and compressed into hard cubes. The mixed liquid is pale brown with the fruit's slightly bitter flavor sweetened with enough sugar to make it pleasant tasting. Lo-han-guo is good for soothing sore throats and cooling an overheated system. Look for Instant Lohanguo Bao Shapai brand with a picture of the fruit and a cup of brewed beverage, Zhonguoming Chan brand, or Kwei Feng Trade Mark with a dozen individually wrapped cubes in a light green or purple box. You will also find bags of three whole dried blackish lo-han-guo fruits. Look for Flower brand.

LICORICE

Gan Cao. This is one of the more extensively used plants in Chinese herbal medicine as it is a harmonizing agent with other ingredients. The dried root is used to make a curative drink for bronchial asthma, peptic ulcers, indigestion, and coughs and it is also used in candies, cough drops, and many herbal blends. You can find Liu Yi San, which is a honey sweetened licorice root tea mixed with other herbs. It is good for combating summer heat (cools the body) and coughs, and nourishing the spleen, stomach, and lungs. Because of its ubiquitiousness, a busybody is often compared to licorice—found everywhere, in everything. You will also find dried roots in bags. To use the licorice root, put 1 teaspoon in a pan with a cup of water and simmer 10 minutes, strain, and drink. Look for Flower and Crown brands.

SHESHE CAO BEVERAGE

sheshe cao

These are boxed plastic packets of brown granules made from sugarcane mixed with two herbal extracts. These are oldenlandia, or sheshe cao, which clears heat, lubricates the intestines, and detoxifies the body, and scute herb (ban zhi lian), which has a natural sweet herbal taste and is a thirst quencher. It helps clean the system of toxins and promotes blood circulation. It also helps combat fatigue from heat, relieves pain, swelling, and difficult urination. Look for a rectangular green and white 7-ounce box made with the outline of a flowering herb plant, made by Yang Cheng Brand from Guangzhou, China. The box contains 10 bags. Mix one bag with a cup of water for a drink.

CANE & IMPERATAE BEVERAGE

These are boxed plastic packets of off-white granules of sugarcane and imperatae extract (bai mao gen). Sugarcane adds a natural sweet flavor and imperatae is good for reducing body heat in hot weather and lowering blood pressure. This drink is a thirst

cane imperatae

quencher and helps stop bleeding, vomiting due to stomach heat, and in clearing edema. It clears heat, cools the blood, and relieves thirst. Mix one small bag in a cup of water to make a drink. Look for a green and white box with a silhouette of sugarcane stalks on it made by Yang Cheng brand from Shantou, China; there are 10 packets within.

Another similar drink is made from water chestnut extract and sugarcane. It too is sold in boxes of granule packets. Look for a pale yellow and lime green box with a flying duck logo and shiny gold Chinese characters. There is also a picture of water chestnuts and sugarcane.

Tea & Chinese Herbs

Several kinds of herb tea blends will be found for helping a variety of ailments and aches. Jasmine with assorted herbs, in a 5.3-ounce, square yellow and red paper packet, comprises a loose mix of dried herbs, medicinal roots, lycium berries, licorice, and jasmine tea. Brew and strain to make a drink good for when you have been out in the sun too much. It is said to reduce hot and cold fevers, ease joint aches, headaches, lower backache, bladder ailments, thirst, and overall tiredness. Also improves appetite and cleans the liver. There is no English on the label, except a paper insert stating Product of China, with a long list of the herbs in Latin.

Other similar herbal teas are Yacht brand Chinese tea in a yellow and green 4.5-ounce bag with a mix of 24 herbs, Yang Cheng brand Chinese herbal beverage in a green box, and Kausing brand Ho Yan Hor herbal tea. When I woke up one morning feeling feverish and so nauseated I couldn't eat, I called the Lins. Mrs. Lin told me to brew the jasmine herb tea. Two pots later, I fell asleep. I woke up drenched in sweat and weak but able to eat some rice porridge and, by the next day, I was fully recovered.

BAMBOO SHEATH HERB TEA

This very unusual herbal mix tea is packed in dried bamboo leaves tied at intervals with threads, making a tube of herb-filled balls. Four tubes of 5 balls each are found in a red and gold plastic bag with a clear gourd-shaped window so you can view the tied sheaths. Look for Sun Wah Foodstuff Co. from Hong Kong. To brew the tea, boil one tube in 5 cups or more water. It has a sweet, slightly bitter taste and is taken as cooling tea, for stomachaches, ringing in the ear (tinnitis), headaches, fever, and loss of appetite.

bamboo sheath herb tea

GUILING-GAO

guiling gao

Boxed packets of sweetened granules made from about 20 medicinal root, herb, and seed extracts, including anteater scale extract. There is usually a picture of a turtle and anteater on the boxes. The granules are dissolved in hot water and taken as a tonic to nourish the blood, strengthen the kidneys, help poor digestion, sexual dysfunction, weakness in back or legs, and promote longevity—thus the turtle, a symbol of long life. It is often served as a jelly (set with agar gelatin) after a hearty meal. It's pretty bitter, so is usually dished up with honey. Look for Yin-Kong brand Guiling Cha in a green box or Guiling-Gao Wuzhou Health brand from Guangxi, China, in a yellow and green box with a turtle on it.

BITTER GOURD TEA

Tra Kho Qua. This mildly medicinal tea is made of dried flakes of the bitter gourd, to be used when the fresh vegetable isn't available. It detoxifies, purifies blood, cools the digestive system, is good for the stomach, heart, and liver, and helps improve eyesight. Not recommended if you have a weak stomach though as it may cause you to vomit. Has a very bitter taste. Look for Cao Nguyen brand of loose tea in plastic bags with pictures of gourds on them. To use, brew and strain.

DRIED WAX GOURD SLICES

Packaged dried winter melon slices are used brewed like tea and taken for clearing the lungs and restoring energy from sunstroke. Look for boxes made by Fenkiang Bridge brand labeled "superior wax gourd slices" with a steaming bowl on a green and orange box.

ESSENCE OF CHICKEN WITH CORDYCEPS

Small glass jars of dark liquid made from chicken essence concentrate and cordyceps (a dried fungus) extract. It is taken by sickly or weak people to boost strength. Said to help bronchitis, reduce anemia, and to be good for the blood and stomach. Look for Yang Cheng brand in a single jar or six to a box.

BAH KUT TEH

Cooling Hot Pot (the name means Pork Bone Tea). Sets of assorted dried herbs, berries, medicinal roots, and flavoring spices available in plastic bags or flat clear plastic boxes. Each herb or root is in a separate small bag and some include a muslin bag of spices. They are added to a pot of water with meat or chicken and garlic and simmered about an hour. Fresh vegetables and salt are added and boiled another 3 minutes. Eaten for energy when feeling weak or fatigued by heat. Look for Golden Flower brand in 3-ounce boxes and Xing Yun Tang brand in aqua bags.

bah kut teh

VITALIZING CONGEE MIX

These are 5-ounce China Wing Group brand bags filled with dried porridge mix, which includes pearl barley and dried lotus seeds, lily bulbs (good for internal organs), longan bits (good for blood and energy), and other Chinese herbs such as dioscorea (a toxin cleanser good for liver and stomach) and polygonatum (which strengthens bones and reduces fatigue and headaches). Boil the mix with water until the barley is soft and it is a thick gruel. Good for restoring energy and easy to digest. Look also for Pine Mark brand in 3-ounce boxes. You will also find Neo Neo Ten's brand congee in soda-type cans.

WHITE GOURD DRINK

Made from wax gourd (also called winter melon) concentrate, water, and cane sugar, this drink is thought to detoxify the body and be good for the lungs, bladder, and intestines, and for eliminating wastes, including phlegm. Sold in 10-fluid-ounce soda cans. Look for Yeo's brand from Singapore with pictures of green gourds on the can.

All of these natural teas and herbal remedies can be taken without any harmful side effects, but are not intended to replace seeing a licensed physician for diagnosis or treatment of illness or serious disease. Use at your discretion. However, thousands of years of tradition and millions of people who use herbal treatments seem reason enough to give it a try.

STOCKING UP

Stock up on at least one of each tea. Good choices would be Orange Pekoe or Lapsang Souchong blacks, jasmine oolong, and a Japanese green tea or Chinese Dragon Well. The best all-purpose healing drinks to keep in stock are chrysanthemum crystals (liver, eye, and lung cleanser), kamwotea (fevers and indigestion), ginseng, ginger, and licorice teas.

17

Cooking with Chinese Herbs

亚洲 烹调方法

Chinese for "Asian cooking techniques"

Can you imagine going to your doctor, getting a prescription, coming home, and tossing the medicine into the cooking pot for dinner? That's the basic concept of Chinese herbal cooking. Food, medicine, and nutrition overlap. The philosophy of Chinese herbal medicine is, as in foods, to balance the body's yin and yang. To be in perfect health, they must be in harmony. When you have too much coolness, or yin, certain herbs are taken and when you suffer too much heat, or yang, other herbs are taken. Cooking with herbs is a way to cure, nourish, adjust, and regulate the body according to seasonal changes and individual needs.

However, many medicinal herbs can taste pretty awful—strong and bitter with unpleasant aromas—so they are combined with everyday foods to create tasty treatments. You don't even realize you're eating herbs! The Chinese have used this as a prescription for health for thousands of years. Now you can too. Everything you need for herbal cooking is found in the Asian grocery. Most preparations are simple. You boil the herbs and make soup, then add flavorful ingredients. Others can be eaten in braised, steamed, or stir-fried dishes. Some can be sprinkled over food.

Following are the most commonly used cooking herbs. The first group are used boiled, with the strained liquid added to recipes or used in soup. The second group are added to dishes and eaten. The Asian grocery is more than a place to buy food—you can also fill your edible prescription—and toss it in the dinner pot!

Boiled Herbs

ANGELICA

There are two different species of angelica used. One is Dang Gui (or Tang Kuei), a sinensis. This is a blood toner and regulator. It makes blood flow more easily and raises the temperature. Also calms nerves, is good for liver, heart, and uterus, and helps control bleeding (internal and external). Use for fatigue, anemia, and to regulate the menses. A good herb for women. It is sold as whole root and as cut slices of the knobby white-brown roots. Bai Zhi, the other angelica, helps with

angelica root slice

blood circulation and alleviates pain. This is sold in pale round chips of the sliced stems. Angelica is good added to soups to increase blood production and ease joint pains. Make a broth by boiling and straining ginseng, Angelica dang gui, and some cinnamon bark. Stir-fry

angelica bai zhi

beef or pork strips in oil with garlic, add a dash rice vinegar, chopped gingerroot, and scallions. Add to broth pot with a skein of bean thread noodles and simmer until meat is tender. Season with salt and pepper. Good mild all-purpose tonic, replenishes chi (vital energy).

ASTRAGALUS

Bei Qi. Also called milkvetch and hoantchy root. The dried roots of this legume plant are used in treating numerous ailments, including the common cold, appetite loss, diarrhea, and nervousness. It has a slightly sweet flavor and is a spleen, lung, and kidney toner. It improves circulation, regulates blood pressure and blood sugar, boosts immunity, helps wounds heal, and improves kidney function. Also helps control excess sweating. Because it's an immune-system booster, it has been used to help cancer patients undergoing chemotherapy and radiation. The cinnamon colored roots are sold sliced on an angle into pale tan slivers. Try making ginger and fish soup with this herb. Cut a whole fish (bass, carp, or catfish are good) in two halves lengthwise. Place in a pot with 4 cups of

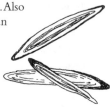

astragalus root

water and add an ounce of astragalus roots, some dang gui angelica, a few slices of gingerroot, a splash of rice wine, and a small handfull of lycium berries. Bring to a boil, then lower heat and simmer until the fish is cooked, about 10 minutes. Good for spleen and stomach, improves appetite, and is delicious!

CODONOPSIS

Dang Shen. This is a type of ginseng and is considered an energy (chi) tonic. The dried pale tan roots look like wrinkled, slightly notched sticks. This herb strengthens the spleen and helps the body produce essential fluids. It is also good for the stomach and lungs and is used to

codonopsis

cure chronic diarrhea. It helps promote digestion, relieves digestive problems and nausea, and is recommended for lack of appetite. While not as strong as Chinese ginseng, it has similiar properties at much less cost. Good in soups with other herbs.

DIOSCOREA

Bei Zie. Also called Long Yam, this is related to the Chinese yam. These dried, sliced yams look like pale wood chips. It aids digestion and is good for the liver, clears toxins from the body, and acts as a diuretic. Add to soup broths with other herbs and strain.

DENDROBIUM

Huo Shan Shi Hu. This is the dried, coiled yellow stems of the tropical dendrobium orchid. They look like little curled-up knots of thick cord. It is good for the stomach and helps the body produce essential fluids. Simmer chicken in an herb stock made from dendrobium, rice wine, ginger, and soy sauce. Chop up the chicken and serve with the stock. Good for strength and helps reduce stomach inflammation.

dendrobium

DRIED CHINESE YAM

Shan Yao. Also called cinnamon vine, this is a long white 2-inch wide tuber cut in slices and dried. They look like thin, flat, oval pieces of chalk. It is good for the spleen and stomach, relieves diarrhea, and helps

dried chinese yam

tone lungs and kidneys. Improves digestion, lowers blood sugar level, and is used to treat diabetes. It is used in soup with beef or pork and can be boiled with ginseng for 30 minutes to make tea. Chinese yam can also be ground into a fine powder and mixed with toasted sweet glutinous rice (which is also ground up), or taken with sugar and black pepper in water daily as a treatment for diarrhea and poor appetite.

GINSENG

Panax Ginseng or Ren-Shen. There are three types of ginseng. They come from China, Taiwan, Korea, and America. Each has slightly different properties from the others. Korean ginseng is thought to be the best. The whole root resembles a little person, with legs split from the root tip and hairs trailing from a head of the thicker root top. Ginseng is used in cooking and made into medicinal teas, often with the addition of ginger, and has a sweet, slightly bitter taste. Dried ginseng roots and the less expensive stem bits (sold in plastic bags) can also be steeped in boiling water to make tea and are good steamed with chicken and rice wine, ginger, garlic, and scallions for a potent broth used to stave off colds, boost immunity, and stimulate energy. Besides tea, ginseng roots are sold preserved in liquid in glass jars.

HAWTHORN BERRY

Shan Cha. Also called haw fruit. This small fruit is sliced and dried. It looks like dark red round, slightly curled chips with a small center hole. This sour, slightly bitter herb helps digestion and prevents fat from entering blood vessels by helping to digest it so that it can be eliminated. It also softens hard substances like the bones in large fish and is often used in cooking tough old chickens, which come out tender. Drink as a tea on a long-term basis to relieve hypertension and cholesterol and prevent coronary heart disease.

LONICERA

Jin Yin Hua. These are dried honeysuckle flowers which are tubular, pale golden petals with flaring tops. It is a cooling and cleansing herb and an antibiotic. Cures fevers and sore throats and is good for clearing skin problems—pimples and itchy allergies. You can add it to soup, congee, and stir-fried noodles and greens. Also makes a liver cleaning tea steeped with dried chrysanthemum flowers and lycium berries.

POLYGONATUM

There are two types, both in the lily family. One is a rhizome called polygonatum odoratum, or Yu Zhu. This is sold in long light yellowish flexible dried strips and is good for energy, affects the heart, lungs, and marrow. The other, polygonatum multiflorum, or Shou Wu is also called Chinese cornbind. It looks like thick slabs of sticky melted tar and nourishes blood, liver, and kidneys, and strengthens sinew, cartilage, and bones. Polygonatum also helps regulate blood pressure and prevents hardening of the arteries. Make a stock from chopped and boiled sho wu, reduce, and marinate peeled shrimp, then steam the shrimp with scallions and ginger and serve with a sauce made from the

polygonatum strips

reduced and thickened stock. Balances internal organs and replenishes chi (vital energy). To make tea, simmer black polygonatum slabs and lycium berries in 3 cups of water until reduced to one. Strain and sweeten with brown sugar. This makes a good natural energy tonic.

PORIA

Fu Ling or Poria Cocos. Called Tuckahoe or Virginia Truffle in English. This edible underground fungus is found on the roots of pine trees and looks like a small potato-sized truffle. Dried and sliced, the compact mass of thread-like tubular spores is sold as off-white or grayish, paper-thin shavings or curled rolls. Poria strengthens the spleen, calms nerves, acts as a diuretic, and is good for the stomach. Considered to be anti-aging, and is taken to

poria

renew youth. In China it is sometimes used in place of yeast in the dough of baozi (stuffed meat buns) and added to soups. Use in pork soup with dioscoria, eurayle, and lotus seeds to make "4 energies soup," good for improving appetite.

SOLOMONS SEAL

A plant in the polygonatum lily family, this is the dried jointed underground stem of a plant native to North America, Europe, and Asia. The name comes from the seal-like scars on the roots. Sold in ginger colored irregular shaped slices. Used in medicinal soups after boiling and straining. Nourishes kidneys, lungs, stomach, and liver, helps body produce essential fluids and is cooling. Helps calm nerves, reduces insomnia, dry mouth, and dry eyes. Reduces thirst. Simmer with Chinese yam in 8 cups of water until reduced to 4 cups. Strain, discard solids, and use to steam a whole chicken with ginger and scallions added to the herb liquid. Steam until tender in a pot on the stove, about two hours. Restores energy and replenishes yin.

solomon's seal

Edible Herbs

COIX SEED

YiYi Ren. Also called Jobs tears. This is an ancient whole grain with a nutty taste which has been grown in China for over 4,000 years. It looks like large white puffy barley grains that have split open. Sold in bags, cooked, puffed, and dried. It is good for the spleen, kidneys, lungs, stomach, and large intestine. Clears heat, promotes urination, and relieves abdominal bloating. It is believed to detoxify and get rid of warts. Also thought to inhibit the growth of cancer cells (boil in water and drink the water daily). Use to make a soup to tone up the stomach and relieve swelling due to water retention—boil equal amounts of coix seeds, peanuts, and brown sugar. Look for Crown brand in 14-ounce plastic bags.

coix seeds

I first experienced Chinese herbal cooking in Singapore at the Imperial Herbal Restaurant. This dark, old-fashioned shop and eating place has staff doctors who recommend and concoct traditional remedies from ginseng, snow frog glands, white fungus, and various roots, tubers, barks, and berries. The menu, in English and Chinese, lists not only dishes (like "cordyceps with snow frog," "jasmine-flower prawns," and "fried venison with wolfberry") but the health benefits too. Waitresses wear pink and white candy stripers' aprons and the feeling is part hospital, part gourmet Chinese restaurant.

DON QUIA SEEDS

Small dried white squash seeds from the winter melon, eaten as a snack and used in medicinal dishes such as red bean, squash seed, and carp soup (nourishing and a diuretic), or added to winter melon soup made with diced melon, the seeds, ginseng, lycium berries, chicken strips, water chestnuts, and chopped black and wood ear mushrooms (regulates chi, beautifies skin). The seeds are good for the intestines and bladder; also are a mild laxative. Look for Peony Mark and Oriental Mascot seeds in 1-pound bags.

EURAYLE

Qian Shi. Also called fox nut. These are seeds from the flower pods of an Asian water lily. The dried, halved, round seeds are white inside and red-brown outside. They are good for the lungs, spleen, and complexion—said to help a person retain youthfulness. Helps joint pain and arthritis. Also a good, easy to digest (and mild tasting) herb to give children. A delicious vegetable soup can be made

euryale seeds

from eurayle and coix seeds with Chinese yam and poria (boil and strain). Stir fry cubes of beancurd, bean sprouts, lily buds, chopped wood ear mushrooms, scallions, and ginger shreds in sesame oil, season with salt and pepper, and add the herb broth, bring to a boil and serve.

Eurayle seeds can also be added to soups and can be cooked until soft and eaten like any bean. A sweet soup is made by simmering lotus roots, euryale seeds, and gingko nuts until the seeds are tender, about 1½ hours. Add red jujubes and dried longan flesh bits and simmer 30 minutes, then add rock sugar and stir until the sugar dissolves. Cool, stir in honey, and serve. Good overall tonic for body.

CORDYCEPS

Dong Cong Xia Cao (literally winter worm, summer grass). Also called chan hua fungus or caterpillar fungus. It is a worm that turns into a plant after being consumed by a fungus which fills the worm's body. The dried plant looks like a small brown caterpillar pod, and is sold in bundles tied with red velvet string that are very expensive. It is used as a medicine in Chinese cooking, adding savory flavor and crunch. It is a tonic for cleansing the system and relieving arthritis, asthma, bronchitis, and sexual dysfunction. Often added to soup made from abalone,

black mushrooms, dried scallops, and sharksfin or boiled with duck, pork, or chicken in soup with herbs. Regarded as being more important for its restorative value than the flavor. They are sold by weight at the counter of Asian groceries where the small bundles are stashed. A whole bundle can cost over $300, but you can just buy a small amount, which won't be more than $10.

cordyceps

JUJUBES

Da Zao. Also called red and black dates. This is a small dried, wrinkled-up, deep red or almost black Chinese fruit from the jujube tree. It has a prune-like taste and is used to sweeten medicinal soups and porridge and slow cooked stews, or with braised chicken or pork. It can also be added to stir-fries after soaking until soft in warm water. If you wish to remove the small pit, pinch with pliers until the kernel cracks and remove it. They are not sweet like palm or medjool dates, but add a slight sweet-tartness to dishes such as beancurd soup or pearl barley and rice porridge seasoned with sesame oil and salt. Soups or gruels with them added are taken as a purifying tonic, believed to build strength, provide energy, help nerves, and improve

red dates

circulation. They are sold in plastic bags or flat boxes. Look for Peony Mark and Flower brands in bags, and Spring brand without seeds in 7-ounce boxes in the refrigerator.

LABLAB BEANS

Bai bian dou. Also called hyacinth beans. Small oval seeds from a legume pod with tan coats and off-white interiors, sold partially split. Good for the spleen, flushes toxins out of the body, and relieves thirst. Also helps cure diarrhea and gastroenteritis (grind beans into a powder, dissolve in warm water, and drink 3 times a day). Can add to soup (they soften in about 30 minutes) or cook with water and sugar. Use as any bean. Look for Crown and Wing Shing brands.

lablab beans

LYCIUM

Qi Zi. Also called wolfberry and boxthorn fruit, they are the dried small red, slightly acidic berries of the Chinese Medlar tree. They have a chewy tart-sweet taste and can be munched like raisins. Good for liver, kidney, and eyesight. One of the most commonly used cooking herbs. They are popped into pork and chicken soups, used as a garnish sprinkled over salads or stir-fried greens, pureed in glazes for poultry, and can be added to braised chicken, duck or pork and steamed with fish. Can also be put into pork stock and vegetable soups. Lycium adds flavor to Chinese clear oxtail soup—a subtle, light broth believed to make the eyes brighter. Lycium are sold in flat clear plastic boxes or bags. Buy ones that are bright red, not overly shriveled and dark (these are old and may be bug infested). Look for Kai Chi brand in 6-ounce bags.

STOCKING UP

The best all-around cooking and soup stock herbs are: Chinese ginseng (ren shan), codnopsis, astragalus, angelica (dong gui), Chinese yam, jujube dates, and lycium (wolfberries). All can be combined as you wish or with coix seeds, eurayle, and lablab beans, good to keep in stock for stews and bean soups.

18

Japanese Food Products

めん

Japanese for "noodles"

When you have a yen to cook Japanese-style food, you don't have to find a Japanese-only shop. The Lins' and most Asian groceries stock all the essential elements to create Japan's minimalist cuisine. Japanese cooking revolves around rice, root vegetables, seafood, and soybean products. Seasonings include soy sauce, mirin (sweet cooking rice wine), seaweed, miso, rice vinegar, ginger, sesame seeds, and wasabi. A varied and balanced

Japanese fish paste

range of dishes can be made from a small number of ingredients dovetailed with well-matched flavorings. In Japan food is not just a functional aspect of life, but a delight to the senses both visually and in taste. Fresh, unadulterated ingredients get only a light touch of seasoning during cooking to bring out their natural flavors. To eat Japanese is to discover little worlds of flavor and texture in artfully arranged morsels.

Everything but the raw fish for sushi can be discovered in the Lins' grocery. Basics like sushi rice are on the rice shelf, while soba and somen are on the noodle shelf. Get your bottled seasonings, dried soup bases and fish flakes, seaweed and tastebud-zapping wasabi in the "Little Tokyo" aisle of Japanese goods. Check the refrigerator cases for fish paste products, pickled plums, radish pickle, miso, and sushi ginger, as well as tofu. You will find containers of fish roe, natto, and mochi (pounded rice cakes) in the freezer. Green tea and ban-cha will be

yama imo

on the tea shelf, and senbei rice crackers are across the way in the snack section. Two vegetables used almost exclusively in Japanese cuisine, burdock (gobo) and mountain yam (yama imo), are found in the produce section. (Soy sauces are discussed in chapter 5 and tofu is in chapter 10 as they are not exclusive to Japanese cuisine.)

S e a w e e d   &   K e l p

Japan is surrounded by sea and many marine plants are cultivated, harvested, and processed in a variety of forms from these waters. The Japanese believe seaweed is good for hair—to keep it, and to keep it black and glossy. Certainly it contains trace minerals and vitamins and makes a healthy addition to your diet.

KONBU

This giant sea kelp resembles starched, olive green strips of dusty cloth. It is used to make soup stock and in flavoring stewed foods. Best quality konbu is dark olive in color, and is frosted with white salt residue. Don't wash this off. Instead, wipe it with a damp cloth before cooking to retain the flavor. Konbu expands as it cooks. Sold in plastic bags, bent or folded. You may also find small squares of salted dried kelp (shio-konbu) in small plastic packets. They are enjoyed as a snack or used as a garnish in soups and simmered dishes. White konbu (shiro-konbu) is pale colored and after reconstituting is used in sushi rolls. There are also packets of semi-soft salt-encrusted strips called tesuki oboro konbu. Soak overnight to use in soup stock or add to salads. For this type, look for JFC brand and Daiei Trading Co. Good brands of dried konbu to look for are Shirakiku, in beautiful black and gold bags, and Tashun Foods with a picture of green kelp fronds on the packet. Both packages are 2 ounces.

WAKAME

Also called fueru (expanding) wakame. This is a deep green leafy kelp tangle that is used in miso soup or vinegared salads called sunomono. It has a chewy texture and delicate ocean-brine flavor. It is good mixed with bamboo shoots in a sweetened soy sauce broth and tossed with cucumber slices in a vinegar dressing, sprinkled with toasted sesame seeds. Salted fresh wakame and a dried form are sold. Both have to be soaked in water before using, about 4 to 6 minutes. The fresh kind triples in size after softening and is found in plastic containers or bags in the refrigerated cases. Assi brand offers fresh salted "nama" wakame in 10-ounce packages. Dried wakame swells up to 10 times or more after soaking and is sold in plastic or paper packages on shelf 6. Look for Orchids, Daiei Trading Co., Shirakiku, and Wel-Pac brands.

wakame seaweed

NORI

Also called laver, it looks like thin sheets of rough black paper. Nori is made by cultivating a mix of marine algae in nitrogen-rich tidal seawater during the cold winter months. After harvesting, nori is washed in fresh water, dried on large frames, and then cut into sheets and lightly roasted. The most common use for nori is as a wrap for sushi and rice balls. Cut strips may also be used as garnishes. In Japan nori is eaten for breakfast with rice and fish, dipped with chopsticks in soy sauce, or crisped in a flame and munched as a snack. Another type of

strip of nori seaweed

nori is iwa-nori, or rock nori. It is much coarser and is made by sun drying seaweed pulp over large rocks. Some nori sheets are seasoned with hot spices or teriyaki sauce. Standard size sheets are 7½ by 8½ inches and are sold flat in packs of 10 in cellophane bags or folded in tin or plastic canisters, both packed with desiccants to retain crispness. After purchasing, store nori in a tightly closed container to keep it crisp and fresh. If it gets damp or stale, recrisp with tongs in a flame on the stove, or microwave. Look for Yamamoto Yama, Daichu, and Takaokaya brands, all in packs of 10 sheets. To try spiced nori, look for Nagai's hot teriyaki nori in plastic canisters with 80 small strips. Use thin strips of nori to garnish the salmon with tea rice recipe on page 216.

HIJIKI

This is a brown, fern-like algae that turns blackish after drying, resembling little licorice twigs. When soaked in warm water for about 20 minutes, it absorbs water and triples in size. Drain and squeeze dry to use. Good when added to salads, tossed in a sesame paste and soy dressing. Often seaweed is sauteed in oil with carrots, tofu, and steamed soybeans with sweetened soy sauce, or added to rice dishes. This is sold in paper or plastic packets in varying amounts. Look for Wel-Pac, Shirakiku, and Daiei brands.

hijiki seaweed

MIXED SEAWEED

You will find bags of several types of dried seaweed mixed together. Soak to soften, drain, and use in salads. The mix will usually include wakame, soft salted konbu, ruffled red tosaka-nori, feathery sugi-nori, and thin strips of clear or green colored agar (kanten, made from cooked and freeze-dried seaweed extract). Look for Shirakiku mix and Kanemasu "healthy tasty" brand.

Pickles

No proper Japanese meal is considered complete without pickles to round it off. There is a popular meal in Japan called the "Japanese flag." It is a bowl of white rice with a red dot in the center made with a pickled plum. Other pickles accompany meals, refresh the palate, and add a crunchy texture to balance other dishes.

TSUKEMONO

This is a collective term for Japanese pickles. This kind of pickle has a clean fresh flavor and crisp texture. All kinds of vegetables—from slim eggplants (nasu) to giant daikon radish—are pickled. The vegetables are salted and weighted down in buckets to pickle in their juices. Miso paste, sake lees, rice bran (nuka), and rice vinegar are also used to preserve the vegetables. In the Lins' grocery you will find whole pickled daikon radish in a yellow brine, packed in sealed plastic bags in the refrigerator case. Called takuan, these are the most popular pickle of all. To make them, daikon are sun-dried, then pickled in rice bran and salt. The origin of the name came from Takuwan-san, a sixteenth-century priest who devised this method of pickling. Traditionally the yellow color was produced by adding dried gardenia flower pods (kuchinash), but most are now dyed with artifical coloring. Takuan is said to be a good digestive and no matter how much raw fish or how many bowls of rice you eat, a few slices of takuan will pull you through. Next to these are pickled turnips and turnip greens, little eggplants, small whole cucumbers, slices of lotus root, and Chinese cabbage in plastic containers or brine-filled pouches.

UMEBOSHI

These are pickled Japanese plums. They are made from small- and medium-sized, soft, wrinkled, deep red, sun-dried, salt-preserved Japanese plums called ume. They are flavored with the leaves of the beef steak plant, which adds a purple color. They have a tart sour-salty taste and are used in making rice ball sushi and added to miso soup or eaten as a digestive. They are found in small plastic tubs in the refrigerator cases and in vacuum-sealed plastic bags on the shelf in aisle 6. Will keep, once opened, for many months. Hime brand in 8-ounce plastic tubs is good.

umeboshi

PICKLED GINGER

Called gari, or sushi ginger, are the translucent pale pink slices that come in a little pile with sushi, and are meant for cleansing the palate between pieces of sushi. They are peeled gingerroot slices, which have been pickled in salt, sugar, and vinegar with a pink dye. They have a sharp, clean, and refreshing taste and are mainly used as a condiment with sushi. You will find pickled ginger in small glass jars or plastic containers in the refrigerator cases and in vacuum-sealed bags on the shelf. Look for Wel-Pac and Shirakiku brands sushi ginger in 5-ounce plastic tubs, and Kame brand in glass jars.

Fish Paste Products

Pureed white fish, primarily cod, pollock, whiting, hake, and shark, is mixed with a starch binder and seasonings, then molded, colored, and steamed into cakes or "sausages." This is sliced and added to soups, one-pot simmered dishes, or noodle dishes, cut into matchsticks to garnish salads, or dipped in soy sauce and enjoyed as a snack. If you have used or eaten surimi, you have tasted a fish paste product—one that has been in existence for centuries in Japan, but only recently mass marketed as "fake crab or lobster." The other most common types are listed below and will be found in the freezer or in vacuum-sealed packages in the refrigerator cases. All types are made by Yamasa and Kibun brands. Wei-Chuan brand offers frozen tubs of fish paste. To use, thaw and shape into cakes and boil.

KAMABOKO

This resembles a pink-coated sponge on a board. It is made from cod or shark paste, which is steamed on thin strips of cedar wood. It has a dense texture and slightly sweet taste. It swells, becoming softer when boiled or simmered.

HANPEN

Fish paste is mixed with yama-imo (mountain potato) and molded into square shapes that are boiled. It has a soft fluffy texture like marshmallow and is used in simmered stews.

CHIKUWA

Fish paste is molded around a metal rod (in the old days a stalk of bamboo was used, which is what the name means) before steaming. The resulting paste cylinder is then grilled and has light brown grill marks on it. Chikuwa is added to soups and stews or eaten as a snack, dipped in hot mustard sauce.

DATEMAKI

This is a sweet-tasting fish paste mixed with eggs and pink sugar. Layers of white fish paste and pink egg mix are rolled up, grilled, and sliced, exposing a pink pinwheel swirl pattern. It is added to mochi rice cake soup for a popular New Year's food and enjoyed anytime as a sweet touch in noodle soups and salads.

Sushi makers have their own language. This jargon developed in the Edo period when sushi was sold by high-spirited (and often sake-fueled) vendors from mobile stalls around Tokyo. In sushi-speak, even numbers are different. For example, itchi (one) is "pin," ni (two) becomes "itchinoji," and san (three) changes to "geta." Rice, usually called gohan becomes "shari." The strips of nori that hold in treats like salmon roe or sea urchin are called "gunkan-maki," or "battleship wraps." The green tea, ocha, sipped between sushi pieces to refresh the mouth is "agari." Shoyu, or soy sauce, is "murasaki," which also means purple. Chopsticks, or hashi, become "otemoto" in a sushi shop.

FISH ROE

The most commonly found type is tobiko, or flying fish caviar. These are the tiny, bright orange, salted eggs of the flying fish which sort of pop in your mouth. It is used in small amounts as a flavorful and decorative garnish on sushi and in salads. You may also find tiny red salted masago (smelt roe), pale pink loaf-shaped tarako (cod roe), and larger jewel-like ikura (salmon) roe. Kazunoko, or herring roe, are salted, yellow, crunchy caviar pieces, usually soaked in water before cooking. It is a delicacy, often called "yellow diamonds" due to its very high price. It is only eaten at the New Year or part of a fancy "kaiseki"—an exquisite multi-course meal based on seasonal foods.

You will find most types of roe in small plastic or styrofoam containers in the freezer case. Once thawed it will keep for several weeks. Look for Wel-Pac brand. Another related product, uni, is the sexual gland of spiny sea urchins and is prized as a sushi topping. It resembles small golden blobs and is not salty but has a sweet nutty taste. It will be found frozen, usually packed in one layer in flat wooden boxes.

Vegetables

BURDOCK ROOT

Gobo. These are long, firm, and woody looking roots, about as thick as your finger. They will be covered with mud and fine root hairs. Sold by the root or tied in bundles. It has a unique earthy flavor and crunchy texture. Used mainly in stir-fries, shaved in small pieces in the same way you sharpen a pencil or in nimono (boiled) dishes or salads. To prepare, scrub well and scrape off the outer skin. Immediately place roots in a vinegar-water solution to soak. This removes the alkaline flavor and retains the crispness and white color. Shaved burdock stalks are good simmered with slices of beef in a soy and rice wine broth bound with beaten eggs. Stir-fried burdock is called kimpira gobo. Kimpira was the name of one of the four guardians for a famous samurai, hence the name is given to anything strong. In this instance, it means shaved pieces of burdock, julienned carrots, and celery stir-fried with soy sauce, rice wine, sugar, and chili peppers in sesame oil. Burdock is believed to be a blood purifier.

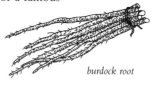

burdock root

MOUNTAIN YAM

Japanese mountain potato or yama imo. These are shaggy brown, bumpy tubers about the size of tiny new potatoes. They are white and slippery on the inside. Peeled and grated, the raw yam forms a thick gooey marshmallow-like sauce eaten with raw tuna, or is mixed with cooked rice and egg. The grated goo is also added to bowls of hot soba noodles called "yamakake," but it is rarely cooked. You will find these little tubers packed in sawdust in crates in the produce section. Store them up to several weeks in the vegetable bin of your refrigerator.

Other Ingredients

DASHI

Japanese dashi

This is instant fish soup base, also called hon-dashi. It is stock for broth made from a blend of dried bonito fish, essence of sea tangle (konbu), and seasonings. Dashi is sold in bouillon cubes, granules, or liquid concentrates, in jars or sachet packets. A good brand to look for is Ajinomoto, with three packets to a package. Use to make quick soup—just add vegetables, seafood, or tofu with hot water and simmer a few minutes. Also Shimaya brand dashi-moto powder in boxes of 16 packets.

MISO PASTE

white miso paste

A thick protein-rich fermented soybean paste that is an important staple in Japanese cooking, it is used in soups, sauces, grilling glazes, marinades, and salad dressing. Miso is made by mixing crushed, boiled soybeans with salt, a special yeast culture called koji, and malted rice, barley, or wheat. The type of malted grain determines the color, aroma, and flavor of the miso. The fermented paste is then allowed to mature for several months and up to three years. The complex, rich flavors enhance, enrich, and bring out the subtle flavors in the foods they are cooked with. You will find three main miso types in most Asian groceries. They are categorized by the grain fermented with the soybeans.

Rice miso is called kome-miso, barley is mugi-miso, and miso made with only soybeans and yeast is called mame-miso. Following are the three main types.

SHIROMISO

Also called amakuchi, chu, or sweet miso. This is a pale to deep yellow color and is made from rice and soybeans. The name means "white miso" because it is the lightest in color and flavor. It has a mild, slightly sweet taste and is used mainly in salad dressings, soups, sauces, and marinades for whitefish such as cod or sea bass and vegetables. Good mixed with sesame or walnut paste to dress blanched green beans or spinach. Delicious smeared on halved eggplants and broiled until the miso bubbles.

AKAMISO

This ranges from reddish-brown to dark brown in color. The name means "red miso" and it is made from barley or rice and soybeans. It is the most commonly used miso in Japan and has a robust, salty flavor. Use this in any recipe requiring miso if no specific type is given. It is best for marinades for meat, poultry, and strong flavored fish such as mackerel, in stir-fries, and in simmered dishes. Dengaku is made by heating a red or white miso with a little sake, mirin, and sugar to make a thick sauce for grilled foods.

MAMEMISO

"Mame" means bean in Japanese and this miso is made from pure, fermented soybeans aged from nine months up to three years. Also called hat-cho miso. "Hat-cho" means eighth street in the town of Okazaki near Nagoya, the place of its origin, but many similiar miso pastes are made throughout Japan. It is a deep red color, chunky in texture, and has an earthy almost meaty flavor. All types will be found in plastic tubs or vacuum-sealed bags in the refrigerator cases. Store in your refrigerator tightly covered, and it will keep almost indefinitely. Brands to look for include Marudai, Marukome, Hana, Shin-Shu, Shishyuichi, Shirakiku, and Yamabuki.

NATTO

This is made of soybeans fermented with a yeast culture called natto-kin into a very pungent smelling and sticky mass. Natto is mixed with hot mustard, chopped scallions, and soy sauce and eaten with rice, added to miso soup, or rolled in sushi. It is very nutritious and said to cure stomachaches and hangovers, plus has a delicious nutty taste and unique slippery texture—once you get beyond the smell! Natto is sold freeze-dried in packets on the shelf. You add hot water and mix into a sticky paste with the enclosed packet of hot mustard and soy sauce. Frozen natto is found in styrofoam containers in the freezer. Also may be found in traditional Japanese straw bundles in the refrigerator case. For dried natto in bags, look for Mitoku brand "hama-natto." Frozen brands include Daiei Trading Co. in styrofoam packs of two, Mitokotsubo and JFC "kumenatto," both in packs of three.

natto

MISO SOUP

Called miso-shiro in Japanese, this is instant miso paste-based soup sold in paper packets. They have a picture or photo of a bowl of soup on the front and come in a variety of flavors. Each package makes three servings and contains three foil pouches of miso paste and three packets of powdered seasonings (scallions, freeze-dried strips or cubes of beancurd, spinach, wakame seaweed, and dried shitake mushroom slices are some). To use, simply mix a pouch of paste with a packet of seasoning in hot water and the soup is ready. Miso should never come to a full boil or it breaks apart. Look for Kikkoman and Shirakiku brands.

miso soup

SEASONING FLAKES

Called furikake in Japanese. "Furi" means shake and "kake" is to sprinkle. They are small flakes of dried egg, plum, and salted salmon or bonito mixed with wasabi powder, sesame seeds, and fine shreds of nori seaweed. Some blends have tiny rice cracker balls, shiso leaf flakes, dried fish roe, and powdered green tea added. They are used sprinkled over plain

seasoning flakes

rice, porridge, omelets, miso soup, and salads, or are rolled into rice ball fillings. You will find a vast variety of mixes in small shaker jars or in strips of small colorful packets sold in paper or plastic packages. Look for Nagatani-En brand in small

Japanese shiso leaf

packet strips and Summit brand in 2-ounce jars. Shirakiku makes packets with three sachets of "noritama" with sesame seeds, dried egg crumbs, nori shreds, and shaved bonito.

AONORIKO

Powdered light green algae used as a seasoning and garnish sprinled over cooked rice, soba, or salads. Found in shaker jars.

KATSUO-BUSHI

katsuo-bushi

These are pieces of bonito, a type of tuna, which have been steamed, smoked, and dried into wood-like hardness, then shaved into paper-thin flakes. The result looks like pinkish-brown wood shavings. These shavings or flakes are used to flavor clear soup and simmered foods or for sprinkling over chilled tofu, boiled vegetables, or omelets. They come in plastic bags of various sizes, and are also sold in very fine feather-light shreds or strips. A good brand to look for is in clear and orange cellophane bags with a logo of two fish in a circle on the label, and five small packets of flakes, imported by Summit Corp. Also Wel-Pac "hana katsuo" brand.

KANPYO

Bottle gourd flesh is machine-shaved into long ribbon-like strands and dried. The pale tan strips are found in plastic bags in folded bundles. To use, knead the strips in salt and wash in water, then boil until soft. Used cut in pieces as a filling for rolled sushi and as decorative ties around parcels or rolls of food, making use of the long flexible form. Kanpyo has a bland taste, chewy texture, and absorbs seasonings. You will also find Hime brand canned "makizushi no-moto." This is seasoned strips of kanpyo and mushroom bits to use in sushi rolls and may be more convenient than preparing dried gourd.

NIBOSHI

These are small, boiled, and sun-dried sardines. This is mostly used for making fish stock by soaking in cold water overnight and straining the liquid. They can also be toasted in a dry pan, seasoned with soy sauce, sake, and lemon juice, and eaten as a snack. Store in an airtight container. Sold in plastic bags. Look for Rokko, Koryeo, and Nishimoto brands.

FUGU-HIRE

Puffer fish (fugu) fins have been dried, salted, and then charred in a flame. They are added to hot sake for a smoky flavor. Sold in flat, plastic, sealed packages of about a dozen fins.

fugu-hire

fu cakes

FU

This is air-dried wheat gluten, also called yaki-fu when baked. It is a hard, bread-like product without any starch. Fu is sold in many shapes and pastel tints. You will find tiny flowers, round balls, pinwheel slices, plums, and bamboo just to name a few. The most commonly used one is called kuruma-fu (wheel) and it looks like an airy bagel or a round slice of french bread. It is added to sukiyaki hot-pots and soupy casseroles. Try it simmered with turnips in a broth seasoned with mirin, vinegar, sugar, and salt. Fu has a bland taste and spongy, but slightly crisp, texture. Soak in hot water to use in vinegared dishes or add dry to hot soup or simmered dishes. Sold in plastic bags with other dried goods on the shelf. Look for Yachiyo brand.

MOCHI

These are Japanese rice cakes made from pounded glutinous rice. They are thick, round white cakes with a dense, chewy texture and slightly sweet taste. They can be added to soup or sukiyaki broth and are delicious toasted in a dry pan and dipped in soy sauce or roasted with miso-sesame seed sauce. Mochi is symbolic of longevity and prosperity, and is closely associated with the Japanese New Year (Oshogatsu). That day is invariably ushered in with a toast of sake and Ozoni—a soup made with mochi, chicken, fish, black mushrooms, and vegetables. You will find mochi in the freezer in plastic packages of four to six cakes. Look for Dai Fuku, Ling Po Mochi, and Hana brands.

> Mochi is symbolic of longevity and prosperity, and is closely associated with the Japanese New Year (Oshogatsu). That day is invariably ushered in with a toast of sake and Ozoni—soup made with mochi, chicken, fish, black mushrooms, and vegetables. And before the New Year, folks gather for all-day rice pounding parties, mashing glutinous rice in tubs with wooden mallets, to make their mochi. The Japanese even see a giant rabbit pounding mochi in the full moon.

KUSHI-DANGO

These are small rice-flour balls on bamboo skewers coated with anko, a paste made of adzuki beans, or grilled and coated in a sticky sauce made from sugar and soy sauce. Sold frozen on flat trays with three dumpling balls to a stick. Look for Shirakiku dango skewers, six to a tray, three of each type. To eat, heat in an oven or microwave on the setting for bread, but be careful not to overheat or they will become hard. If they are in vacuum-sealed packs (or any air-tight pack) with separate packets of paste, dip the unopened pack in a pan of boiling water. Remove and squeeze the hot paste over them.

KONNYAKU

Also called yam cake and devil's tongue jelly, this is sold in blocks of greyish-brown,

Japanese jelly noodles

speckled, semi-transparent (unrefined) kuro-konnyaku and thin, clearish-white (refined) noodle strands called shiritaki ("white fall"). It is made from the starchy roots of the yam-like devils tongue plant. The roots are peeled, dried, and ground into a fine powder. This is then dissolved in water with a coagulant and formed into rubbery blocks or jelly noodles. Eaten for its texture, which is slippery and gelatinous. The block-type is cut into chunks and added to simmered and braised dishes or is boiled and served with a sweet miso sauce. Jelly noodles are always added to sukiyaki hot-pots and used in vinegar dressed salads.

Konnyaku is a laxative and has no calories, so is used by dieters. Sold in liquid-filled, sealed plastic bags or plastic cartons in the refrigerator case. Look for Giant Explorer and Shirakiku brands for both types.

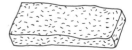

konnyaku cake

WASABI

wasabi

This is a Japanese horseradish resembling a small celery root. The root is peeled and grated on sharkskin to make fresh, pale green, nose-tingling wasabi dip. As the root is hard to find fresh, what you will usually find is a powdered "mustard" in tiny cans, or small tubes of bright green paste in boxes. To reconstitute powdered wasabi, mix a small amount with a few drops of water. It will turn into a pungent paste. You can add soy sauce to make a dip for sashimi (raw, thinly sliced fish) and sushi. It is very hot, so use sparingly. The powdered form is generally more potent than the tube-type. Keep the tube-type refrigerated after opening. Look for S & B, Kinjirushi, and Kaneku brands in cans and tubes. Wasabi is added to the salmon with tea rice recipe on page 216.

SANSHO

Japanese pepper—it is not really a chili pepper but a reddish-brown powder made from the pod of the prickly ash tree. It has a tangy rather than hot flavor, and is sprinkled over hot soba noodles or in soup. Sold in small shaker top jars. Look for S & B or brands imported by JFC.

SHICHIMI TOGARASHI

This Japanese seven-spice hot pepper is a powdered combination of aromatic seasonings, including dried hot peppers, rapeseeds, poppy seeds, sesame seeds, mustard seeds, pepper leaf, and dried orange or lemon peel. Has a pungent fragrant flavor and is used to add spice to soba noodles and soups or is sprinkled on grilled meats and fish to counter balance fatty tastes. It is sold in small tins and spice jars. Look for House Foods Corp., S & B, and JFC "Yagenbori" chili flavored seasoning mix in a small red and black can.

178

SAKE

The national beverage of Japan, also called Nihon shu, seishu, or rice wine. It is a made from rice fermented with koji (a yeast) and water. Sake is a clear, slightly sweet tasting drink with a 15–16% alcohol content. It can be served heated or chilled. The thousands of types are classified into three grades according to its body, or "koku." The grade will be stated on the label. The top grade is tokkyu, followed in order by ikkyu and nikkyu. Tokkyu is about twice as expensive as nikkyu. Sake is sold in glass bottles in a variety of sizes from both Japan and California. Sake is usually served in small ceramic flasks (tokkuri) and drunk from little china cups. When serving, the host fills each guest's cup and keeps them filled. You should never fill your own cup—allow your host to do this. Also, the sake should never be poured into a cup resting on the table (in proper Japanese etiquette). Lift your cup for filling. To signal you don't wish to drink anymore, turn your empty cup upside down. For a toast, everyone raises their cup and yells "kampaii!" or "cheers!" Keep in mind, sake does not improve with age—once a bottle is opened, it's best to finish it fairly quickly. To warm sake, fill a tokkuri flask and place it in a pan of water over low heat for 3 to 4 minutes. Sake is also an important cooking ingredient used for balancing salty ingredients and for flavoring and tenderizing in marinades.

MIRIN

A sweet, pale, syrupy rice wine used only in cooking, with a 12–14% alcohol content. It is made from fermented glutinous rice and shochu (distilled grain alcohol). Mirin has a high sugar content, adds a rich flavor and translucent sheen to cooked dishes, and is used in teriyaki and sukiyaki sauces. Tenderizes meats in marinades, glazes grilled foods, and is added in small splashes to soups and simmered dishes. Sold in glass bottles. Look for Kikkoman.

mirin

RICE VINEGAR

Called "su" in Japanese, this is a clear to pale golden vinegar made from distilled fermented rice. It has a stronger acidity than other vinegars. A seasoned variety has sugar added and is used to flavor sushi rice. Both types are used in salad dressing, marinades, and mixed with soy sauce to make dipping sauces. Sold in glass bottles. Look for the excellent Marukan and Mitsukan brands. Rice vinegar is used to make the lotus root pickle recipe on page 219.

PONZU

This vinegary dipping sauce is made from the juice of a bitter orange called sudachi. It has a pale citrus green color and sour tangy taste. It is mixed with soy sauce and dashi soup stock to make a dip for grilled seafoods and is served in tiny saucers with shabu-shabu to dip the beef into. Sold in small- and medium-sized glass bottles. Look for Mikusan brand in 5- and 12-ounce bottles.

NOODLE DIPPING SAUCE BASE

"Men-rui" is the general term for noodles in Japanese. Soba, somen, and udon are dipped in a variety of seasoned soy broths. These dark liquids are sold in 10- and 12-ounce glass bottles. Memmi noodle soup base is one to look for, made by Kikkoman from soy sauce, sugar, seasonings, and bonito fish extract. It can be diluted with hot or cold water—instructions are on the back label of the bottle—or used "straight" (undiluted). Other soup and noodle dipping bases include JFC Ajisenryu, Momoya, Nippon Marutten, Shimaya, and Mitsukan brands.

noodle soup base

TAMARI SAUCE

A thick dark soy sauce made without wheat or sugar. It has a stronger flavor than regular soy sauce and is used in yakitori sauce. Yakitori are skewers of grilled chicken (yaki means "burn or grill" and tori is "chicken") and other meats or vegetables brushed with a glaze made from tamari, sake, sugar, and mirin. Look for Kikkoman and Wan Ja Shan brands.

TERIYAKI SAUCE

Used in luster grilled foods, marinades, and Japanese-style barbecue sauces. It is made from soy sauce, enriched with mirin, sake, sugar, and spices—usually garlic and onion powder. The sugar in this sweetened sauce tenderizes foods, adds flavor, and gives a pleasing sheen to grilled or baked meats and fish. They are found in tall 10- and 12-ounce bottles. Look for Kikkoman regular and roasted garlic flavor, and JFC Ebara teriyaki and marinade sauce.

TEMPURA DIPPING SAUCE

Tentsuyu. A thin pale brown dipping sauce for batter fried foods. It is made from dashi (kelp and dried fish base), mirin, and light soy sauce. Add grated daikon radish or fresh ginger when serving tempura. Look for Kikkoman brand.

TONKATSU SAUCE

Tonkatsu sosu. A thick sauce served drizzled over breaded, deep-fried pork cutlets or other fried foods, croquettes, and even hamburgers. It is made from tomato ketchup, Worcestershire sauce, dark soy sauce, mustard, and sake and has a tangy sweet-sour taste. Look for Bull Dog brand and Kikkoman in tall plastic squeeze bottles. Chuno sauce is a thicker sauce, with apple, carrot, onion, garlic, caramel, and tamarind added, also made by Kikkoman.

Regardless of the season, you can discover the special ingredients of traditional Japanese cuisine right in your local Asian grocery. Go ahead and make your poetry of edible art, delicate "sense of season" dishes, and Zen gardens on a plate. Slurp your chilled somen noodles or seaweed soup, crunch crisp lotus pickles with a bowl of rice, and roll some sushi in a sheet of nori. Or skip the tradition and feel free to mix and match Japanese flavors with western ones. Experiment and break the rules! Why not wasabi mayonnaise on a hamburger, seven-spice powder in your clam chowder, or a natto-stuffed omelet?

STOCKING UP

To create authentic Japanese recipes you should stock up on the following basics: instant dashi soup base, at least one seaweed (I suggest nori if you plan on making sushi rolls), a miso paste, wasabi, mirin, rice vinegar, and teriyaki sauce. Extras, if you plan on really "going Japanese" would include some crunchy pickles, pickled ginger, noodle dipping sauce, and seven-spice powder. Don't forget some sake to serve with your Japanese meal.

19

Exotic Items for the Cultivated Palate

珍品

Chinese for "unusual items"

Now let's journey into the world of unusual ingredients—those things you may have seen, but had no idea what they were—or their use. Some of these are acquired or cultivated tastes, others are definitely not for the squeamish. However, forays to the Asian grocery should include a level of risk-taking, as well as learning—nothing compares with trying totally new-to-you ingredients. On each trip, pick something you've never tried before. In some of your ventures, you might find delicious flavors and pleasing textures—adding depth and diversity to your cooking. Of course there are some things that you just can not ever like, but at least you will have tried them. And you will know what it is when you spy it in the grocery the next time.

BIRDS' NEST

Yanwo. This is one of the most sought after and expensive delicacies in Asia. Served to affluent customers in exclusive Bangkok, Hong Kong, and Taipei restaurants, it is the regurgitated spittle of a tropic swift, collected from large mountainside caves throughout Southeast Asia. Climbers risk their lives scaling bamboo scaffolding to retrieve the nests. The dried, hand-cleaned, teacup-shaped nests are very costly, and they are believed by Asians to be good for the complexion and for curing various illnesses. The best grades are "white" nest and pink, or "blood," nest. Birds' nest is coveted mainly for its texture, which is a bland, soft, crunchy jelly. The nests must be soaked before using in special broths and to flavor sauces or soups. Definitely an acquired and expensive taste.

Found on the shelf or behind the front counter in some stores, along with other exotic and expensive items. Look for Kwong Cheong Swallow's Nest Co. in ornate boxes with a picture of two lovely Chinese ladies taking a bath, Tai Loong brand packed in Hong Kong in round boxes inside a pale peach box with a phoenix on it, and Golden Bell brand in a red box.

SHARKSFIN

Yuchi. This is another exotic luxury item throughout Asia. There are restaurants that serve only sharksfin on the menu and eating at them is a conspicuous symbol of extravagance as it is extremely expensive. It is the cured, sun-dried dorsal or "comb" fin or two ventral fins of a number of species of shark. Sharksfin is available in two forms: the whole dried fin with cartilage, or as fin needles. The price is an indicator of the quality, and complete whole fins are always more expensive than shreds. Preparation of either involves an elaborate process of soaking and boiling in many changes of water, but you can sometimes find already prepared sharksfin in the freezer. It has little flavor, but is prized for its absorbency, clear gelatinous strings, and texture.

Sharksfin is often served in a rich stock as sharksfin soup, in red-braised dishes, or added to poultry stuffing; also scrambled with eggs and crabmeat. Look for Diamond brand in clear hard plastic boxes with rolls of dried sharksfin shreds. Manila yellow, from the Philippines, is considered the best. Dried whole or shredded sharksfin is often behind the front counter and in the freezer.

sharksfin

DRIED FISH MAW

This bubbly textured tissue is removed from the stomach of a type of fish. They resemble puffy oblong cream-colored pieces of polyurethane. It is an Asian delicacy exalted for its texture, which is light, spongy, and chewy when cooked. Air bladders, or swim bladders, are inflatable organs in the stomach of large bony fish and they regulate the fish's hydrostatic pressure at different depths in the ocean. After being removed and cleaned, the maw is deep-fried, which expands the sac's membrane and forms crunchy balloons. Maw must be soaked in warm water for at least 6 hours before using; weigh it down in a bowl or pan. You should trim off any yellowish

membrane, cut in pieces, and heat in a saucepan of water with a splash of vinegar. Let it cook a few minutes, drain, and soak in cold water until ready to use. Often called Thai or Chinese "soul food," maw is simmered in thickened chicken stock with garlic, black mushrooms, and bamboo shoots, and seasoned with chili-vinegar sauce, scallions, and cilantro, or it is added to stews. Look for Wang Derm, Combine Thai Foods,

fish maw   and Hua Feng Food Co. brands in 3-ounce bags.

FISH LIPS

These are the mouth section of certain very large fish which have been sun-dried into hard brownish sheets. To prepare, place a sheet in a pan of water and bring to a boil. Simmer 3 to 4 hours, then remove from heat and rinse in cold water. Scrub with a soft brush, return to the pan, and cover with water. Simmer again, until tender, with a splash of rice wine and some slices of ginger and spring onion. Remove from the water, pull out any bones and discard them, then trim off the jagged edges and soak in cold water until ready to use. Prepared fish lips are used as an ingredient in seafood dishes and rich soups. It has a soft, gelatinous texture and a mild, but distinctly fishy flavor. Look for Hang Loong Marine Products or Lion and Globe brand in 8-ounce plastic bags.

RICE PADDY CRABS

Ba khia. These tiny, dark blue-gray crabs are caught in the rice paddies of Thailand and Vietnam and preserved in a pungent solution of fish sauce, sugar, water, garlic, and crushed red chilies, making them very

hot and pungent. The whole crabs are lightly smashed and added to pounded green papaya salad (see recipe on page 205). The uncooked pickled crabs have a salty tasting, creamy interior, which is meant to be sucked out. Definitely an acquired taste, these are found in 14-ounce plastic tubs in the freezer case. The label will say "crabe sale congele." Look for Cawaii Trading Co. and Papaya Tree brands.

rice paddy crabs

BLOOD PUDDING

Although not to be confused with the sausage of the same name, this is also made from pigs' blood. The Asian version is made from congealed pigs' blood cut into cubes, and it resembles reddish-brown soft tofu. It has a rich, creamy texture, mild taste, and is very nutritious, and is used mainly in Chinese soups and hot pots. It can be used to make blood pudding, or to make the Filipino specialty called dinuguan—pigs' innards in blood sauce. Pigs' blood pudding is found freshly made on styrofoam trays wrapped in plastic in the refrigerator case. It is also sold frozen in plastic containers. Look for Gold Medal brand in 11-ounce tubs.

SEA CUCUMBERS

Haishen. Also called iriko in Japanese, these are a strange vegetable-like, soft-bodied marine slug with the texture of firm jelly. When dried they resemble large fat blackish-green knobbed tubes or cucumbers. They are used to add texture as they have almost no flavor. You need to soak them in warm water and slice to add to soups or stir-fries or soak and marinate in rice vinegar and soy sauce and serve as an appetizer. They are found in plastic bags on the shelf or in plastic baskets behind a glass counter in some stores, where they are weighed and sold by the piece. Other stores in large Chinatowns may sell fresh ones in buckets of water in the produce section or at the meat counter, sold by weight.

CHICKEN OR DUCK FEET

This is yet another delicacy eaten mostly for its texture. Barbecued duck feet and tongues dangle on metal hooks over Mrs. Lin's deli counter and are found frozen in the freezer if you want to make your own. Pale yellow or black chicken feet (the color depends on what type of chicken they are from) are often served for dim sum or enjoyed as a snack. The rubbery skin becomes soft and succulent after boiling in a rich soy-seasoned stock and literally melts off in the mouth. Not bad once you get past the concept of eating bird feet! Look for Dim Sum King brand seasoned chicken feet in 12-ounce plastic packs.

BLACK MOSS

Also known as hair vegetable or fatt choy in Cantonese (fa cai in Mandarin), this algae symbolizes prosperity—the name "fatt choy" sounds like the last two words in the Lunar New Year greeting "kong hei fatt choy!" (wishing you happiness and prosperity). Thus it is often added to a vegetable dish served during the new year celebrations. Almost tasteless, it absorbs other flavors and adds a slippery texture. Popular uses include Buddhist vegetarian dishes, glass noodle and vegetable stew, and the Cantonese New Year dish of dried oysters, stir-fried pork, and mushrooms with hair seaweed. This is sold in plastic packages. You need to soak in water before using and add one teaspoon of vegetable oil to the soaking water to help separate the fine black strands. Look for Peony Mark brand dried sea moss in small bags. You may also find small glass jars of a salt preserved variety of black moss.

KOREAN TOTORI MUK

Also called acorn curd. This is an off-white or beige colored creamy slab of gelatinous curd made from muk (a silky starch that comes from a non-bitter Korean acorn) mixed with water and a coagulating agent. Looks like tofu and has a smooth texture and tastes like green tea. It is served with spicy sauces.

The list of exotic things I've eaten in my travels includes all of the above, plus a whole lot more. Crispy fried ant eggs, raw cod sperm, caterpillars, scorpions, cow eyes, snapping turtle blood mixed with rice wine and balut—the Filipino delicacy of an unhatched duck embryo eaten straight from the shell. Suddenly the exotic contents in your typical Asian grocery seem pretty tame, don't they? Why not add some chicken feet, black moss, or rice paddy crabs to your shopping basket?

20

The Mosaic Melting Pot: The Rest of the Asian Market

珍品

Chinese for "unusual items"

Here we will discover miscellaneous bits and pieces scattered throughout the grocery, reflecting the melting pot of Asian cuisine. We'll check on types of sweeteners, bouillon cubes, instant soup stock, and convenience spice and sauce mixes, and examine frozen or packaged ready-to-use items—from shrimp balls to dumplings and stuffed buns. Lastly we will check out wrappers for egg and spring rolls, wontons, and pot-stickers plus some leaf wrappers for steaming rice dumplings, spicy fish paste, or meats in.

Sweeteners

Sugars are used sparingly in Asian cooking, yet they play an important role as a balancing element to other flavors in various sauces and savory dishes. Sour lime juice, hot chilies, and pungent fish sauce are tempered by palm sugar in Thai recipes, and a pinch of sugar balances rice vinegar, ginger, and garlic in stir-fries. Sugar is added to hot-and-sour soups, curries, marinades, and satay sauces to mellow the spiciness. It is an important ingredient in Chinese red-cooked foods: sugar caramelizes and glazes and adds a translucence and luster in slow-braised dishes or sauces. Sugar is used to season sausages, fish paste, and meatballs. In Japan sugar and soy sauce add a salty-sweet flavor to many grilled and teriyaki-style dishes. Sugar is used to make fruit liquor and mirin, a sweetened sake used only in cooking, and it is added to pickling brines. Of course sugars are also used in desserts as well as to sweeten hot or cold drinks.

PALM SUGAR

This creamy tan colored sugar has a mild caramel-like flavor and distinctive fragrance. Called gula melaka in Malaysia and nam tan peep or maprao in Thailand; it is also sometimes labeled "coconut sugar" as it comes from the coconut palm or sugar (palmyra) palms. The sap is boiled down to a semi-soft paste and then formed into hard cakes, slabs, or cones. It is used in desserts and to balance flavors in hot-and-sour dishes, dips, and dressings.

This sugar is commonly sold in hard round cylinders, two to a package, or small round discs in a bag. If the slabs or cylinders are very hard, use a small garlic or cheese grater to shave off bits. Look for Caravelle brand in round slabs wrapped in plastic with a red palm on a gold label. Siamese Coins brand has little swirled sugar palm cakes in 1-pound plastic jars, handy when you just need a little. For semi-soft, thick, creamy pastes look for Tropico, Eastland Thai, and Lucky Man brands in 1-pound tubs. You can substitute light brown sugar with a few drops of maple syrup.

palm sugar

BROWN SLAB SUGAR

layered brown slab sugar

This caramel-colored sugar is made from compressed layers of partially refined brown sugar, white sugar, and honey. It tastes like refined brown sugar and looks like slabs of candy. It is used in any dish requiring a bit of balancing sweetness, roasted meat sauces, or in desserts. The slabs are 3 to 5 inches wide and sold in 1-pound pieces, sealed in plastic wrappers. Look for Crown brand from China in 14-ounce bars with a yellow and green label and red crown logo or Pearl River Bridge brown sugar in pieces. Crush with a rolling pin to use.

ROCK SUGAR

These are large crystal lumps of sugar with a slight yellow color, also called yellow lump. It has a richer, more subtle flavor than refined granulated white sugar. It is used as a sweetener for soups and in sauces, for cooling herbal teas, and to give a good luster or glaze to braised dishes. Rock sugar can be reduced with water to make a sugar syrup or boiled with mung, adzuki, or white fungus to make a dessert soup. Sold in plastic bags and boxes. Look for Pearl River Bridge Yellow Lump brand in a white box with a photo of sugar crystals, and Narcissus or Peony Mark in bags. If the lumps are very large, break into smaller pieces with a hammer or rolling pin.

rock sugar

MALTOSE SUGAR

Also called malt sugar, this is a thick, amber colored liquid made by fermenting germinated grains such as millet or barley. The process converts the grain's starch into maltose and dextrose sugars. Used mainly in preparing roasted meats—this is what gives Peking duck its lacquered look. It is not as sweet as other sugars and is often diluted with water, then mixed with vinegar and soy sauce to make sauces. It may get hard and sticky in the container, so dip a spoon in hot water before scooping out the amount you need. It is sold in glass jars or chubby plastic tubs and most brands are from China. Look for Great Wall or Best Quality brands.

HONEY

Several types of honey may be found in Asian groceries—most are from China, and are either clear, creamy, or scented. Pure Chinese honey is the most common type and it is a clear pale golden color. Look for Bee's Queen brand from Shanghai in 10-ounce glass tumblers with a yellow plastic seal around the top and a bee logo. Use straight from the jar or dilute with water in sauces. Honey can replace sugar in most recipes or be used as a beverage sweetener. Creamed honey, often labeled as "regular flavor syrup," is condensed or crystallized honey. There will be a thick cream color layer on the bottom and a clear amber syrup on the top. Lychee honey is made from the blossoms of lychee fruits and it is dark gold with a fragrant smell. Sold in 3-pound glass jars in a pink plastic net and pink label with a picture of lychee fruits on it. Look for Tick Shing Hong brand for both types, also in 12-ounce glass jars.

Frozen Fast Foods

In the freezer case of most Asian groceries you will find plastic-wrapped packages of frozen abalone, squid, octopus, oysters, mussels, fish, clams, snails, broiled eels, and pig brains, tails, intestines, hearts, and tongues along with whole ducks, duck tongues, chickens, squab, frogs' legs, and beef tripe. There may also be pork paste, liver pate, and rolls of cooked pork hock, used sliced like lunch meat for sandwiches or chopped for dumpling fillings. Then there will be a section of ready-made convenience products, including meat balls, fish cakes, spring rolls, banana leaves for steaming foods in, fruit pulp, grated coconut, and whole vegetarian lobsters sculpted from wheat gluten dough!

Here are some of the frozen products you might want to select from and keep in your freezer for quick snacks, appetizers, and noodle or soup additions.

FISHBALLS & MEATBALLS

These are made from ground pastes rolled into small balls, from a variety of white fish, shrimp or cuttlefish, minced pork or beef. They are seasoned and bound with egg-whites and a starch and are used mainly in noodle soups and hot pots. They can be boiled and sliced to add to stir-fries and hot-sour salads or grilled with barbecue sauce. You may also find tubs of fish meat paste to make fish patties or balls from and fried fish bars made of seasoned fish paste and tapioca starch, which can be sliced and added to soups or stir-fries. They are sold in vacuum-sealed plastic packages. Look for CTF Thai, Oriental Mascot, and Wei-Chuan brands. Shirakiku has fried fish cakes called satsuma age, while Shungkee Food offers fried fish cakes. Kaizen has Thai fish patties with long beans and red curry paste. For meatballs look for Asia Foods or BMC Thai brands. Westlake, Saigon Foods, and Huong Duyen make Bo Vien Gan Tay Ho—cooked beef meatballs with beef tendons.

BUNS, DUMPLINGS, & SPRING ROLLS

These are convenient ready-made items that just need reheating (steaming, pan-frying, or microwaving) to use. Serve them with hot mustard or soy-chili sauce dips. Buns are sold in packs of four to five, dumplings and wontons come in 1-pound bags of 28–32 pieces, and spring rolls or egg rolls are found in flat boxes of a dozen. Following are types to look for:

Char siu bao are dome-shaped soft steamed buns filled with chunks of barbecued pork. Bao means bun.

Siu mai are round or cylindrical dim sum dumplings, open on top and filled with ground pork or shrimp.

Gow choy gao are chive dumplings wrapped in a thin translucent dough and steamed.

POT-STICKERS

Kuoteh, these are pan fried and steamed dumplings stuffed with meat, shrimp, or vegetable fillings. You will also find buns stuffed with lotus paste, ground peanuts, or small plain ones dusted with pink sugar (for birthdays). There will also be Vietnamese spring rolls, egg rolls, crab, pork, and shrimp stuffed wontons, scallion pancakes, and Mandarin shredded bread rolls (silver thread buns). Brands that make a broad range of these frozen goodies include Cawaii, Doll, Laurels, Little Chef, May-May, Hunsty, and Wei-Chuan. For Vegetarian lobster, look for Kuan Tien Farm Co.

CHINESE DUMPLINGS

Fun gao are crescent-shaped, wheat starch dumplings stuffed with a minced shrimp, pork, mushroom, and bamboo shoot mixture.

Jien dui are chewy, sesame seed covered dough balls filled with sweet red bean paste.

Hom soi gok are sticky rice flour dumplings stuffed with minced pork, shrimp, bamboo shoots, and mushrooms.

Woo gok are deep-fried, egg-shaped croquettes of mashed taro root stuffed with a minced mixture of pork, shrimp, bamboo shoots, and mushrooms.

Nor mai are steamed lotus leaf packets, filled with sticky rice, chicken, Chinese sausage, pork, and black mushrooms.

Soup Bases

You will find cubes or powdered forms of concentrated fish, vegetable, chicken, pork, and beef stock in all Asian markets. There may also be packets of popular types of Southeast Asian and Chinese soup mixes. They work as spice packets. You dissolve them in water or coconut milk and add meat, seafood, vegetables, or noodles. Recipes and cooking instructions are printed on the back of most packets or on the small boxes of cubed concentrate. Soup bases are usually found with spices on the dried goods shelf. In the Lins' grocery look for them on shelf 3.

SOUP STOCK

Concentrated cubes or powdered bouillon are used to make clear, intensely flavored broths. Look for Thai-made Knorr brand cubes or small jars of powdered concentrate in fish, chicken, pork, beef, and vegetable flavors (use the cartoon pig, bull, fish, or chicken to identify the flavor as the label is all in Thai). Hot-and-sour soup stock cubes are made by Rivon and CPC/AJI Thailand Ltd.

Vietnamese Soups

The fragrant, spice infused broths of Vietnamese soups are easy to duplicate at home by choosing from the variety of instant cubes, powders, and spice bags available.

PHO

soup powder

Rice noodle soup flavored with a rich beef (bo), chicken (ga), or Duck (vit) stock. Look for Saigon Food Company brand "Bunbo Hue" beef flavor base and Thanh Loi "Pho Pasteur," which comes in a red 2-ounce box with two filter bags of spices to boil with beef or duck to make soup. Bao long has chicken flavor in small boxes of four cubes.

CANH CHUA

These are spicy-sour broths flavored with tamarind and lemongrass to which seafoods are added. Look for Vifon brand tear off strips of one-bowl servings of bon canh tom (shrimp flavor), and Cawaii Trading Co. canh chua in boxes of four cubes. Dissolve and simmer a cube, then add tomatoes, pineapple, shrimp or fish, and rice noodles to make a tangy soup.

KOREAN DASHIDA

Dashida is basic Korean soup stock, infused with beef or fish concentrates. Use it to make light, clear soups. Cheil Foods of Seoul sells pouches of Sogogi beef flavor stock and Myulchi, an anchovy and tuna soup stock. Assi brand makes clam powder soup stock and kim chee flavor base for noodle soup. (Japanese dashi, which is similar ,in chapter 18.)

SOUP MIXES

soup mix

These will be found in paper packets with powdered pastes in plastic pouches or powdered concentrates inside. They range from Japanese miso and seaweed soups to Filipino guava and tamarind seasoning mix for Sinigang (a tangy sour seafood soup), Szechaun hot-and-sour soup, Chinese egg flower soup, and Penang sour laksa soup. There is Tom Yam Gung, a Thai hot sour prawn soup, Tom Gai Kha, a chicken coconut ginger soup, and Indonesian chicken soup.

Some common brands to look for include Kikkoman (miso, egg flower, and seaweed soups), Mama Sita's (a full range of Filipino soups), Bamboe (Indonesian beef and chicken soup mix), Caravelle, Lobo, and Asian Gourmet (for Thai and Chinese soups).

CONVENIENCE PACKAGED MIXES

You will find a variety of packets of semi-soft pastes and prepared spice, sauce, and marinade mixes to make dishes from fried rice to roast duck. You supply the main ingredients but add authentic flavor with the spice blends. These range from spicy coconut curries, Southern Thai salad mixes, satay sauces, Thai sausage seasonings, noodle sauces, and mixes for Indonesian chicken and beef dishes, to gado-gado peanut dressing, agar jelly desserts, custards, and coconut macaroons. Popular brands to look for are: Asian Home Gourmet, Lobo Thai, Bamboe (Indonesian mixes), Kikkoman, Mama Sita's (Filipino specialties), and Noh brand of Hawaii (kim chee pickle mix and roast duck spices).

instant mix

Wrappers & Skins

You will seek out different areas to find a variety of wrappers and skins made of rice, wheat, and egg-and-flour doughs, both fresh and dried. Dry brittle rice papers will be in the rice noodle section of the noodle shelf but for fresh wonton, gyoza, and egg roll wrappers look in the refrigerator cases. Check the freezer for lumpia, wonton skins, or moo-shu shells. Following is a list of the kinds of wrappers to look for, where in the store to find them, how to identify by size and shape, and tips on use. Generally the round wheat flour wrappers are used for boiled and steamed dumplings, square egg dough ones for boiled or deep-fried wontons, and rice papers for fresh or deep-fried rolls.

EGG ROLL WRAPPERS

These are thin sheets of pliable dough made from wheat flour, eggs, and water, similar to wonton skins but larger. They are sold in 6- to 7-inch squares in little piles ranging from 40 to 60, wrapped in plastic. Found fresh in the refrigerator case or frozen. You can stuff them with a variety of fillings, roll up, and deep fry until the surface becomes bubbly, golden brown, and crisp. Can also be stuffed and steamed. Look for Twin Marquis, Oriental Mascot Gold Label, and Dynasty brands.

WONTON SKINS

Also called yun tun, meaning "to swallow clouds," or pi, a general term for pasta skins. They are made from the same wheat flour, egg, and water dough as egg roll wrappers and noodles, and come in two thicknesses. You can stuff them with minced meats and seafood and deep-fry, pan-fry, or steam. Thin skins are used in soup wontons and thick for steaming or frying. Found fresh or frozen in refrigerator cases or freezer. They are sold in small 3-inch squares in piles of 30 to 40 wrapped in plastic. Look for Twin Dragon, Yung Kee, Twin Marquis, TYJ's "Spring Home" label, and Wonton Specialist brands. Twin Marquis also makes

wonton wrappers   pale green vegetable-flavored wonton wrappers.

GYOZA WRAPPERS

Also called jiao or ji pi, they are thin, 3-inch wide circles of pasta dough made from wheat flour, eggs, and water. These round dumpling wrappers are used to wrap fillings for Japanese gyoza, pot-stickers, and siu mai dumplings, then deep-fried, pan-fried, or steamed. Sold in 1-pound plastic-wrapped packages containing 80 to 100 skins, fresh or frozen. Look for Dynasty, Twin Dragon, Fortune, Golden Dragon, and Twin Marquis brands.

gyoza skin

SPRING ROLL WRAPPERS

Also called chunjuan pi, they are thin square or round pliable sheets made from a wheat flour and water batter, about six to seven inches in diameter. Two types will be found—Cantonese, which are smooth, like noodle dough, and Shanghai, which are transparent, like rice paper. Both can be used to wrap fillings or be stuffed, rolled, and deep-fried until crisp. When fried, spring rolls have a smoother texture than egg rolls. Wraps can also be steamed or the sheets can be cut in strips and used as fresh pasta in stir-fries and soups. Sold fresh or frozen, in sealed plastic packs of 20 to 50. Frozen ones pull apart easily when defrosted. Look for TYJ's "Spring Home," Caravelle, or Wei-Chuan brands in the freezer.

LUMPIA WRAPPERS

Also called poh-pia, they are thin Filipino and Southeast Asian crepe-like skins in round or square sheets made from a cornstarch, wheat flour, egg, and water batter, about 6 to 7 inches wide. They are made by rubbing the thin batter over a hot grill or wok and peeling the cooked soft lacy skins off. Use as a wrapping for raw vegetable or cooked fillings, or roll up, seal, and deep-fry. Turrones are deep-fried Filipino banana rolls stuffed with sugar and banana chunks. When deep-fried, lumpia skins stay crisper longer than others. Sold in plastic-wrapped packages of 20 to 40, fresh or frozen. Look for Pacific Isles or Newton brands.

rice paper

RICE PAPERS

Called banh trang in Vietnamese. They are brittle translucent paper-thin sheets sold in both round and triangular shapes. The rounds are about 6 inches across, triangles are the four quarters of one round paper. They are made from rice flour, salt, and water, then dried in the sun on bamboo mats which create the faint imprinted pattern on them.

rice paper

To use, carefully dip one sheet at a time in warm water to moisten until pliable and keep damp on a kitchen towel. They then can be used to wrap summer rolls, "nem," which are softened papers filled with lettuce, fresh herbs, and meat or seafood fillings; or cha gio— Vietnamese spring rolls stuffed with a minced filling, deep-fried, and wrapped in lettuce, then dipped in a sweet-and-sour hot sauce. Wrapped rice papers can also be steamed or sauteed. Another type has black sesame seeds embedded in grayish sheets. Both kinds are sold in round 12-ounce hard plastic containers or sealed plastic bags with 50 to 100 in a package. Good brands are from Vietnam or Thailand. Look for Caravelle, Asian Boy, Erawan, or Family Elephant. For the sesame type, look for The Duck brand. They will be on the noodle shelf, near rice noodles and vermicelli.

MOO-SHU SHELLS

Also called Mandarin or Peking pancakes, they are round griddle- or pan-cooked flat bread made from wheat flour and water, about 6 inches across. Use smeared with plum sauce to roll up Peking duck or moo-shu ingredients such as pork, scallions, mushrooms, shrimp with seasonings, and cut-up vegetables. Think of Chinese fajitas. Almost always found frozen. Defrost and heat in a dry pan or microwave to use. Look for Wei-Chuan and Oriental Mascot brands. You can substitute flour tortillas.

Leaf Wrappers

A variety of leaves from plants that grow throughout China and Southeast Asia are used to wrap rice cakes, dumplings, meat, fish, and pounded pastes before steaming, boiling, or grilling. The leaves protect the contents from heat while adding flavor. In Asia they are picked fresh, but you can find frozen or dried ones in the grocery.

PANDAN

Bai toey in Thailand or duan pandan in Indonesia is the long, slim spiky leaf of the screwpine tree (pandanus). This is used for its distinctive flavoring and as a green food coloring in Southeast Asia. It tastes slightly like butterscotch and is used in both savory and sweet dishes. The leaf is best used fresh, either raked with the tines of a fork to release its fragrance or tied in a little knot before being added to the cooking pot or sticky rice steamer. The leaves are used

pandan leaf knot

to wrap pieces of marinated chicken or shrimp before steaming or grilling, infusing the meat with a delicate flavor. Frozen leaves can be used, but won't be as fragrant as fresh. Look for Eastland brand frozen pandan leaves. The leaf is also pounded to extract the juice to flavor and tint cakes, puddings, and sweet Thai iced tea. You will find tiny bottles of pandan essence in the sweets section or among the spices.

FROZEN BANANA LEAVES

These are a common wrapper for steaming and grilling fish, chicken, and sweet or savory rice. The leaf protects the food, seals in the juices, and imparts a subtle grassy flavor. In Cambodia, Laos, and Thailand warm sticky rice flavored with coconut milk, sugar, and salt is grilled with a chunk of jackfruit or banana in banana leaf envelopes. Malaysian otak-otak is spicy seasoned fish paste wrapped in banana leaf strips (or coconut leaflets) and grilled over coals. Look for Eastland brand.

DRIED LOTUS LEAVES

These come from the lotus plant, which grows in muddy ponds. The leaves resemble large round scallop-edged lily pads. They are used to steam sweet and savory sticky rice in. Loh mai gai are dim sum dumplings made of glutinous rice, chicken, mushroom, and Chinese sausage, steamed in a lotus leaf. A must for Tet, the Vietnamese New Year, are banh chung—pretty pale green square cakes of sticky rice filled with mung beans and pork, wrapped and steamed in lotus leaves.

A very famous dish using lotus leaves is Beggar's Chicken. The chicken is seasoned and wrapped in herbs and grasses. This is then wrapped in a lotus leaf and the entire package is smeared with mud. Traditionally it was buried in the ground and baked under a fire. This dish is said to have been created by a beggar who stole a chicken and found himself with no pot to cook it in. In fancy Chinese restaurants the dish is prepared by wrapping a stuffed chicken in lotus leaves and sealing it in pastry dough and parchment or newspaper.

BAMBOO LEAVES

These are the long, spear-shaped fronds of bamboo stalks—the staple food of the Giant Panda. They are used for steaming sweet or savory rice cakes and dumplings. No Chinese Dragon Boat festival in China, Hong Kong, or Singapore is complete without sticky rice dumplings wrapped in bamboo leaves. They are served up in tribute to the spirit of the ancient poet and statesman Qu Yuan, who drowned himself in the Mi-Lo River in protest against government corruption. Peasants went in their boats looking for his body and when they couldn't find it, they beat drums and flung rice dumplings in the water to keep the fish from making a meal of him. To use dried leaves, soak in warm water until soft enough to fold (about 20 minutes) and pat dry before stuffing. Look for Caravelle and Heritrade brands in 1-pound bags or unwrapped folded-in-half bundles of lotus leaves tied with fiber strings. For bamboo, look for Yacht brand, Hang Tai Marine Products, and Happiness brands in 1-pound plastic bags.

Wrappers encircle, encrust, and enclose small bursts of flavor in neat little parcels of tactile, fun food. Use your imagination and appetite as to what morsels can be enveloped in any variety of the doughy, sticky, crisp, or soft translucent skins, sheets, papers, and leaves available. Join wrap mania—Asian style—by borrowing from the Lins' grocery and making your own package deal. It's a wrap!

STOCKING UP

Palm sugar, convienence soup and spice paste mixes, frozen fish, shrimpballs or meatballs, dumplings, and wonton or egg roll wrappers. Rice papers for making easy salad rolls.

frozen fish balls

Epilogue

I hope you,ve become more familiar with the contents of Asian grocery stores with the help of this guide—and by actually walking yourself through a store. If you love Asian flavors, but have been too intimidated to cook them at home, now there is no excuse! Head for the nearest Asian grocery with this guide and begin putting together your personalized collection of basics.

While no two Asian groceries are exactly the same, they all follow the logic of the Lins' little store. The best strategy is to find an Asian grocery near you and learn its layout. After repeated trips, you will be as familiar with the aisles as you are with your local supermarket. And you will probably have made friends with the owner, who will be more than glad to assist a loyal customer—and like the Lins, give you advice and recipe suggestions.

While I could not possibly cover each and every one of the thousands of products stocked in Asian grocery stores, I hope a lot of your questions have been answered. When in doubt you can slip this guide out of pocket or purse and look up what you don't recognize. Certainly, I hope I have inspired you to go into an Asian grocery and explore with confidence.

· Appendix 1 ·

Basic Utensils

Or a large skillet. There are three basic sorts of woks: teflon-coated non-stick, heavy cast-iron, and the light black or stainless steel ones. A traditional Asian cook would always choose the cast-iron one as it is most lasting and gives the best results. If possible, buy a domed cover for your wok. This is useful for steaming and braising. The modern teflon woks come with matching covers.

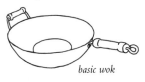

basic wok

A new wok must be seasoned before use. To do this, scrub it well to remove any machine oils from its manufacture. After this, dry the wok and place it over low heat. Add 2 tablespoons of cooking oil and rub the oil over the inside with paper towels. The entire surface should be lightly coated with oil. Heat the wok slowly for another 10 to 15 minutes, then wipe thoroughly with clean paper towels. There will be black machine oil and grease on them. Repeat this process until the towels wipe clean. A seasoned wok should not be scoured with scouring cream, and must always be dried after washing or it will rust.

A Chinese cleaver or good thin-bladed, medium-sized, all-purpose, stainless-steel chef's knife is important for chopping, slicing, and mincing vegetables, seafood, and meats. Keep clean and dry and sharpen periodically.

MORTAR

A stone mortar and pestle is ideal for pulverizing and grinding spices and herbs into seasoning pastes and spice mixtures. Purists insist that this allows the natural oils to be released and makes for better flavors. A convenient alternative is to use a mini processor or spice grinder.

STEAMER

This can be either a bamboo basket with lid or an aluminum one. A steamer is used for cooking dumplings, vegetables, and whole fish over boiling water. It is possible to use a wok that has a fitting cover as a steamer, by placing the dish on a pair of chopsticks or a small wooden rack over boiling water in the wok.

bamboo steamer

OTHER HELPFUL TOOLS

It is most useful to have a wood spatula or metal slice for stir-frying and a wire mesh skimmer or slotted spoon for lifting food from hot water or oil. You might also like to have a pair of long cooking chopsticks or tongs to remove items from the wok as they are cooked. You could get a bamboo brush for cleaning the wok without spoiling its surface. Finally you might like to have a semi-circular metal grill for draining foods over the wok and wok stands—a metal wire utensil for holding steam plates in woks over the boiling water.

Bamboo strainer

· Appendix 2 ·

Basic Asian Cooking Techniques

Have everything at hand, pre-cut, chopped, measured, and ready to go. Foods, especially meats, should be cut into bite-sized pieces. Before turning on the heat, combine your sauces and group piles of ingredients in a logical cooking order according to the recipe directions. Read the recipe all the way through so you have a good idea of what you are going to do.

STIR-FRYING

Probably the best known and most popular Asian method of cooking. Food is kept in constant motion by stirring and tossing to ensure even cooking. The wok should be preheated over a high flame until it almost smokes. Add in the oil and, when it is hot, then toss in and stir the flavoring ingredients (onions, garlic, ginger) until they smell fragrant. When the recipe uses meat or seafood, these are added next. They should be tossed quickly in the hot oil to seal in the juices, then removed and set aside. The dense or tough textured vegetables (such as cauliflower, carrots, broccoli, and cabbage) are now added to the oil. The smaller, more delicate vegetables are added later, since they need only a short cooking time so they won't lose their crispness. When vegetables have been cooked, the pre-seared meat or seafood is returned to the pan. Toss until everything is glazed in the sauce. If you are using any binders, such as cornstarch, add last to thicken the wok liquids.

BRAISING

This technique is used to cook large, tough cuts of meat which become tender in long term, low temperature cooking. It is also used for poultry and some seafoods. Good for make-ahead dishes that need only to be reheated. First add a little oil in a preheated wok or deep pot, heat it until it almost begins smoking then add meat and lightly brown it to seal its juices. Add in seasonings and flavoring liquid, then cover tightly and let everything cook on the stove top (or in the oven) for several hours at a low temperature. The meat will be succulent and tender.

RED COOKING

A method of simmering food gently over low heat in a liquid sauce made with soy and sugar. This creates a dark reddish-brown colored glaze, thus the name. Red-cooked meats, poultry, and seafood come out tender and juicy with the flavor of the sauce imparting a deep richness. The cooking liquids range from a simple soy, sugar, and water mix to complex mixtures made from rice or other wines, rock sugar, and seasonings such as cinnamon, star anise, ginger, five-spice powder, garlic, tangerine peel, and onions. Sauces can be strained and saved to use over and over, becoming richer each time. Allow the sauce to cool, remove the fat, and refrigerate or freeze it. Thaw or melt slowly to reuse.

STEAMING

Ovens are recent additions to the typical Asian kitchen, so the old technique of steaming was and is a popular cooking method. It is also a very healthy one, using little or no added oil or fats. Nutrients are retained and the subtle flavors of ingredients are brought out. To steam foods, bring water to a boil in a wok or wide skillet. Put ingredients in a heatproof dish and place the dish on either a steamer rack or two parallel chopsticks about ¾ of an inch above the boiling water. Make sure the steam circulates freely. Cover with a tight-fitting lid

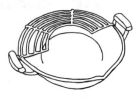

drainer for wok

and steam to desired doneness. You may need to add more hot water for certain foods if they need to steam longer. When removing lid, be careful to tilt it away from you to prevent yourself getting scalded by the escaping steam.

DEEP-FRYING

This method produces a moist interior and crisp golden crust. Foods prepared this way should be well drained of the oil after cooking and served hot. In order to obtain a perfect result, the oil should be of good quality, pure and clean. In the cooking pot the oil must be several inches deep and very hot. To test that it is hot enough, drop a small bit of uncooked food in the oil. If the oil is at the correct temperature, the bit will immediately sizzle and bubble. Do not try to cook too much at once. Frying in small batches allows for even cooking and keeps the oil temperature constant. Crowding causes the temperature to drop and produces the dreaded result—oil soaking into and saturating the food. Remove cooked food with a wire strainer or slotted spoon and drain well on paper towels.

GRILLING

Roasting and baking are new to Asian cooking, where, except for the Indian tandoor, ovens are practically unheard of. Grilling was done over an open charcoal pit. Meats, poultry, and large fish are marinated and then grilled on a rack. Satay, barbecued pork, and roast suckling pigs are some of the more common grilled foods.

· Appendix 3 ·

Recipes

Rice

Before cooking any rice, rinse the grains in several changes of water. Swish the rice around with your hands and pour off the cloudy water. It is ready to cook when the water drains clear. This is done to remove any talc from the polishing process, to get rid of any impurities, and allow the grains to separate during cooking, making a fluffier final product.

PLAIN WHITE RICE

When combining ingredients, add enough water (once the rice is in the pan) to come up to the first knuckle on your index finger.

> 2 cups long-grain rice
> pinch of salt
> 2 cups water

In a deep saucepan bring rice, salt, and water to a boil over high heat.

Cover the pan and turn heat to low. Simmer 20–25 minutes or until all the water is absorbed—try not to peek.

Remove from heat, checking that the water is absorbed—you will see little holes, or craters, in the surface of the rice. Let sit to steam 10 minutes, tightly covered.

Remove the lid and fluff rice with a fork. Serve immediately.

Makes 4 servings.

STICKY RICE
(KHAO NEEO)

> 3 cups Thai long-grain glutinous or "sticky" rice
> cold water

Place rice in a bowl large enough to hold twice the volume of rice (about 6 cups). Pour in cold water until the rice is covered by about 2 inches of water. Leave the rice to soak at least 8 hours or overnight. The longer it soaks, the more flavor it develops.

Drain the rice and transfer into either a Southeast Asian rice steamer basket or a sieve placed over boiling water in a large pot or kettle. The rice must not touch the boiling water.

Cover the pot with a tight-fitting lid and steam the rice for about 25–30 minutes or until the rice looks shiny and is tender. You should check the water level occasionally to ensure it doesn't boil away. Add more boiling water if necessary.

Transfer the cooked rice to a serving basket (also sold in Southeast Asian markets) or bowl, breaking up any large lumps. Cover the rice with a lid or clean kitchen towel, since it will dry out when exposed to air as it cools.

Keep in the steamer container to keep warm. Eat warm, rolled into small balls.

Makes 6 servings.

SUSHI RICE

It is used for nigirizushi (finger size pieces), maki rolls, temaki rolled cones, chirashizushi (sushi rice in a bowl scattered with seafood, pickles, and boiled vegetables), or to make o-bento lunch boxes—a portable container filled with sushi rice and other foods. You can also stuff sushi rice in pockets of fried tofu skin (abura-age) to make inari-sushi.

    2 cups short-grain rice
    2 cups cold water
    ¼ cup rice vinegar
    2 to 3 tablespoons sugar
    1 tablespoon mirin (sweet cooking wine)
      pinch of salt

Place rice in a bowl, add enough water to cover and wash rice by swishing it around with your fingers. Repeat several times until the water drains clear. Pour rice into a strainer, drain and let sit 10–15 minutes.

Place rice and water in a heavy saucepan (a 2–3 quart pan). Bring to a boil and reduce heat. Cover tightly with the pan lid. Simmer about 15 minutes or until all the water is absorbed. Turn off heat and let rice stand for 10 minutes covered with a kitchen towel.

While rice is cooking, combine vinegar, sugar, mirin, and salt and heat in a small saucepan until sugar dissolves.

Empty the rice into a large wooden or plastic bowl. Pour vinegar mixture over the rice. Fold in with a wooden rice paddle (shamoji) or big wooden spoon. Run the paddle or spoon through the rice in slicing motions to separate the grains. While you do this, fan the rice (or have a helper do this) with a paper and bamboo fan (uchiwa) or piece of cardboard. This brings out the luster of the grains. Continue folding and fanning until rice absorbs all the vinegar mixture, about 10 minutes.

Cover with a damp towel and let stand until ready to use. Do not refrigerate. Sushi rice will last one day and does not do well as a leftover.

Makes 4 cups.

Salads

THAI GREEN PAPAYA SALAD
(SOM TAM)

Serve this unique salad as a side dish with rice and other foods to aid digestion. The raw enzymes of green papaya can give you a bellyache.

- 5 leaves lettuce
- 2 sprigs cilantro, cut into 1-inch lengths
- 1 medium-sized green (unripe) papaya, grated, soaked in iced water (to retain crispness)
- 2 cloves garlic, peeled
- 2 tablespoons roasted peanuts, roughly ground or chopped
- 1 tablespoon dried shrimp, ground or shredded
- 2 medium-sized green or red fresh chilies, chopped
- 4 to 5 green beans, coarsely chopped
- 1 medium or 2 small plum tomatoes, diced
- 1 tablespoon palm or light brown sugar
- 2 tablespoons fish sauce (nam pla)
- 2 to 3 tablespoons fresh lime juice

Line a serving dish with the lettuce and cilantro sprigs.

Drain the papaya shreds and pound together with the garlic, preferably in a stone mortar and pestle. If you don't have one, use a heavy can to smash the ingredients in a wide plastic bowl.

Stir in the rest of the ingredients, adding liquids last.

Alternate pounding and turning with a spoon until the mixture is thoroughly blended.

Adjust seasonings to taste. Pour into the serving dish.

Variation: 2 cups grated cabbage and carrot or jicama can be used instead of papaya. You can add 4 to 5 whole rice paddy crabs (to a khia) to make the salad heartier. Crush them into the mixture just before you adjust seasonings.

Makes 2 to 4 servings.

GRILLED EGGPLANT SALAD
(YAM MAKEUA YANG)

I enjoyed this with Thai friends in the patio garden of Silom Village Restaurant in Bangkok. It was one of the side dishes accompanying rice.

Sauce

    1 tablespoon fresh coriander (cilantro) root, chopped coarsely

    8 cloves garlic, 6 chopped coarsely

    1/2 teaspoon salt

    1 tablespoon rice vinegar

    1 medium mild fresh green chili, such as poblano, seeded and chopped

    4 fresh, small red chilies, seeded and chopped

    1 tablespoon palm or light brown sugar

    2 tablespoons fresh lime juice

    1 1/2 tablespoons fish sauce (nam pla)

Salad

    3 pounds eggplants, sliced lengthwise 1/2 inch thick (preferably the long, pale purple Asian variety)

    1/4 cup vegetable oil

    pinch of salt

Garnish

    2 cloves garlic, finely minced

    2 shallots, sliced thinly

    3 tablespoons dried shrimp, lightly browned in 1 teaspoon oil

    10 to 15 sprigs cilantro

Crush the coriander root and the coarsely chopped garlic in a mortar or grind in a processor until it forms a paste. Pound or grind in the salt, vinegar, and chilies. Stir in palm or brown sugar, then add lime juice and fish sauce. Set this sauce aside.

Light a grill or preheat a broiler.

Brush eggplant slices on both sides with oil and sprinkle with salt. Grill or broil over low heat, turning once, about 3 minutes per side or until browned and tender.

Arrange grilled eggplant on a platter and drizzle the sauce over each piece. Garnish with the reserved minced garlic, shallots, sauteed dried shrimp, and cilantro sprigs. Serve warm or at room temperature.

Makes 4 to 6 servings.

Side Dishes
CHILI PEANUTS WITH ANCHOVIES

This is a Malaysian snack or side dish to accompany rice and other dishes. Even breakfast packets of nasi lemak (wrapped in banana leaves) are garnished with a dollop of chili sauce and a sprinkling of these peanuts.

4 dried red chilies, soaked in water

1 shallot or small red onion, sliced finely

1 tablespoon cooking oil

$^1/_2$ teaspoon salt

1 tablespoon sugar

$^3/_4$ cup roasted peanuts, with skin on

$^1/_2$ cup dried anchovies or silver fish (ikan bilis), heads removed and fried until crisp

Blend or pound chilies and shallot or onion together.

Heat oil and gently fry the blended mixture with salt and sugar for one minute. Add in the peanuts and anchovies.

Stir-fry for 3 minutes and remove from heat. This can be served immediately or stored, when cool, in a tightly closed jar in the refrigerator for up to three weeks.

Makes 4 to 6 servings.

BALINESE TOMATO
& LEMONGRASS BROTH

This light, fragrant soup makes a good starter before a rich meal or buffet.

Soup

 1 1/2 cups chicken stock or water

 3 stalks lemongrass, tender center part only, chopped

 6 large ripe tomatoes, chopped

 2 shallots, chopped

 10 to 15 large sprigs cilantro

 3 slices fresh gingerroot, peeled

 2 cloves garlic, peeled and crushed

 10 kaffir lime leaves (or 1 tablespoon grated lime zest)

 1 to 2 tablespoons fish sauce (or to taste)

Garnish

 4 tablespoons cucumber, finely diced

 4 tablespoons tomato, finely diced

 cilantro leaves, chopped

 bean sprouts, blanched if desired

 lime wedges

Bring stock or water to a boil and add all soup ingredients except fish sauce.

Reduce heat and simmer over low heat for 45 minutes.

Strain soup through a fine-mesh sieve. Discard the solids. Add fish sauce to taste.

Serve in individual bowls. Place 1 tablespoon of diced cucumber and tomato in each bowl before ladling in the hot broth. Sprinkle cilantro leaves and bean sprouts on top. Have lime wedges on the side.

Makes 4 servings.

BEANCURD CABBAGE

This mild mix of soft beancurd and slightly crunchy Chinese cabbage is based on an ancient temple recipe from Hangzhou in southern China.

  1 pound firm beancurd
  1/2 cup, plus 1 1/2 tablespoons peanut oil
  3 tablespoons green onions, chopped
  2 cloves garlic, chopped coarsely
  1 pound napa cabbage, cut in 1/2 -inch shreds
  2 tablespoons rice wine or dry cooking sherry
  1 tablespoon soy sauce
  1/2 teaspoon ground white pepper
  1/2 teaspoon salt
  2 teaspoons sugar
  1 tablespoon crushed red pepper flakes, optional
  1 tablespoon sesame oil

Cut the beancurd into 1-inch cubes. Let it drain on paper towels for 10 minutes.

Heat a wok or large skillet until hot. Add ½ cup of peanut oil. When it is hot, fry beancurd cubes on both sides until golden brown. Drain on more paper towels. Set aside.

Reheat pan and warm up 1½ tablespoons peanut oil. Toss in green onions and garlic and stir-fry 30 seconds.

Add the cabbage and all the seasonings except the sesame oil. Continue to stir-fry another 2 minutes.

Return the fried beancurd cubes to pan and cook over high heat about 5 minutes or until cabbage is tender. Add sesame oil, toss to coat, and serve.

Makes 4 servings.

Main Dishes
THAI FRIED NOODLES
(PAD THAI)

In Thailand, pad thai is a fast food enjoyed as a snack between meals. As part of a meal, it would be served with a soup, several other vegetables, fish or meat dishes, plus rice.

Noodles

- 4 tablespoons peanut oil
- 2 cloves garlic, finely chopped
- 1 egg
- 1 package long thin rice noodles (sen lek in Thai), soaked in water for 20 minutes
- 2 tablespoons fresh lime juice
- 1 1/2 tablespoons fish sauce (nam pla)
- 1/2 teaspoon sugar
- 2 to 3 tablespoons tamarind juice (or vinegar)
- 2 to 3 tablespoons roasted peanuts, chopped, divided into 2 portions
- 2 tablespoons dried shrimp, ground or shredded, divided into 2 portions
- 1 teaspoon red chili, crushed (or chili powder)
- 2 tablespoons preserved turnip or radish, finely diced
- 2 to 3 green onions (scallions), sliced into small pieces

Garnish

- 1 cup fresh bean sprouts, blanched if desired
- cilantro sprigs
- lemon or lime wedges

Heat the oil in a wok or skillet. Add the garlic and fry until light golden brown. Break the egg into the wok and stir quickly for a few seconds. Add the rice noodles and toss well.

Add in the lime juice, fish sauce, sugar, tamarind juice or vinegar, one portion of the peanuts and dried shrimp, the chili pepper, preserved turnip or radish, and green onions. Stir quickly and toss constantly.

Test noodles for tenderness. They should be springy, not mushy or falling apart, and the ingredients should be well mixed in. When done, turn onto a serving plate and garnish with the reserved peanuts and dried shrimp. Add beansprouts and cilantro sprigs. Serve with lemon or lime wedges on the side.

Makes 4 to 6 servings.

SHRIMP COCONUT CURRY
WITH RED CURRY PASTE

This dish has a rich creamy taste and can include a variety of seafood such as firm white fish cut into chunks, squid, crab, lobster, or mussels.

    2 tablespoons cooking oil
    1 small onion, finely chopped
    1 large clove garlic, finely minced
 1 1/2 tablespoons red curry paste (see recipe on page 217 or use ready-made paste)
    1 can (13.5 fluid oz) unsweetened coconut milk
    2 tablespoons fish sauce (nam pla)
    1 stalk lemongrass, sliced in several pieces
    1 teaspoon sugar
   12 large or 24 small uncooked shrimp, shelled, deveined, but tails left (or other seafoods)
    2 lime leaves, finely sliced (or 1 tablespoon grated lime zest)
    1 to 3 small red chilies, seeded and chopped finely
   10 holy basil leaves

In a wok or deep pan, heat oil, add chopped onion and garlic, and fry until light golden.

Add the curry paste, and cook briefly.

Gradually add half the coconut milk. Add fish sauce, lemongrass, and sugar, stirring constantly. Mixture will begin to thicken.

Add shrimp (and/or other seafood) and cook until they turn opaque. Then add the rest of the coconut milk, lime leaves or zest, and chilies. Continue to cook for another few minutes.

Sprinkle on the basil leaves and serve the curry hot over steamed rice.

Serve as a main dish along with a noodle or vegetable side dish and crunchy cucumber and onion salad or an assortment of achar (pickles). It can also be served as a light but spicy lunch with just rice.

Makes 4 to 6 servings.

VEGETABLE STIR-FRY

A snappy, delicious, easy-to-make stir-fry. You can add any of your favorite vegetables, beancurd, nuts, meat, or seafood to make a heartier dish.

Sauce

   1/4 cup chicken or vegetable broth (you can also use the water the mushrooms were soaked in)

   3 tablespoons soy sauce

   dash of rice vinegar

   1 1/2 teaspoons sugar

   1 teaspoon ground white pepper

   1 teaspoon sesame oil

Stir-fry

   1 tablespoon cooking oil

   4 whole dried red chilies

   1 small onion, chopped

   1 clove garlic, minced

   3 thin slices gingerroot, peeled and cut in fine shreds

   1/4 cup dried black fungus (cloud ears), soaked in warm water for 30 minutes

   8 dried Chinese black or shitake mushrooms, stems removed, soaked in warm water 30 minutes, sliced finely

   1 green bell pepper, cut in strips or chunks

   1 cup fresh button mushrooms, wiped clean and sliced

   1/4 pound sugar snap peas or snow peas, ends and strings removed

   6 baby bok choy, cut in half lengthwise

   1 small can whole water chestnuts, drained

   1 teaspoon cornstarch, dissolved in 2 teaspoons water

Combine the sauce ingredients in a small bowl and set aside.

Heat oil in a wok or skillet over high heat. Add chilies, onion, garlic, and ginger and stir-fry for 30 seconds.

Add cloud ears and black mushroom slices and stir-fry for 1 minute.

Add the rest of the vegetables and the water chestnuts. Cover and cook another minute.

Add the sauce and let it heat through before pouring in the cornstarch solution and stirring until the sauce boils and thickens. Remove from heat and serve with rice.

Makes 4 to 6 servings.

VIETNAMESE-STYLE STEAMED FISH
(CA HAP)

You can use sole, cod, haddock, snapper, or any firm-fleshed white fish. As it steams the fish remains delicate and flavorful and the vegetables stay fresh and crunchy.

steamed rice

2 pounds fish fillets, cut into bite-sized pieces

2 tablespoons fish sauce with 1 teaspoon sugar dissolved in it
black pepper to taste

2 to 3 slices fresh gingerroot, peeled and chopped finely

1 clove garlic, minced

1/2 cup fresh button mushrooms, wiped clean, stems removed, cut in thick slices

3 stalks celery, cut diagonally into wide slices

1 red bell pepper, cut in strips or chunks

1 tomato, cut in chunks

1/2 cup water

Garnish

3 to 4 green onions (scallions), chopped

mint leaves

dill, with stems removed

bean sprouts

lemon or lime wedges

fresh cilantro

nuoc cham sauce

Make steamed rice for 4 (see page 203). Set aside.

Mix fish pieces with all the other ingredients except water and garnish ingredients in a heat-resistant bowl.

Place water in a steamer, wok, or deep pan and bring to a boil over high heat. Place bowl with fish mixture in steamer. Cover and steam over medium heat for 9 to 10 minutes.

Lift cover and allow steam to escape before removing bowl carefully with hot gloves.

Garnish with the chopped scallion, mint, dill, bean sprouts, and cilantro. Serve over steamed rice with lemon or lime wedges on the side. You can also serve this with huoc cham sauce (see page 217) spooned over the fish.

Makes 4 servings.

SINGAPORE-STYLE CHICKEN CURRY
(KARI AYAM)

This is a richly seasoned curry inspired by the gastronomic mix of Singapore Indian and Malaysian spices and cooking styles. Serve this with steamed rice or crusty bread to soak up the rich gravy. Have a cucumber-yogurt salad, mint or fruit chutney, and pineapple relish to complete the meal.

1 whole chicken (about 3 1/2 pounds)

3 tablespoons cooking oil

1 medium onion, chopped

1 to 2 small red chili peppers, seeded and chopped

4 large cloves garlic, chopped coarsely

1 inch piece gingerroot, minced

2 cinnamon sticks

3 cardamom pods

2 whole cloves

1 whole star anise

3 tablespoons curry powder, made into a paste with a little water

1 1-1/2 pound potato, peeled and cut into large chunks

4 cups unsweetened coconut milk

2 teaspoons salt

3 medium tomatoes, cut in wedges

Cut up chicken, discarding wing tips. Separate thighs from drumsticks. Cut breast in half lengthwise, then crosswise, discarding bone if desired. Remove any excess lumps of fat.

Heat oil in large deep pan or dutch oven. Add onion, chilies, garlic, gingerroot, cinnamon sticks, cardamom pods, cloves, and star anise. Saute for 3 minutes.

Stir in the curry-powder paste and cook for 2 minutes.

Add in the chicken pieces and potato pieces. Stir well to coat with the spices.

Pour in coconut milk and add salt. Bring to a boil, then reduce heat, cover loosely, and simmer for about 45 minutes.

Add in the tomato wedges, then cook uncovered for 15 minutes more.

Makes 6 servings.

SWEET SESAME RICE NOODLES

This is a cross between a dessert, a snack, and a side dish. It is often eaten in Asia as a between-meal snack, and can be purchased at street stalls.

Noodles

    1 pound fresh rice noodles or wide, thin rice sticks

    1/2 cup chicken stock

Sauce

    5 tablespoons sesame paste (or peanut butter)

    3 tablespoons sugar

    5 tablespoons warm water

Garnish

    3 to 4 green onions (scallions), chopped finely

    2 to 3 tablespoons dried shrimp, soaked until soft, drained, and fried crisp

    sugar

If using packaged noodles, soak them in warm water for 20 minutes.

Heat chicken stock in a wok or large skillet. Add in the noodles and cook until soft and most of the liquid has evaporated. Turn noodles out on a warm platter.

While noodles are cooking, prepare the sauce. Put the sesame paste, sugar, and warm water in a blender or food processor, and blend until smooth. Add more water if the sauce is too thick.

Pour sauce over noodles in the serving platter and sprinkle with sugar (if desired), the green onions, and fried shrimp. Serve warm or at room temperature.

Makes 4 to 6 servings.

SALMON WITH TEA RICE
(OCHAZUKE)

This Japanese homestyle dish dates to the old days when cooked, crusty rice left in the pot was softened with boiling water or tea for another meal. It is often eaten at the end of a full course meal or an evening of drinking to soothe the stomach and as a late night snack. You can use freshly cooked rice or cold, day-old rice, reheated.

> 2 salmon fillets (about 8 ounces), lightly salted
> 3 cups steamed rice (to make fresh, cook 1 1/3 cups raw rice)
> 4 cups hot Japanese green tea (or other type) or boiling water
> 1 sheet nori seaweed, cut into thin strips
> 2 to 3 teaspoons wasabi

Grill or boil salmon about 4 minutes per side until the flesh turns opaque and pale pink. Be careful not to burn.

Remove the skin and bones and flake the meat with a fork.

Divide the rice into 4 deep bowls. Top each rice bowl with a portion of flaked salmon.

Pour 1 cup of hot tea or water over each serving. Top with nori and a dab of wasabi, then serve.

Makes 4 servings.

Condiments
RED CURRY PASTE

8 dried red chilies, soaked, seeded, and chopped

1 teaspoon coriander seed

1/2 teaspoon cumin seed

1 teaspoon kaffir lime skin or leaf, chopped
or shredded

1-inch piece of galangal or gingerroot, chopped

2 teaspoons shrimp paste

1 teaspoon salt

Blend all the ingredients, using a mortar and pestle, food processor, or spice grinder, into a smooth paste. You might want to double or triple the recipe in order to have extra on hand for another recipe. Leftovers may be refrigerated or frozen for future use.

Makes 4 to 5 tablespoons.

NUOC CHAM SAUCE

The Vietnamese use this liquid the way we use salt; it is on the table at every meal.

1/2 cup fish sauce (nuoc mam or nam pla)

1 large clove garlic, minced

1 teaspoon crushed red pepper flakes or 1 thinly sliced, fresh, hot
red chili

3 tablespoons fresh lime juice

2 teaspoons sugar

2 teaspoons rice vinegar

1 finely shredded carrot, optional

Combine the ingredients in a medium-sized bowl, stirring to dissolve the sugar. Add extra water to thin the sauce, if needed. Adjust to taste with more fish sauce and lime or sugar. Store in a glass jar or bottle, refrigerated.

Makes about 1 cup.

PINEAPPLE RELISH
(ACAR NENAS)

This is a delicious Malaysian relish and goes well with spicy curries and bar-becued meats or grilled skewers of satay.

   1 large cucumber
  1/2 medium or 1 small red onion, sliced thinly
   3 cups fresh pineapple pieces, sliced thinly (do not use canned)
  1 1/2 teaspoons salt
   1 clove garlic
   1 small fresh red or green chili, seeded and chopped
   2 tablespoons sugar
   2 tablespoons rice vinegar or white vinegar

Peel cucumber and cut in half lengthwise. Scoop out seeds and cut into ¼-inch thick slices.

Combine the cucumber and onion with the pineapple in a bowl. Sprinkle with salt and let stand 1 hour. Pour mixture into a sieve and squeeze out excess liquid. Pat dry with paper towel. Put pineapple mixture back into the bowl.

Pound garlic and chili in a mortar or spice grinder to form a paste.

Dissolve the sugar in the vinegar and stir in chili paste.

Pour dressing over the pineapple mixture. Mix in well, cover, and leave to marinate in the refrigerator for at least 2 hours.

Makes 2 cups.

LOTUS ROOT PICKLES

A favorite all-purpose Japanese pickle, good as a side dish, with rice, in salads, or eaten as a snack.

> 1 large lotus root (ha su or renkon in Japanese)
> 2 cups water
> 1 tablespoon of rice vinegar

Dressing
> 4 tablespoons rice vinegar
>   pinch of salt
> 1 tablespoon sugar

Peel lotus root, soaking it in the water and vinegar as you peel to prevent discoloration. Remove peeled root and cut in half lengthwise, then into slices a little over ½-inch thick.

Transfer lotus pieces and water-vinegar mixture to a pot and boil until tender (about 30 minutes). Meanwhile, mix the dressing ingredients well.

Drain and slice the lotus pieces very thin. Coat them with the dressing and leave to marinate in a glass or plastic container for several hours (or overnight).

The pickles can be stored for several days in the refrigerator.

Makes 4 to 6 servings.

Herbal Soups

The following recipes make use of the herbs listed above in various combinations to make soups. All are old, time-tested Chinese remedies. It is fine to estimate the amount of herbs—I have provided exact amounts, but feel free to measure by eye. Many Asians (and myself) cook this way with herbs—you may wish to even add more of one especially beneficial to you. It is important to know which combinations are complementary and which fight each other. The classical soups below are all "correct combinations," so use these as a guide as to which commonly used herbs go with one another.

Then just estimate the amounts used in a recipe. One other tip, never use daikon (Chinese radish) with any herbs—it is believed to negate any value of the herb. A note on Chinese soup: Always wait until the water is boiling before putting in the chicken (a small whole one or necks, wings, and backs), meat, or pork bones. Because Chinese soups are simmered for hours (at least 3!) the meat is quite tasteless. This is the time to save all your leftover bones and use them for soup. Add a little meat in the last hour of cooking if you want to eat the meat too.

Likewise, veggie soups involve meat stock with the vegetable (only one is used in Chinese soups) added in the last half hour, or less if it's a delicate one. Chinese believe the essence of the soup is in the drinking, not the eating. Your dog (or cat) can have the scraps!

All of these soups can be used as a liquid ingredient in other dishes.

GINSENG TONIC SOUP
(GINSENG QUING BU TANG)

A very nourishing soup meant for convalescents. It improves immunity and body resistance and helps blood circulation.

- 1 ginseng root (any type)
- 10 strips of polygonatum yu-zhu
- 3 to 4 pieces dioscorea
- 2 tablespoons lycium berries
- 15 red jujube dates
- 8 cups water
  chicken parts (use necks, backs, and wings if not eating the chicken; use legs or thighs if you want to eat the meat)

Simmer all ingredients in a covered pot until chicken is tender, about 2 hours.

Let the herbs and chicken settle to the bottom, skim fat, and strain. Discard chicken parts and drink the liquid.

Makes 4 servings.

SIX FLAVOR SOUP
(LIU WEITANG)

For general health, so it can be an everyday soup.

  6 strips of polygonatum yu-zhu
 20 lotus seeds
  1 ounce each dried longan fruit flesh, dioscorea, lily bulb (bai he), and eurayle seeds
  1 pound of beef tenderloin, cut in small 2-inch cubes (or 5 chicken legs with skin on)
  8 cups water

Cook all ingredients in a covered pot until eurayle seeds are tender (about 1 ½ hours). Since this soup is not simmered for hours the meat can be eaten along with the other ingredients.

Variation: for a sweet soup, use rock sugar instead of meat.

Makes 4 servings.

ANGELICA BLOOD TONIC SOUP
(DANG GUI DA ZAO)

Improves general circulation in body.

  5 pieces of angelica dang gui
 10 codonopsis sticks
 15 red jujube dates
  1 ounce dried longan fruit flesh
  2 tablespoons lycium berries
  1 pound of pork bones (or if you want to eat the meat, 8 ounces of lean pork, cut into bite-sized pieces)
  8 cups of water

Simmer all ingredients in a covered soup pot for for 2½–3 hours. Skim fat, then strain. If using lean pork, return to the strained liquid.

Makes 4 servings.

BLOOD AND SKIN TONIC SOUP
(BU XUE YANG YAN TANG)

Nourishes blood and skin, builds strength, and improves circulation.

  4 ounces of raw peanuts
  8 cups of water
  2 pieces of dried tangerine peel
 15 red jujube dates
    a few slices of ginger
  2 pounds of beef shank
    pinch of salt

Chop or grind peanuts coarsely.

Bring water to a boil, add peanuts, peel, and dates. Add ginger slices and beef, bring back to boil, skim foam, and reduce heat.

Cover, simmer 3 hours, and add salt to taste. If you want to eat the meat, remove from broth and when cool enough to handle, slice. Eat the slices with a soy and vinegar dipping sauce or return to broth.

Makes 2 to 3 servings.

TASTY DOUBLE-BOILED CHICKEN SOUP
(XIANG WEI DUN JI TANG)

 1 ounce codonopsis
 1 ounce angelica dang gui
 1 ounce lotus seeds
 1 ounce lycium berries
 1 ounce dioscorea
 1 ounce polygonatum yu-zhu
 1 ounce astragalus
 1 ounce chuan xiong (ligustrum rhizome, a dried dark brown root which is an immune system booster)
 6 cups water
 2 chicken legs with thighs attached (or 5 chicken legs with skin on)

Simmer all above ingredients in a covered pot for about 2 hours. Cool, skim fat, strain, and reboil.

You can save the chicken to eat with rice and a soy-chili sauce.

Makes 3 to 4 servings.

ASTRAGALUS-CODONOPSIS SOUP
(BEI QI DANG SHEN TANG)

This is a sweetish soup meant for improving overall health and alleviating tiredness.

   15 red jujube dates
   2 tablespoons lycium berries
   6 pieces of dioscorea
   1 ounce dried longan fruit flesh
   6 slices of astragalus root
   5 codonopsis sticks
   8 cups water
   1 pound beef brisket (or 5 chicken legs or 1 pound of pork bones)

Put all ingredients into a large covered soup pot until reduced to 4 cups (about 2½–3 hours). Strain.

If you want to eat the beef, remove, and when cool enough to handle cut into small chunks and return to the broth. The chicken can be shredded and added too.

Makes 2 to 4 servings.

LUNG TONIC SOUP
(ZI YIN RUN FEI TANG)

Make this soup for convalescense from prolonged illness. Especially good for lungs.

   2 ounces codonopsis
   2 ounces lycium berries
   2 ounces poria
   2 ounces polygonatum yu-zhu strips
   1 ounce ground rehmaunia (shu di, a root for tonifying blood)
   1 ounce ophioposon (mai dong, winter wheat)
   8 cups water

Simmer several hours over low heat in a covered pot and strain.

It can be eaten as a soup or you can use it as stock for other recipes.

Makes 4 servings.

WHITE FUNGUS DISPELLING PHLEGM SOUP
(XUE ER RUN FEI TANG)

Treats yin deficiency, improves digestion, stops cough, and clears phlegm.

- 1 ounce dried apricot kernels (xing ren)
- 1 ounce white fungus
- 1 ounce polygonatum strips (yu zhu)
- 1 ounce dried figs
- 1 ounce honeyed dates
- 4 cups of water
- 8 ounces of lean pork or chicken, cut into bite-sized pieces

Simmer all ingredients over low heat in covered pot for about 2 hours. Remove meat and serve separately.

Makes 2 to 4 servings.

SPICED PORK BONE TEA SOUP
(BAH KUT TEH)

- 12 cups of water
- 1 pound of pork ribs, cleaned and cut in pieces
- 6 ounces of lean pork (in one piece)
- 5 licorice slices
- 1 luo han guo fruit (dried)
- 3 codonopsis sticks
- 6 angelica dang gui slices
- 4 whole star anise
- 2 cinnamon sticks
- 1 piece of tangerine peel
- 10 cloves
- 1/2 cup of light soy sauce
- 1/4 cup dark soy sauce
- lump of rock sugar
- ground white pepper

Bring water to boil, add ribs and lean pork. Add all the herbs and spices. Add soy sauces and sugar. Lower heat and simmer about 2 hours.

Season with the ground pepper. Remove whole pieces of pork, slice into small bits, and return to soup. Discard the pork bones.

Makes 6 servings.

Glossary

Abura-age—Thin slices of tofu fried in oil

Achar/Acar—Salted, sun-dried vegetables pickled in a vinegar, sugar, salt, and spice brine

Amaranth—Leafy green Chinese vegetable similar to spinach with reddish-purple-tinted leaves and red roots

Amazu shoga—Pale pink slices of pickled ginger

Assam—Tamarind

Bagoong padas—Filipino fermented anchovy sauce

Biriyani rice—Indian rice dish mixed with meat, seafood, or vegetables and flavored with spices

Cephalopod—Mollusk with tentacles attached to the head

Chinchalok—Shrimp sauce made in Malacca, Malaysia, from salt cured, pickled, tiny whole shrimp

Claypot dishes—One-pot stew or rice cooked in a covered earthenware container

Corm—Water tuber; the bulblike base of a water plant's stem

Cycad—Palmlike non-flowering trees with a thick trunk, a crown of feathery leaves, and large cones with exposed seeds

Galangal—Ginger-like rhizome with a hot, peppery taste

Goreng—Deep-fry or stir-fry

Gula melaka—Palm sugar

Juk song—Dried bamboo pith

Kanpyo—Dried bottle gourd strips

Kencur—Lesser galangal

Kinako—Flour made by roasting and grinding soybeans

Kuih—Sweet Malaysian cakes

Laksa asam—Rice noodle soup in a fragrant hot-and-sour fish broth

Laksa lemak—Rice noodle soup in a spicy coconut milk broth

Lap cheong—Chinese sausage

Liquor—A tea term meaning brewed, poured tea

Mee siam—Rice vermicelli in a hot-and-sour sauce

Mooncakes—Sweet, round cakes representing the moon that are stuffed with sugar, nuts, spices, dates, pureed beans, salted egg-yolks, or lotus seeds

Moon snail—Edible sea snail with a round spiral shaped shell

Nam prik—Very hot, thin Thai chili sauce

Obento—Japanese lunchbox with compartments packed with rice and other foods

Ochazuke—Rice in a bowl with green tea (or boiling water) poured over the top

Pancit—Noodles (Filipino)

Petis-udang—syrupy, slightly sweet, blackish-brown shrimp paste used to flavor soups, sauces, and rojak salad dressing

Pho—Vietnamese rice noodle soup in a rich meat broth

Pomfret—Roundish oval shaped fish with pointed triangular fins and sweet, firm white flesh; about 1 inch thick and 6 inches long

Rhizome—Root-like underground stem

Radix—Root

Rojak—Salad combining tart fruit, vegetables, and crispy fried bits in a pungent sauce made from dark shrimp paste, sugar, chili, tamarind water, and crushed peanuts

Sambal—Any moist, chili based condiment or relish

Samosa—Turnover; crispy triangles of deep-fried pastry dough stuffed with a meat or vegetable filling

Sinensis—Meaning it comes from China (e.g. Sino); Latin for the complete genus-species name of a thing (plant, animal, mineral, etc.)

Sotong—Squid in Malay

Sunomono—Japanese salad dressed with rice vinegar

Sukiyaki—Japanese one-pot meat and vegetable dish quick-cooked at the table

Tamari—Thick, dark soy sauce made without wheat or sugar

Tandoori paste—North Indian spice used to marinate meats roasted in a clay oven at high heat

Tauhu goreng—Deep-fried tofu

Temper—Tone down; work spice mixture into the proper consistency

Trefoil—Three-lobed flower or leaf

Toen-jang—Korean fermented soybean paste

Toddy palm—Tropical palm yielding toddy, a thin sap that is fermented into an alcoholic drink

Tokkuri—Sake flask

Tsukemono—Japanese pickles

Tuk prahok—A Cambodian fish sauce made from diluted fermented mud fish

Zest—Small strip of grated citrus peel used for flavoring

Index

· Notes ·

Notes

· Notes ·

· Notes ·

About the Author

Linda Bladholm is a regular contributor to the *Miami Herald*. She is also a designer, illustrator, and photographer who has contributed to *Singapore and Asia Pacific Magazine* and *Big O Magazine*. A graduate of the University of San Francisco, she has designed books for Noto Publishing and designed and illustrated for FEP/McGraw-Hill, Gunze Company, and World Books International. She has appeared on the National Television Network (NHT) of Japan in conjunction with a series on Japanese art and culture. She has published two books, *Kanzawa, the Heart of Japan* (Noto Printing Co.) and *Singapore Memento* (FEP International). For ten years she lived in and travelled throughout Asia as a teacher, photographer, and representative of the Japan National Tourist Office. She resides in Miami Beach, Florida, where she and her husband are directors of World Island Design.

WHAT'S INSIDE
OF ENGINES?

by
HERBERT S. ZIM

illustrated by
RAYMOND PERLMAN

WILLIAM MORROW & CO.
New York   1953

Foreword

The great machines that make things we use every day are run by powerful engines. Everyone is curious about what is inside these engines and how they work. The youngest readers of this book can learn from the pictures alone. Better readers can make use of the captions and the large-type text. The more detailed text in smaller type is for adults who are using the book with children, or for young people who can read for themselves.

Grateful thanks are given to William L. Hull, Professor of Mechanical Engineering, University of Illinois, for checking the manuscript and the illustrations for this book.

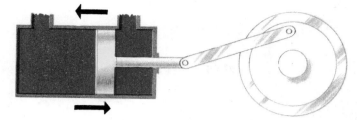

In some engines a piston pushes back and forth

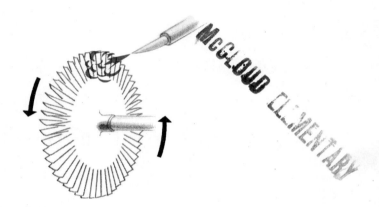

In some engines a rotor spins round and round

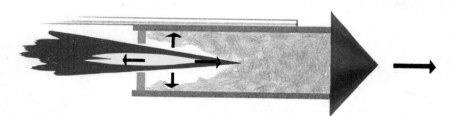

In some engines no parts move. Changing
pressure inside the engines makes them go

Engines are machines for changing heat into motion. They make something move, or move themselves. Your body is an engine. The food you eat furnishes heat. As you run and jump, you move and work. In this way you are like a steam engine, a gasoline engine, or a rocket. The engines that men have invented work for us. They run the machines that plow fields, carry loads, lift weights, and do other jobs we used to do by hand. Some engines, but not all, are large. All burn some kind of fuel.

WHAT'S INSIDE A STEAM ENGINE?

EARLY STEAM ENGINES

John Stevens' locomotive - 1825

a steam tractor

A steam engine has two important parts. One is a boiler where a hot fire turns water into steam. The steam goes through a pipe to the other important part—the steam chest, which contains a cylinder and a piston. Steam enters one end of the cylinder and pushes the piston back. Then it enters the other end, shooting the piston forward again. After the steam has pushed the piston, it is cooler and has less energy. As the piston is pushed again by fresh steam, the waste steam goes out through an exhaust pipe.

INSIDE A STEAM ENGINE

boiler

steam

firebox

water

steam chest

piston   cylinder   piston rod

HOW THE REVERSING VALVE WORKS

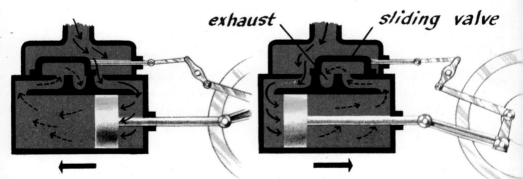

exhaust   sliding valve

steam enters one end
of cylinder, pushing
piston forward

steam enters other end
of cylinder, pushing
piston back

The steam engine was the first high-speed engine ever invented. It pumped water from deep coal mines. It ran mills to grind grain and spin cloth. It ran trains and boats. The idea behind the steam engine is simple. When water is boiled, it changes into steam. If steam is kept inside a closed tank or boiler, it pushes against the sides. The more the steam is heated, the more push, or pressure, it has. If the steam pressure should get too high, the boiler might explode. It is the pressure of steam that we put to work.

In the steam engine, steam from the boiler goes through a pipe to the steam chest. This chest has a heavy tube, or cylinder, containing a tight-fitting steel piston which can move back and forth. In the chest are valves, or openings, which let steam in first at one end, then at the other. As the piston moves in the cylinder, it opens and closes the valves automatically, so that fresh steam enters just when the piston has reached the end of its stroke. The piston forms a tight but movable wall in the cylinder. As the steam enters and expands, it pushes the piston. As the piston moves back, it pushes the used steam out through another valve.

A rod from the piston is connected to a balanced drive wheel about halfway out from the center of the wheel. When the piston goes forward, the wheel makes half a turn. As the piston goes back, the wheel turns the rest of the way. Once steam engines ran farm machinery and many kinds of factories. We even had steam automobiles. Now locomotives are the only common steam engines, and fewer steam locomotives are being made each year. Someday they will be seen only in museums.

WHAT'S INSIDE
A GASOLINE   ENGINE?

DIFFERENT KINDS OF GASOLINE ENGINES

The fuel burns inside the cylinder of a gasoline engine—not in a separate boiler. Gasoline vapor and air are sucked into the cylinder and are exploded by a spark. When things are heated, they get bigger, or expand. That is what happens to the gases in the cylinder during the explosion. The heat is so great that they expand rapidly, pushing the piston down and spinning the shaft to which it is connected. Gasoline engines have from 1 to 28 cylinders. The explosions come fast—one right after the other.

INSIDE A GASOLINE ENGINE

spark plugs

valves

cylinder

crankshaft

piston

THE FOUR-STROKE GASOLINE CYCLE

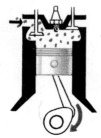

gas and air come in

mixture is compressed

explosion makes power

waste gases pushed out

When wood, coal, oil, or gasoline burns, gases are formed. In gasoline engines these gases do the work of pushing the pistons. Gasoline vapor and air are mixed in the carburetor before they go into the cylinder. When touched off by a spark, this mixture explodes. Billions upon billions of explosions take place every day in the millions of gasoline engines that run cars and planes and boats.

In most gasoline engines the piston pushes, or gives power, in only one stroke out of four as it moves up and down in the cylinder. In the first stroke the piston moves down the cylinder, sucking in the fuel mixture through an opening, or valve. The valve shuts, and in the next stroke the piston moves up, squeezing or compressing the vapor fuel. At this instant, a spark leaps across the spark plug, exploding the fuel mix-ture. The gases from the explosion are heated tremendously just as they are formed. With more push than hot steam has, they shoot the piston down in the third, or power, stroke. In the last stroke before the cycle starts again, the piston moves up, pushing the waste gases out through another valve.

So much power is produced by each explosion that the motion of the pistons spins the heavy shaft to which they are attached. This spinning crankshaft sends each piston up and down till the next power stroke. When an engine has more than one cylinder, the power strokes are timed to come one after another so the engine can turn wheels or propellers smoothly and steadily. Automobiles usually have 4 to 8 cylinders. Large airplane engines may have 20, 24, or even 28, arranged in one or more large circles.

WHAT'S INSIDE A DIESEL ENGINE?

DIESEL ENGINES IN USE

Diesel engines (named for the inventor) are like gasoline engines but simpler. They are usually larger and can do more work. In a diesel engine, only air is sucked or blown into the cylinder. It is compressed by the piston till it becomes very hot. At that instant, oil is squirted or injected into the compressed air. The air is so hot that the oil explodes immediately. It does not need a spark to set it off. The explosions push the pistons and turn a crankshaft, as in gasoline engines.

INSIDE A DIESEL ENGINE

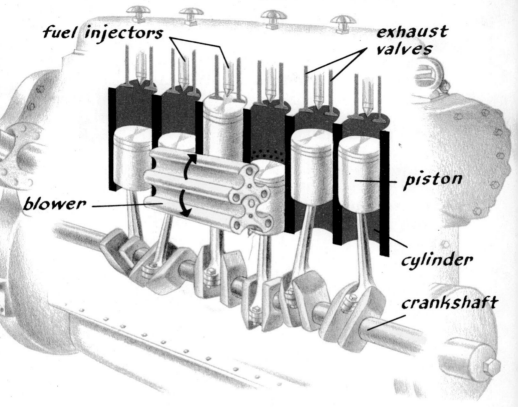

fuel injectors

exhaust valves

blower

piston

cylinder

crankshaft

THE TWO-STROKE DIESEL CYCLE

ir blown in pushes
out waste gases

air is compressed
and heated

fuel is injected
and burned

Trucks, bulldozers, trains, and ships are powered by diesels. These big brothers of the gasoline engine are of several kinds. A four-stroke diesel engine works in about the same way as a gasoline engine, except that the fuel explodes as soon as it is injected into the hot compressed air inside the cylinder. No spark plug is used. Many diesels made today are the two-stroke type. Every second stroke is a power stroke. This is a real advantage, since the engine gives more power for its size.

In a two-stroke diesel, as the piston moves down, a powerful fan, or blower, blows air through valves into the cylinder. As it comes in, the air pushes out the waste gases from the last explosion. The valves shut and the piston moves up, compressing the air and raising its temperature to about 1000° F. At that instant a fine spray of fuel oil is injected by a small, powerful pump. The fuel oil explodes and the hot gases thrust the piston down. As it comes up again, air is blown in and waste gases are pushed out once more.

Diesel engines are harder to start than gasoline engines, but once they are going, they run as well or better. They use a cheaper kind of fuel and give more power for each gallon of fuel burned. Diesels are built heavier than gasoline engines and do not run as fast, so they often last much longer.

In our newest trains and ships, diesel engines run large generators which make electricity. The electricity runs motors connected to the wheels of the train or to the ship's propellers. Diesel-electric combinations are powerful and easier to control than other engines.

WHAT'S INSIDE A STEAM TURBINE?

A HOMEMADE
STEAM TURBINE

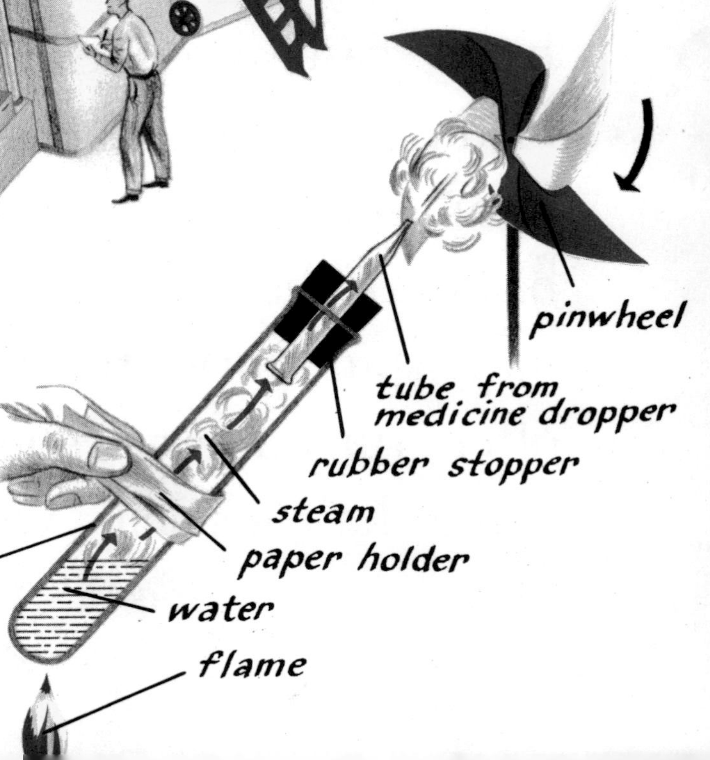

pinwheel

tube from
medicine dropper

rubber stopper

steam

paper holder

test tube

water

flame

A steam turbine is like a pin-wheel or a windmill. But its metal blades, pushed by hot steam under great pressure, spin much faster. A thick shaft runs through the turbine. On it are thousands of curved blades set in circles. This shaft, the rotor, turns inside a heavy case also lined with curved blades. These blades send the steam shooting against the moving blades of the rotor. A rotor, which may spin 3600 times a minute, often runs huge generators that make the electricity we use.

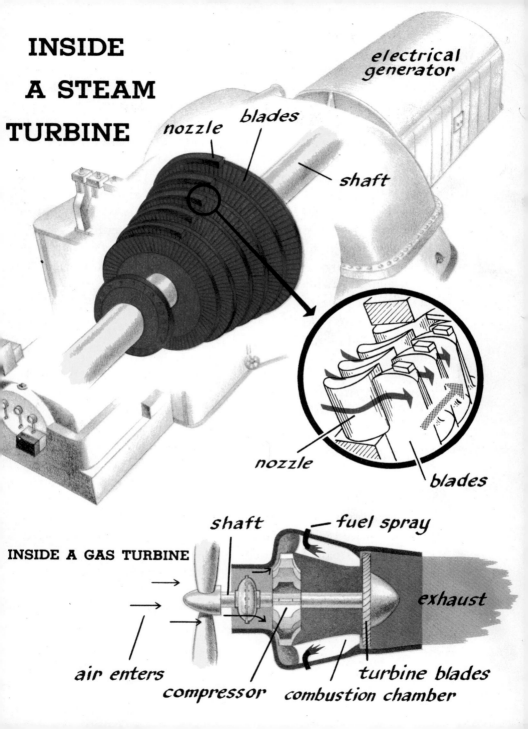

INSIDE A STEAM TURBINE

electrical generator

nozzle

blades

shaft

nozzle

blades

INSIDE A GAS TURBINE

shaft

fuel spray

exhaust

air enters

compressor

combustion chamber

turbine blades

Since pistons go back and forth in steam, gasoline, or diesel engines, they must come to a full stop before they go the other way. That is why something spinning steadily in one direction makes a better engine. In a steam turbine, the rotor, a shaft with many curved blades, spins steadily at high speed without stopping.

A spinning wheel makes an excellent engine. Windmills and water wheels are the oldest spinning, or rotary, engines. But these wheels turn slowly and produce little power compared to a modern steam turbine. Steam turbines are mainly used to run electric generators. The water in the huge boilers must be specially pure. The fires under them sometimes use as much as 50 tons of coal an hour in changing water into steam. The steam is heated under pressure till it is several times as hot as boiling water. At sea level, water boils at 212° F. The steam may be as hot as 700° F.

Steam turbines are often funnel-shaped. The circles of blades are smaller where the steam enters at high pressure. As the steam strikes the blades and loses some of its energy, it is sent against larger and larger blades which have more surface against which the steam can push. By the time the steam has reached the end of the turbine and has pushed against the largest blades, it has very little pressure left. It is changed back to water, which returns to the boiler again.

A gas turbine is a newer kind, in which the fuel (oil or gas) is burned in a chamber just in front of the turbine blades. The hot high-pressure gases from the burning fuel spin the blades just as steam does in steam turbines. Gas turbines are smaller than steam turbines. They run at higher temperatures and at faster speeds.

WHAT'S INSIDE A JET ENGINE?

A RAM-JET

Pressure
equal in
all
directions

Pressure
less toward
back - balloon
goes forward

A jet engine is a large tube, wider at the middle. Here a spray of oil burns rapidly, aided by a blast of air. Hot gases from the burning oil shoot out from the jet at high pressure and at great speed. As the gases go out, the pressure at the back of the jet chamber becomes lower than at the front. As if caught in an unequal tug of war, the jet moves toward the high-pressure end. A toy balloon, full of air, acts like a jet. Air rushing from the balloon's mouth sends it flying forward.

INSIDE A JET ENGINE

fuel spray

air intake

compressor

combustion chamber

turbine

tail cone

exhaust

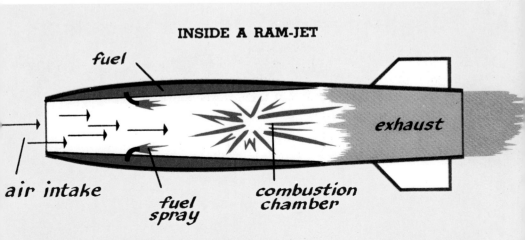

INSIDE A RAM-JET

fuel

air intake

fuel spray

combustion chamber

exhaust

The simplest jet (a ram-jet) has been called a "flying stovepipe." It is nothing but a tube, a fuel tank, and wings. It must be started by a plane towing it at high speed. This forces air through the jet tube. Then the pilot closes an electric circuit, and the spark lights the oil spray. As the oil burns with a roaring flame, the hot gases rush out the jet exhaust much faster than air enters at the front. This makes the pressure in the jet chamber higher in the front where the fuel is burning, and lower in the back where the gases shoot out. So the ram-jet moves forward under its own power.

The more common kinds of jet engines do not have to be started at high speeds. A shaft runs through the jet chamber. At each end is a circle of blades somewhat like those in a steam turbine. As the hot gases roar out the back of the jet, they spin the rear blades rapidly. The rear of the jet is partly a gas turbine. The spinning blades at the rear of the jet spin the shaft and the blades at the front end. These blades act like a fan. They force air into the jet chamber at high pressure so the fuel can burn.

A jet is one of the simplest kinds of engines. It could be used on cars, trains, or boats, but it is best suited for high-speed use—as in planes. Jet engines are both old and new. The idea has been known for centuries, but until planes were invented and improved, there was little use for a practical jet engine. Even today, jet engines are far from perfect. Newer and better kinds are being made. At first jet engines were used only for fighter planes. Now bombers and passenger planes use jet engines. In the next ten years you will see more of them—and better ones, too.

WHAT'S INSIDE A ROCKET?

an ordinary skyrocket

V-2 rocket

DIFFERENT KINDS OF ROCKETS

Jato

WAC-Corporal

guided missile

Rockets and jets are very much alike. Hot gases shoot out of the rear of a rocket, sending it ahead just like a jet. A jet needs air to burn its fuel. A rocket does not. It carries oxygen—the part of the air that makes things burn—or a chemical which gives out oxygen. With its own fuel and oxygen, a rocket can travel to heights where there is no air. It is the only engine we could use to go to the moon or to Mars. Rockets big enough to carry people have not yet been built.

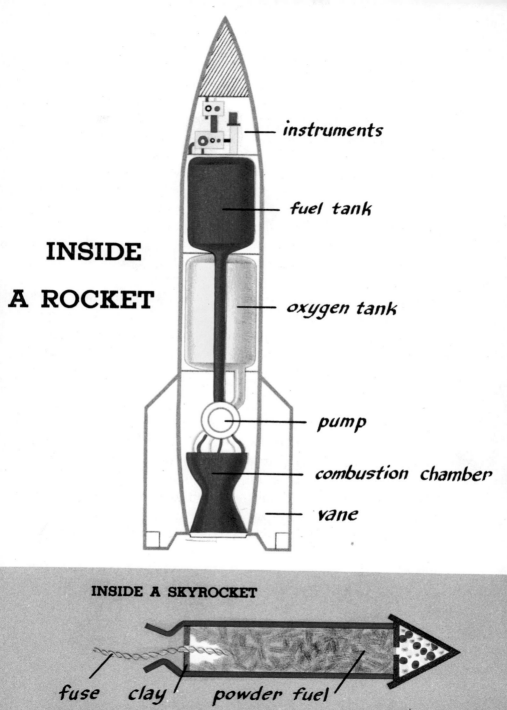

INSIDE A ROCKET

instruments

fuel tank

oxygen tank

pump

combustion chamber

vane

INSIDE A SKYROCKET

fuse   clay   powder fuel

The Fourth of July rocket is a simple and wonderful engine with no moving parts at all. It has a solid fuel made of powdered charcoal, sulfur, and a chemical that supplies oxygen as soon as the mixture begins to burn. The burning powder makes gases so rapidly that the rocket would explode if there were no way for the gases to escape. As the gases rush from the rear of the rocket, they provide the thrust or push that sends the rocket up into the air. As long as burning fuel keeps the pressure in the rocket chamber up, the rocket will go higher.

Modern rockets usually use a liquid fuel that is sprayed into the rocket chamber. They carry a tank of liquid oxygen or a liquid chemical that easily gives up the oxygen in it. These fuels are explosive and dangerous. Just the right amounts must enter the rocket chamber to give the hottest flame. Rockets use a lot of fuel and burn it very fast. The temperature in the rocket chamber might get so high that ordinary metals would melt.

Experiments with rockets are going on all the time. New kinds are being made. Ways to steer and control rockets by radio are being worked out. Engineers are making new fuels and are finding ways to burn them better in the rocket chamber. The first modern liquid-fuel rockets traveled only a few hundred feet; now they go 250 miles up into the air. Already a rocket-driven plane launched from underneath a giant B-29 has flown at a speed of nearly 1300 miles an hour. It flew 15 miles high to break the record. Not too many years from now, rockets will circle the earth. The next step will be rockets to go to the moon, and later to Mars and to other planets.

WHAT'S INSIDE AN ATOMIC PILE?

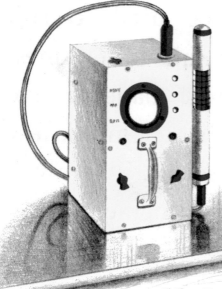

GEIGER COUNTER

warns workers of dangerous radiation

In all engines fuel is burned to make heat. The engine then changes this heat into motion. An atomic pile is not an engine and it does not burn anything. It makes heat in a new way. One kind of uranium changes into other chemicals in such a way that a great deal of heat is formed. This heat can be used to run turbines or other kinds of engines. Atomic piles can be made to give out more or less heat. Only a few have been made so far. There will be more in years to come.

INSIDE AN ATOMIC PILE

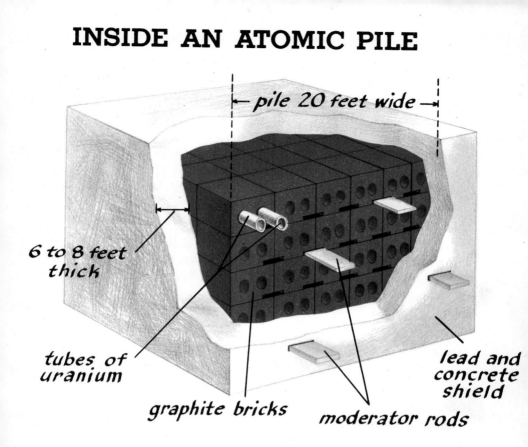

← pile 20 feet wide →

6 to 8 feet thick

tubes of uranium

graphite bricks

moderator rods

lead and concrete shield

ATOMIC PILE USED TO MAKE ELECTRICITY

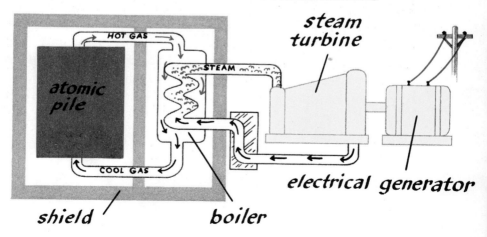

HOT GAS

atomic pile

STEAM

steam turbine

COOL GAS

electrical generator

shield

boiler

Engines burn fuel to get the heat they need to run. Without coal, oil, gas, or gasoline, an engine is of no use. In years to come, the atomic pile will take the place of some of the fuel we use to heat boilers or to burn directly in engines. The atomic pile may operate large electric plants, run submarines and other ships—and perhaps even airplanes. Atomic piles are already heating houses and running electric generators, but they are not yet practical for everyday work.

Different kinds of atomic piles can be made. In one kind, Uranium 235, a rare kind of uranium, changes into other chemicals and gives off heat while doing so. This change is different from burning. When gasoline is burned, the gases that are made weigh *more* than the gasoline. In an atomic pile, the new chemicals weigh *less* than the Uranium 235. The slight loss in weight means that a bit of the uranium has become a great deal of energy. This energy is the heat which is set free.

The rays and particles shooting around inside an atomic pile are so dangerous that heavy walls of lead or concrete must be used to protect the workers. Rods of carbon or other chemicals are pushed into the atomic pile to slow down the change from matter into energy. If the atomic pile could not be controlled, it might become as dangerous as an atomic bomb. Every day we are learning more and more about how to control and use atomic piles. Already they are being used in the manufacture of valuable chemicals which are needed in science and medicine. Before very long they will be running engines in regions where coal, oil, or other kinds of fuel are hard to get.

SOME EARLY

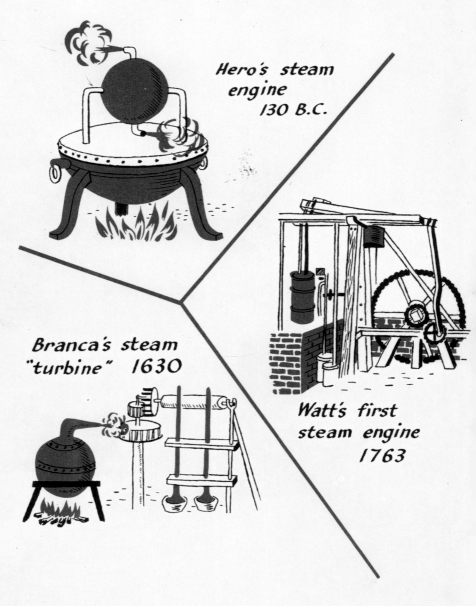

Hero's steam engine 130 B.C.

Branca's steam "turbine" 1630

Watt's first steam engine 1763